The Epic of Cuba Libre

New World Studies
Marlene L. Daut, Editor

The Epic of Cuba Libre

The *Mambí*, Mythopoetics, and Liberation

Éric Morales-Franceschini

University of Virginia Press
Charlottesville and London

University of Virginia Press

Printed in the United States of America on acid-free paper

First published 2022

9 8 7 6 5 4 3 2 1

Library of Congress Cataloging-in-Publication Data
Names: Morales-Franceschini, Eric, author.
Title: The epic of Cuba Libre : the *mambí,* mythopoetics, and liberation / Éric Morales-Franceschini.
Description: Charlottesville : University of Virginia Press, 2022. | Series: New World studies | Includes bibliographical references and index.
Identifiers: LCCN 2021061602 (print) | LCCN 2021061603 (ebook) | ISBN 9780813948140 (hardcover ; acid-free paper) | ISBN 9780813948157 (paperback ; acid-free paper) | ISBN 9780813948164 (ebook)
Subjects: LCSH: Cuban literature—20th century—History and criticism. | Revolutionaries in literature. | Revolutionaries in popular culture. | Archetype (Psychology) in literature. | Cuba—History—Insurrection, 1868–1878—Literature and the insurrection. | Cuba—History—Revolution, 1879–1880—Literature and the revolution. | Cuba—History—Revolution, 1895–1898—Literature and the revolution.
Classification: LCC PQ7378 .M67 2022 (print) | LCC PQ7378 (ebook) | DDC 860.9/3587291064—dc23/eng/20220310
LC record available at https://lccn.loc.gov/2021061602
LC ebook record available at https://lccn.loc.gov/2021061603

Publication of this volume has been supported by *New Literary History*.

Cover art: La Caballería, Cuba, Raúl Corrales Forno, 1960. (Museum of Fine Arts, Houston, gift of the estate of Esther Parada, 2006.471)

For Cintio Vitier (1921–2009),
exegete of the impossible
&
la Virgen mambisa,
quien me pidió este libro

Contents

Acknowledgments

LIKE ANY book worth the trouble to write (let alone read!), this one has its debts, scholarly and otherwise. Scholars, citizens, artists, family, friends, and, yes, even foes have had their hand in its fruition and fulfillment, and I am thankful to them all.

Miguel Martinez-Saenz, a doctoral student at the University of South Florida when I came to know him, was instrumental. It was he who recommended I read Alejandro de la Fuente and Louis A. Pérez Jr., whose judicious works were revelations. For me, raised in the vicinity of many Cuban Americans, friends and (extended) family alike, there was no nuanced talk of Fidel or Revolution. Only that of a dictator, loss, repression, and poverty. And so Cuba was a mystery, and I, incorrigibly curious, wanted to understand it. I was also drawn to Cuba as Boricua, born on the sister island of Puerto Rico with its many affinities yet worlds apart: the one an anti-imperialist state that has defied the United States for decades, the other a US colony for over a century. How could I not be seduced by the revolutionary epic?

It would take years of study and research, however, to be able to write anything not cliché or redundant about Cuba—let alone revolutions. That trajectory began in earnest at Duke University, where I was introduced to decolonial theory and Latin American subaltern studies in seminars with Valentin Mudimbe, Walter Mignolo, Romand Coles, Diane Nelson, Wahneema Lubiano, and Irene Silverblatt. After that, at UC, Berkeley, where I earned my PhD in rhetoric with a designated emphasis in critical theory, I made the most of an anti-disciplinary curriculum and wrote a somewhat heterodox dissertation on Cuba, cochaired by the world-renowned intellectuals Judith Butler and Trinh Minh-ha and with the brilliant Wendy Brown and Samera Esmeir as readers. That dissertation and their feedback served as the stimulus for this book.

The project I would eventually write did not, however, come about for years. Much work had yet to be done, and for that I am thankful to LACSI at the University of Georgia, whose Faculty Ambassador Grant enabled further research in Havana and Santiago de Cuba. I am also forever indebted to the Ford Foundation for the 2018–19 postdoctoral fellowship, which afforded me an indispensable year to reformulate and (re)write this project. A special thanks to Maurice Daniels, dean emeritus of the School of Social Work, and to Richard Gordon, former director of LACSI, who supported my hire at UGA; to Amy Ross, current director of LACSI, for her enthusiastic support, especially when it came time to revise this manuscript; and to all my colleagues in LACSI: Pablo Lapegna, Cassia Roth, Diana Graizbord, Jorge Derpic, Derek Bentley, Paul Duncan, and Sergio Quesada. A special thanks, too, to the UGA English Department. The mentorship of Barbara McCaskill, Cody Marrs, and Ed Pavlić has been crucial, as has the collegiality and camaraderie of Christopher Pizzino, Channette Romero, Esra Santesso, John Lowe, Jason Payton, Susan Rosenbaum, LeAnne Howe, Maggie Zurawski, Aruni Kashyap, and Casie LeGette, among others. A heartfelt thanks to my cherished compañero Josh Barkan, interdisciplinary scholar and critical thinker, who read this manuscript in its entirety with unusual care and rigor—and did so without receiving an honorarium or official credits for service! A thank-you to other colleagues across campus, not least Rielle Navitski, Lesley Feracho, and my beloved colega Sharina Maillo-Pozo. Also, a thank-you and saludo to the poet and Venceremos brigadista Ben Olguín; to the scholar and internationalist Anne Garland Mahler; to Louis Pérez Jr., for weighing in on this project in its earliest stages; and to Ada Ferrer, for her insurmountable *Insurgent Cuba*.

Needless to say, my debts to those in Cuba are considerable. My trips between 2010 and 2018 were never for as long nor as frequent as I would have liked, but they sufficed to conduct or partake in interviews, ethnography, archival research, pláticas, and tertulias of inestimable worth. A special thanks to those who have generously hosted me over the years: Zoé, Rogelio, and Tania Jiménez; Maritza and Manolo Lamane; and Niurka Laudelina; to the staff at the Biblioteca Nacional José Martí, Casa de las Américas, ICAIC, Fernando Ortiz Institute, University of Havana, Center for José Martí Studies, the Plaza de la Revolución Antonio Maceo Grajales, Museo Casa Natal de Antonio Maceo Grajales, and Centro de Estudios Antonio Maceo Grajales; and to the countless Cubans whom I have casually met and talked to about their epic history and the *mambí*, whether taxi drivers, waiters, vendors, teachers, doctors, engineers, soldiers, docents, retirees, veterans, or dissidents. And, lastly, a special thank-you (and apology) to the late Roberto Fernández Retamar, former president of Casa de las Américas, for his keen interest in my project, if only its premise. I regret that I could not finish this book sooner for him to read, critique, and maybe even endorse. In any case, the errors of this study are uniquely mine.

At the University of Virginia Press, I would like to thank editor in chief Eric Brandht and New World Studies series editor Marlene Daut for their prompt and reassuring endorsements; assistant editor Helen Chandler, project editor Morgan Myers, and copyeditor Jane Curran, for fostering the book through to its end; and the anonymous reviewers, whose feedback have made for a smoother read and conceptually tighter thesis.

And, lastly, to my family, boricuas and cubanxs alike; to Paloma, lover of fantasy and nature; and to Rebecca, my one true comrade in this hostile world.

The Epic of Cuba Libre

Introduction

Epic of the Dispossessed

Yo soy bueno, y como bueno/moriré de cara al sol

—José Martí, *Versos sencillos*

In defense of the July 26, 1953, assault on the Moncada barracks, in what would amount to the storied manifesto *History Will Absolve Me,* a twenty-seven-year-old Fidel Castro proclaimed:

> We are Cubans, and to be Cuban implies a duty: not to fulfill this duty is a crime, a treason . . . We were taught from early on to venerate the glorious example of our heroes and our martyrs. Céspedes, Agramonte, Maceo, Gómez, and Martí were the first names engraved in our minds; we were taught that the [Bronze] Titan had said that liberty was not begged for, but conquered with the blade of the machete . . . we were taught that October 10th [1868] and February 24th [1895] are glorious events worthy of patriotic rejoice because they mark the days on which Cubans rebelled against the yoke of an infamous tyranny; we were taught to love and defend that beautiful, solitary-starred flag and to sing every afternoon a hymn ["La Bayamesa"] whose verses say that "to live in chains is to live in disgraceful and opprobrious submission," and that "to die for the patria is to live."[1]

Like Pericles or the Homeric poet, Castro dictated what was in effect a funeral oration, one that rhetorically cast his fallen comrades as heirs to the grandeur and transcendence that was the nation's "glorious epic" (*epopeya gloriosa*).[2] For history had not just "absolved" those who took up arms and sacrificed their lives for the nation (*pro patri mori*): it had come to *exalt* them.

And not superfluously so. Between 1868 and 1898, Cubans fought and died in what amounted to the most deadly and destructive of all wars for independence in the Americas. The Ten Years' War (1868–78), the

Little War (1879–80), and the War for Independence (1895–98) resulted in as many as six hundred thousand casualties, approximately one in every five Cubans. Entire towns and villages were destroyed, estates and crops scorched, livestock systematically slaughtered, civilians interned and starved, families irrevocably torn apart, and the economy ravaged. "The losses were incalculable, the suffering was unimaginable," says historian Louis Pérez Jr.[3] And a pyrrhic, or at least equivocal, victory it was. Not only because of the extraordinary costs, but also the dubious outcomes. The United States had militarily intervened in 1898 and all but unilaterally ended the war with Spain. They then occupied the island until 1901 and left in their wake a so-called republic subservient to American "interests," as it is blandly put.

That said, Cubans did not look to their wars as melancholic or dismal affairs. For not all was sheer misery and humiliation. Loss could readily be narrated as "sacrifice" and their dead as "heroes." Indeed, Cubans now had battles to commemorate and martyrs to revere, a flag to salute, and an anthem to cheer. They, especially veterans, had an emboldened sense of dignity and entitlement. And if nothing else, they now had a founding myth, the story of all people who sacrificed everything to found a republic "with all and for the good of all." The story of Cuba Libre (Free Cuba).

That story would become familiar to all Cubans, from its most hallowed surnames and battles to the nation's archetypal hero, the *mambí,* as the rank-and-file independence soldier came to be known. No other story is as ritualistically retold, no other archetype as beloved. Not then. Not years later. Not now. And why wouldn't it be? The wars are a bountiful "archive" for storytellers (and audiences) who wish to rejoice in motifs as sacred as creation and as seductive as redemption. And rejoice Cubans have. Whether in town festivals or school plays, comics or films, museums or monuments, hymns or textbooks, on logos or the national currency, the mambí and his quest for a Cuba Libre have reigned in the popular imaginary and borne quite decisively on national identity and revolutionary ethos.[4] So much so, evidently, that its mythical aura has not aroused much scrutiny. For rarely has the mambí been analyzed as a *rhetorical* or *mythopoetic* referent and, rarer still, as a referent in the twentieth century. An excellent historiography does, to be clear, exist.[5] Be it military strategy, demographics, social history, or international relations, the wars have been amply researched. But the ways in which the wars have been *aesthetically rendered* has received far less scrutiny, least of all when it comes to its twentieth-century iterations. And while this is typical of studies on wars and revolutions, it is regrettable. For neither the mambí nor Cuba Libre became any less salient in the postwar years, and never have they conveyed just one emancipatory possibility. A past so intensive and extensive can, after all, easily foster a multiplicity of stories and, accordingly, a multiplicity of "lessons" bequeathed to future generations. Those stories told and lessons bequeathed are the subject of this book.

In so doing, what we learn is that the stories told about the mambí and Cuba Libre do not seamlessly abide by the epic, classically conceived. How, for instance, does one account for a hero that is not a demigod or a noble, but a racially stigmatized other? Or for tactics more sly than virtuous? Speech more colloquial than decorous? For deaths that could not credibly be narrated as "sublime"? And what of the epic heroine, the *mambisa*? This study elaborates on what these idiosyncrasies bespeak and how they have come to edify as well as vitiate emancipatory possibilities in Cuba. To do so, it draws on an ensemble of artifacts—be it poetry, plays, memoirs, monuments, songs, speeches, or films. For there is no single canonical text titled *The Epic of Cuba Libre,* much less an epic poem written in hexameter verse or its equivalent. What there is, is a copious "archive" left behind by generations of Cubans who have reckoned with those wars and their mythical aura. This inquiry is, thereby, a critical exegesis of the cumulative and salient "text" (Latin *texere,* "to weave, braid") that is the mambí epic. It takes into account the contexts in which it has been (re)created and the ends to which it has been (mis) appropriated. And it does so in order to illuminate the idiosyncrasies and vicissitudes of an aesthetics, if not ethics, of liberation. But such a project calls for unique theoretical criteria. In this introduction, thus, I spell out the *mythical, catachrestical,* and *obediential* attributes that characterize, whether promiscuously or precariously, what we can call a subaltern or decolonial epic. Thereafter, I summarize the book's chapters and its scholarly contributions.

The Mythical Text as Promissory Note

To reckon with the mambí is to reckon with the mythical: "What *mambí* can we know," asked Cuban historian Blanacmar León Rosabal, "other than the mythical one?"[6] So much of what has been written and said about the mambí is, after all, akin to dramatized fantasies and sacred tales. But even the most sober historical accounts can bear elective affinities with the mythical, and this fact ought not be neglected.

Myths can be defined as "stories" (Greek, *mythos*) that "explain" how a given reality came into existence. They are usually set in what Mircea

Eliade called "sacred time" and dramatized by divine or supernatural entities.[7] They are, accordingly, fantastical and metaphysical in their capacity to articulate events that, as Northrop Frye said, touch on the "conceivable limits of desire."[8] Or as Claude Lévi-Strauss put it: "with myth everything becomes possible."[9] But to their adherents they are true and sacred. And this is what distinguishes myths from other narratological artifacts such as novels and folktales, which can be purely fictional and are rarely, if ever, deemed sacred.

Myth's sacral profile and its capacity to flout limits are said to distinguish it from history as well. For with history, in the secularized modern(ist) sense, not everything becomes possible. In fact, with history the possible is held hostage to the sober realm of that which *verifiably* occurred. But certain "stories" about the past can be empirically true and, even if avowedly secular, endowed with sacred and redemptive salience or "natal" capacities. This is especially the case when it comes to revolutions. As Hannah Arendt pointed out, revolutions are "inextricably bound up with the notion that the course of history suddenly begins anew, that an entirely new story, a story never known or told before, is about to unfold."[10] Whatever its content, the story of revolution is usually a story in which the collective desire called liberation becomes the decisive "plot."[11] This means that no matter how wedded to the verifiable past, to tell the story of a revolution is to narrate the *possibility* to initiate something new—to say nothing of the jouissance embedded in that creative act. That such "stories," even if restricted to the realm of mortals, are endowed with sacred and redemptive attributes should come, thus, as no surprise.

Nor should it strike us as a scandal that such mytho-historical accounts are dramatic and, as such, endowed with *literary* and *rhetorical* attributes. Literature and history are of course presumed to be incommensurate, at least insofar as literature enjoys a license to the fictional and a proclivity toward the dramatic. But the astute reader knows that, insofar as it *narrates,* history draws on literary and rhetorical resources, even when impeccably documented or bound to the materially real. No other critic has argued this case more persuasively than has Hayden White. In order to render intelligible the random and innumerable series of events that is the totality of the past, White argued, the historian recounts the past in terms that are not only chronological but also narratological: her account tells a *story.* And that story is rarely told without a "plot," that which organizes events in such a way as to communicate *why* this or that occurred and is noteworthy amid so many other occurrences that *could have been* narrated. In order to do so historians draw on narrative tactics

White called *mythoi* or "modes of emplotment." To nineteenth-century European historiography, four mattered most: romance, tragedy, comedy, and satire. But other modes of emplotment do exist (e.g., the idyll, the pastoral, the epic), and all are liable to permutations (e.g., tragicomedy, the epic romance). Granted, the mythoi at the historian-as-storyteller's disposal are, in Northrop Frye's words, "artistically exhaustible"—only as far, that is, as one's cultural and aesthetic repertoire permits—but, all the same, narrate historians must and (aesthetic) choices they make.[12]

There is, after all, no already formulated—much less conclusive—story in the "archives" inasmuch as an ensemble of documents and variables that can accommodate a multiplicity of stories. How one chooses to meaningfully organize and communicate such "facts" are not decidable on purely "scientific" or "logical" criteria. For insofar as we narrate and wish to tell a story that *edifies,* such choices are no less aesthetic and ethical. This is not to say that history is (solely) moralistic or that mythoi are sheer stylistic artifice. For what White called the "poetics of history" (i.e., mythoi, narrativity, tropes, etc.) bear on history's *explanatory* power. Albeit elliptically, a tragically emplotted story "explains" to the reader why this or that event was (in)consequential or why this or that choice was (un)wise precisely because a tragedy is also an account of how the (social) world operates and what, thereby, can be reasonably expected of like circumstances and choices.[13]

Yet history's elective—if not ineradicable—affinities with myth are not often welcomed. For such drama, pathos, and "inventiveness" are deemed synonymous with "ideology," repressively construed. No critic, in this regard, has been more influential than Roland Barthes. For Barthes, myth is a mode of "interpellant speech," one that hails the subject to identify with its account of the world—an account that conveys itself "as if for all time." It is an account of history, in other words, paradoxically *deprived* of history, history as trite tautology: "This is so because it's always been so." Myth is thus, for Barthes, tantamount to false consciousness. One need only look to the incriminatory vocabulary with which he characterized it: as "perpetual alibi," "stolen language," "larceny," "arrest," "robbery," "duplicity," as that which "corrupts," "distorts," "masks," etc.[14]

Myth is not, however, only "interpellant speech," but also "lived reality," at least for its adherents. Anthropologist Bronislaw Malinowski characterized myth as a "pragmatic charter," one that bears within it "moral wisdom" and fulfills any number of functions: to codify belief, safeguard morality, satisfy metaphysical curiosities, glorify social hierarchies, keep the peace, etc.[15] Granted, such sacred tales and their accompanying rituals can be repressive. René Girard famously theorized myths as stories that *symbolically* reenact an archaic rivalry and its violent resolution. A myth tells the story, accordingly, of how a collectivity restored order by recourse to a "scapegoat." It is as such a *cathartic* story, a story that *pacifies.*[16]

But the universality with which Girard expounded his theory of myth and sacrifice is, as Terry Eagleton has noted, "absurdly hyperbolic."[17] To wit, it forecloses the possibility that myth and sacrifice can *engender* emancipatory desires and projects. For French anarcho-syndicalist Georges Sorel, myths should be judged not by their fidelity to the past but by their capacity to act on *the present.* No other myth proves this more poignantly, Sorel tells us, than does the Christian apocalyptic myth. It tells of the imminent return of a Messiah, a catastrophic event that spells the end of the pagan world and inaugurates the new Kingdom, where the lamb shall lie peacefully with the wolf. The early Christians believed it so, even if this meant an ascetic life or a tortuous death at the hands of the Roman Empire. That the myth never came to pass did not dissuade millennial Christians. Their persecuted brethren were taken, in fact, to be all the saintlier and their credo all the more sublime. As Sorel pointed out, Christianity did not wither in their wake inasmuch as flourish.[18]

Sorel accordingly inferred that the myth of the General Strike could yield the "innumerable sacrifices" it would take to render socialism a feasible and formidable force in the world. Whatever its feasibility, the myth of workers who heroically stand off against capital could engender the "serious, formidable, and sublime work" that revolution calls for in the unsavory present. And with each revolutionary that falls, that myth and its attendant credo becomes all the less abstract and all the more heroic. And "heroic" is the word of choice. The myth of the General Strike is no workers' idyll. It is, in Sorel's words, an "economic epic," and its heroes the proletarian strikers. Not surprisingly, thus, Sorel invoked the Homeric epics and the "warlike spirit" of the Spartans as exemplary for modern revolutionaries. The strike is a "phenomenon of [revolutionary] war," and like all wars can arouse the "forces of enthusiasm" that foster valor, honor, sacrifice, and martyrdom.[19]

Peruvian intellectual José Mariátegui concurred: "The strength of revolutionaries is not in their science; it is in their faith, in their passion, in their will. It is a religious, mystical, spiritual force. It is the force of myth."[20] That said, other myths can and have just as readily vied to enchant the masses—none, arguably, as consequential as the *national* myth. In Ernest Renan's insurmountable words:

> Of all cults, that of the ancestors is the most legitimate, for the ancestors have made us what we are. A heroic past, great men, glory (by which I understand genuine glory), this is the social capital upon which one bases a national idea. To have common glories in the past and to have a common will in the present; to have performed great deeds together, to wish to perform still more—these are the essential conditions for being a people. One loves in proportion to the sacrifices to which one has consented, and in proportion to the ills that one has suffered. One loves the house that one has built and that one has handed down. The Spartan song—"We are what you were; we, will be what you are"—is, in its simplicity, the abridged hymn of every patria.[21]

Yet the corollary of this is not that *national* and *revolutionary* myths are irreconcilable. Insofar as that "heroic past" bespeaks the "plot of liberation," it can arouse virtuous conduct. As Cuban poet Cintio Vitier put it, such heroic tales can foster a "redemptive impatience" with *contemporary* injustices.[22] The tale of a dignity and decorum that once was (or was to come) can, in short, become a potent stimulant for emancipatory futures.

This would be to read myth, or the mythical text, *dialectically,* as Frederic Jameson would recommend. The mythical text is for Jameson a "symbolic act," whereby contradictions in social reality are only *aesthetically* resolved. The mythical text can as such "mystify" the interpellated subject because it fosters the believe that contradictions have been surmounted "on their own terms." And in this regard, it functions as a *substitute* for emancipatory politics. That same text, nevertheless, bears within it "utopian impulses."[23] For insofar as it posits a harmonious "unity," it bespeaks a desire for a world liberated of those contradictions: the mythical text as collective wish fulfillment. Utopian desire does not, of course, in and of itself dictate a form or a horizon. It might be expressed, as Ernst Bloch documented, in the most trite artifacts, and its dreamed "solutions" may in fact be eerily vulgar.[24] The "unity of collectivity" in which utopian desire revels is, after all, haunted by its constitutive other, namely the excluded.[25] Utopian desire presupposes an unpleasant stimulant, an "evil" (scapegoat?) for which to blame the *lack* of harmonious collectivity, such that utopian desire is, at its most rudimentary, a "clarion call" to root out this evil.[26]

The mythical text is seductive and "beautiful," accordingly, because it can *indict* a disagreeable reality and *postulate* a harmonious horizon beyond it: the mythical text as "promissory note," to cite Herbert Marcuse. Marcuse, after Freud, theorized the aesthetic as an erotically sublimated affair. It is an activity that gives voice to "taboo" desires, desires buoyed by the memory of an edenic "once upon a time." And this is precisely the sense in which the *no longer* can constitute a stimulant for the emancipatory *not yet.* Allegorically, thus, we could look to the story of Cuba Libre as a "promissory note" that bespeaks the collective desire for a harmonious unity—that republic "with all and for the good of all" that national martyr José Martí famously intoned. It is a story that hailed and roused subjects to tender all manner of untold sacrifices and was rendered, thereby, all the more venerable. For insofar as it is taken to be a historically true account, it is not just a "promise" per se but a remembrance of things past, in which case it postulates (or recalls) a horizon not only desirable but also possible—because it once was (believed to be) so. But it is only ever thus: an *aesthetically* or *rhetorically* inflected memory whose emancipatory possibilities the present is not obligated to redeem. For as Marcuse stoically confessed, "reality offers no promise, only chances."[27]

Epic Emplotment as Catachresis

Utopian "unities" have historically borne names like "Eden," "Philadelphia," "Kingdom," and "commune." Relative to our inquiry, it has borne the name Cuba Libre. Cubans dared not, that said, use words such as "myth" or "utopia" to name the historic event that was their wars for independence. Such words are the colloquial equivalents to "superstition" and "fantasy." To use them would be to trivialize (or worse) the *veracity* of what happened and the *exceptionality* of what was at stake. Instead, Cubans have habitually used the word "epic" (*epopeya*) to dignify as much as denote the scale and significance of their wars for independence.

For an epic is more than *just* a story. As Paul Innes has pointed out, "Epic was once considered to be the highest literary form[. . . .] Its cultural importance was such that entire societies could be defined by and through it."[28] Homer's *Iliad,* Virgil's *Aeneid,* the Hindu *Ramayana,* the Malinke *Sundiata,* the Scandinavian *Beowulf,* the French *Song of Roland,* and the Spanish *Song of Cid* are such canonical texts. Each is a narrative that, in C. M. Bowra's words, "gives a special pleasure because its events and persons enhance our belief in the worth of human achievement and in the dignity and nobility of man [*sic*]."[29] The formal attributes of the epic themselves connote glory and grandeur. Classic epic texts or (oral) performances are *extensive,* whether hundreds of verses or several evenings to recite. And such scale connotes much is at stake. The events that occur within an epic narrative are *events of consequence.* They are narratives frequently set in the context of war and what is understood to be a formative period. The protagonist's choices and heroic deeds are decisive to the fate of a city, race, or civilization. He is entrusted to fight perilous battles and secure his peoples' glory, often dying in the event. Little wonder the *solemn tone* and *lofty diction* so characteristic of the genre. For what else would befit events and deeds presumed to be so momentous and, as Aristotle put it, "marvelous"?[30] The epic narrative thereby memorializes a heroic ethos that transcends time and finitude and comes to constitute the archetypal and the venerated. Hence, its explanatory powers: the epic "explains" from whence a people came and what greatness they (allegedly) possess.[31]

Folklorist Eleazar Meletinsky was not misled, thus, when he said that national epics preserve a "mythological substratum."[32] Like myths, epics are set in the structurally analogous times of creation and the chaotic battles out of which is born a new harmonious order. Theirs are wars waged against foes who—like the demons, monsters, or rogue gods of myths—are believed to be unimaginably evil and possess powers near to magic. The "shamanic aura" of the mythical hero cedes herein to the chivalric aura and martial aesthetic of the epic hero, whose death in combat is, as Dean Miller put it, "the currency in which heroism deals."[33] The epic narrative is, accordingly, a historical and dramatic narrative but so, too, an edifying one. Or more exactly, it comes to constitute *the* edifying narrative, whose creed to the living is that of piety to and emulation of one's ancestors.

Mikhail Bakhtin argued that this was precisely why the epic is a hopelessly antiquated and oppressive genre. The pious relation to the past that it extorts holds the present—and its futurity—hostage to what once was. For the epic past is not just chronologically but also *morally* first. With it comes the "founders" and "fathers" whom descendants compulsively, if not compulsorily, revere and against which their conduct is judged. In that heroic past there is no space for "open-endedness, indecision, indeterminacy." There is only ever an already finished narrative and ancestors to memorialize.[34] Whatever uniqueness (and future possibilities) the present might possess is confined, thereby, to ritualistic recitations of the epic past. Hence Bakhtin's famous thesis: the epic narrative is cast in "marble or bronze," whereas the novel is molded in "clay."[35] The latter has no obligations to the past. It can dwell in the present (let alone a fantastical future), be articulated in familiar speech, and take on the most profane and "unheroic" of subjects. It can revel in the laughter, travesty, irony, or debauchery that enable us to see the world "realistically" and divine a future not already prophesied—or, rather, *foreclosed*—by the epic past. The "hero" of the novel is not, thus, the virtuous and beautiful subject bound to a national tradition inasmuch as a fallible and improvisational subject with an "unrealized surplus," one that anticipates new beginnings.[36]

Bakhtin's critique of the epic is no doubt seductive. Postmodern critics of "master narratives" have found it irresistible.[37] But not all are as amenable to its polemical charms. Joseph Farrell insisted that Bakhtin discredits the epic tradition's "capacity for self-questioning and for the radical reinterpretation of its own generic roots."[38] Indeed, there are epic texts and translations that cannot so easily be dismissed as unimaginative "marble" or obtuse "bronze," so to speak. John McWilliams Jr. has pointed to the rebellious iterations that are Herman Melville's *Moby Dick* and Walt Whitman's *Leaves of Grass;* A. K. Ramanujan to the diverse iterations of the *Ramayana* throughout Southeast Asia; Jonathon Repinecz to those West African epics that have been subversively "reinvented" to address contemporary issues; and Sneharika Roy to the "dialogical" and self-reflexive techniques that thrive in "postcolonial epics" such as Amitav Ghosh's *Ibis Trilogy* and Derek Walcott's *Omeros.*[39] These are no idle exceptions to the "marble" versus "clay" dichotomy. For if the epic was once considered the "highest literary form," it was also the literary form of choice for empires.[40] What the *Iliad* was to the Macedonian empire, *Aeneid* was to the Roman empire. Nor incidentally did European intellectuals doubt the existence—indeed, *the possibility*—of epics in Africa and the indigenous Americas.[41] To do so would be to dignify a people presumed to have no history—or, at least, no history of any scale and significance. Such peoples have been cast in a perpetually "primitive" present or as the "undeveloped."[42] In Frantz Fanon's apt words: "The colonist makes history. His life is an epic, an odyssey. He is invested with the very beginning: 'We made this land'. He is the guarantor for its existence: 'If we leave all will be lost, and this land will return to the Dark Ages.'"[43]

That said, attributes such as scale, war, a formative past, and a virtuous hero do not preclude an epic that is anti-imperialist and anti-racist—among other progressive or radical "promises." Epic emplotment is not, in other words, immune to subaltern appropriations and emancipatory plots. None other than Fanon discerned how the epic, with its "typified categories" and "inert episodes," was conjured anew in the midst of the Algerian Revolution (1954–62). Storytellers who were once "stereotyped and tedious to listen to, completely overturned their traditional methods of storytelling and the contents of their tales." The epic formula that once read, "This happened long ago," was amended to read, "but it might well have happened here today, and it might happen tomorrow." The epic thereby became an "invocation" and its drama a drama attuned to the people's "struggle."[44]

On this count, the true epics of the modern era are not poetic verses about conquests inasmuch as carnal acts of revolution. Such events are awash in variables amenable to epic emplotment: scale, foundational stakes, a context of exceptional violence, and the motifs of heroism, sacrifice, and redemption. But, to be clear, the conjuncture of epic and revolution is not without its idiosyncrasies. For all its affinities to the classical epic, the modern epic known as "revolution" modifies the *profile* of the hero and *plot* of the drama: the epic protagonist becomes "the people" and the drama's plot imbued with emancipatory "promises." One readily thinks of the French Revolution, that "new story" whose emancipatory promises stimulated the "serious, formidable, and sublime work" of revolutionaries in the historical present and its radical futures.[45]

That said, the small islands of the Caribbean proved themselves no less worthy of epic history—or, at least, laid claim to it. The Haitian Revolution (1791–1804) was not narrated as an epic of the dispossessed, not amid those who profited from commodified and enslaved Black lives. Rather, it was sensationalized as a racial apocalypse, one in which Black "savages" massacred and defiled respectable whites. That Black subjects could be endowed with revolutionary desires and capabilities was, as Michel-Rolph Trouillot has argued, "unthinkable."[46] They were not deemed worthy of the words "revolution," "citizen," and "republic." Any claim to such names was itself a rebellious act, or, more exactly, a *catachrestical* act.

Catachresis refers to the "misuse" of a word, whether because it is applied in a context or to an object not "properly" associated with it. Gayatri Chakravorty Spivak has looked to catachresis as the rhetorical trope that best conveys the postcolonial predicament, namely if the subaltern is to speak—let alone be heard—she must "wrench" and "wrest" such names away from their Occidental provinces and "seize," or outright "displace," the value attributed to them. To do so is to lay catachrestical claim to the power, dignity, and respectability attributed to beloved words and, accordingly, to "tamper" with the "authority of storylines"—including, no doubt, the epic storyline.[47] To say that epic emplotment is catachrestical is to point, however, to an ineluctable referential predicament: the subaltern cannot *unequivocally* occupy or employ the sovereign's names. But such referential precariousness is fecund because one need not understand catachresis as, to quote Spivak, a "word for which there is no adequate referent to be found."[48] One could just as readily understand it vice versa: a referent for which there is no adequate word to be found. In the catachrestical "text" that is the *subaltern* epic such words either could, if not had, to be (re)invented or novelized. A case in point are the words "Haïti" and "Haitian," derived from the Arawak word for "land of mountains." These words had no real political—let alone aesthetic—salience prior to 1791. It was in the midst and wake of that revolutionary war and the abolition of slavery that such words came to supersede "slave," "negro," "Saint-Domingue," etc. For the latter could not possibly accommodate these new referents that were the Black revolutionary subject and a Black republic—let alone this new story that was (or could be) the Haitian Revolution.[49]

A similar catachrestical revolt occurred by virtue of Cuba's nineteenth-century revolutionary wars. In Roberto Fernández Retamar's words:

> The most venerated word in Cuba—*mambí*—was disparagingly imposed on us by our enemies at the time of war for independence [. . .] in the mouths of Spanish colonists [it] implied the idea that all *independentistas* were so many black slaves—emancipated by that very war for independence—who of course constituted the bulk of the liberation army. The *independentistas,* white and black, adopted with honor something that colonialism meant as an insult. This is the dialectic of Caliban. To offend us they call us *mambí,* they call us black; but we reclaim as a mark of glory the honor of considering ourselves descendants of the *mambí,* descendants of the rebel, the *cimarrón, independentista* black—*never* descendants of the holder.[50]

Retamar, too, wrote within a revolutionary context and to catachrestical effect. Published in 1971, his essay-cum-manifesto "Caliban" took Shakespeare's anagram for "cannibal," etymologically derived from the Amerindians known as the *caribs,* and proudly laid claim to it as the name for the "valiant and warlike" peoples of the Americas. They and the literary monster Caliban become (like the mambí) the name for a rebel and that rebel's dignity.

At stake, thus, in epic emplotment as subaltern catachresis is vindication.[51] It was not just poetic license for Aimé Césaire to christen the Haitian Revolution the "first epic of the New World" or for C. L. R. James to anoint its heroes with the (catachrestical) title *The Black Jacobins.*[52] To vet that history as a *revolutionary epic* was to testify to the esteem it and Haitians deserved in league with the French Revolution and the *white* Jacobins. As a consequence, the narrative's interpellated readers (i.e., the subaltern) could identify with the grandeur and solemnity that epic emplotment and the name "revolution" can afford, just as Retamar and countless other Cubans have done vis-à-vis the mambises and the epic of Cuba Libre.

But, of course, neither the Haitian Revolution nor the mambí epic ended triumphantly. They were wars rife with brutality, misfortunes, betrayals, discord, and unpleasant outcomes. This is the sense in which the specter of tragedy haunts epic emplotment. Indeed, none other than C. L. R. James rendered Toussaint more akin to Hamlet than to Achilles. Toussaint was the tragic hero whose hubris and lack of faith in the Black masses condemned him to his inglorious death in that cold Fort-de-Joux prison cell.[53] As David Scott has argued, tragedy bears within it sobering lessons that the romantically construed epic does not.[54] Whereas the one flaunts salvation and redemption, the other dwells on fallible humans and unlikely odds. The point, however, at which tragedy bespeaks the *futility* of liberation is the point at which it becomes irreconcilable with the epic. For, as J. B. Hainsworth said, "in the epic there must be achievement and therefore hope."[55] The epic bespeaks the hope that an "evil" shall be surmounted and tells the story of a heroic willingness to wager one's life on that hope. The epic postulates as such that, despite tragic loss, life did and can flourish. It is not sobering inasmuch as empowering, and its subaltern iterations abound in catachrestical possibilities. For the subaltern epic is an opportunity to exploit referential equivocations. It is an opportunity to rearticulate *who* and *what* kinds of deeds count as "heroic" or "sublime" and *to what end* liberation. Such possibilities are not, surely, without their risks. The dignifying and explanatory powers that the epic can afford are likewise incentives to make, in Spivak's words, a "catechism of catachresis."[56] Or as Cuban scholar Marial Iglesias Utset has warned, there is always the risk that epic memory and its icons of rebelliousness will be rendered an "antiseptic" ritual of assent—one that depicts liberation as consummated fact, rather than a timely call.[57]

Obediential (and Necrophilic) Aesthetics

As said, the mythical text that is the epic of Cuba Libre can be read as a classical epic: its scale, heroes with epithets, momentous battles, potent foes, dramatized deaths, and formative stakes all recommend it. Yet so, too, can that epic be narrated (and it has been) with emancipatory "plots" and catachrestical audacity, not least the audacity of colonized subjects to lay claim to the grandeur of "revolution." The epic of Cuba Libre can also be read, thus, as a decolonial epic. This is the case especially insofar as that epic tells the story of what philosopher Enrique Dussel calls *obediential* power, a power enacted by "the people."[58] For Dussel, the category of "the people" (*el pueblo*) is not the equivalent to "the nation" inasmuch as a coalition of the dispossessed, or what he calls "the social bloc of the oppressed." They are the victims to *fetishized* power, that which is parasitical. Fetishized power is power that "corrupts" those institutions that ought to serve the people—be it the state, the church, or any other such vested authority. That said, the people are always already endowed with the capacities (*potentia*) to provoke a "state of rebellion."[59] As a series of dissident and collective acts that disarm fetishized power, the state of rebellion constitutes that "event" through which liberation becomes possible. The horizon of a conscious people in a state of rebellion is not, however, only liberation *from* fetishized power; so, too, is it a "courageous and creative" act to *institute* obediential power, a power that, as the Zapatistas say, "governs by obeying" (*mandar obedeciendo*).[60]

The corollary of this is that any aesthetic of liberation should be an obediential aesthetics. This, too, must be understood in relation to fetishized power, for aesthetics in the Americas was consolidated within a modern world system that has looked to Europe as the citadel of the beautiful. The indigenous arts (and phenotypes) of the Global South, by contrast, have been routinely coded as exotic and folkloric, when not barbaric.[61] An aesthetics of liberation is thereby one that critiques this aesthetic regime and recuperates the "beauty" of the people. It listens and is attuned (*a la escucha*) to those who have been rendered the embodiments of "ugliness," so to speak. In doing so, it strives to cultivate a new sensorium and the critical sensibilities that reflect, indeed *obey,* the people's "will-to-live" (*voluntad-de-vida*). For, as Dussel reminds us, aesthetics in its purest sense is devoted to the "criterion of life."[62] Herein Dussel works from the speculative premise that humans are endowed with a faculty (*áisthesis*) that enables us to marvel at and judge a perceived object as beautiful. The wonder (*asombro*) with which we recognize the object as beautiful is indebted to the criterion of life because that object is "available" to life (*disponibilidad*). In other words, the object is interpreted as a *mediation* for life, that which contributes to life's sustenance and flourishment.[63] The technical craft we call "art" thereby conveys the enthrallment and value we attribute to such objects or experiences of the beautiful. But such judgment and craft are situated within historical contexts and cultural endowments that likewise prefigure our perceptions of the beautiful. It is not, that is, only existential needs or sheer pleasure that dictate the terms of the beautiful; so, too, do cultural endowments and institutional power. In a paraphrase of Marx's famous formula, we could assert that humans receive and render the beautiful, but not as they please.[64] And precisely in this sense has aesthetics in the Americas fetishized that which is European and vulgarized that which is not. An *obediential* aesthetics, thus, decolonizes this fetish and "subsumes" whatever is worthwhile to liberation within a "new horizon," one in which the beautiful is consonant with life and the people.[65]

In this regard, the mambises are the "delegates" and "servants" of *el pueblo* (the people) and the collective desire called Cuba Libre a project to institute obediential power. Yet the epic that is a revolution—or, so to speak, a "state of rebellion"—is never without its intimacies with violence and death. And this is no frivolous point. Dussel's own logic deduces that the beautiful is to life as ugliness is to death.[66] Arguably, then, we should invoke not the beautiful but the *sublime* when it comes to the revolutionary epic. For whereas the beautiful arouses pleasure, the sublime arouses awe and terror.[67] That a revolution arouses terror is rather self-evident. The violence that is consequent to radical antagonisms makes this so. But as Arendt stipulated, violence does not in itself suffice to conceptualize revolutions. Only where that violence is exercised to liberate the dispossessed and build a "new house" in which justice can dwell can we speak of revolutions.[68] And it is this historic transcendence that arouses awe, not just terror. For in revolutionary epics, violence transcends the mortal body and singular life of the epic hero (or heroic generation). Rhetorically at least, epic violence is rendered equivalent to sacrifice (not murder) and the purveyors of that violence heroes and martyrs. Whatever abject privations and untold losses were suffered were not, consequently, "tragic" inasmuch as courageous and honorable. For catastrophic wars and tragic deaths are among the mortal drama that confers on national (and revolutionary) epics an aura of gravitas and the sacral. Homer's *Iliad* and Virgil's *Aeneid* are, for instance, riddled with calamities that befall loved ones, nobles, and innocent civilians. Such morbid spectacles and bereavement are consistent with the fact that, as Benedict Anderson pointed out, nations write their "biography" not in terms of births inasmuch as deaths: "exemplary suicides, poignant martyrdoms, assassinations, executions, wars, and holocausts."[69] Deaths of a "special kind." Such storied deaths and exceptional violence have the capacity to evoke awe and kinship between peoples with no "natural" (i.e., blood) ties. The dead, the living, and the unborn are all liable to its charms and its passions, which have roused millions throughout history to tender all manners of "colossal sacrifices."[70] And as anthropologists Marcel Mauss and Henri Hubert once said, "there is no sacrifice into which some idea of redemption does not enter."[71]

In this respect, it is telling that Vitier characterized the "Cuban sublime" in terms of sacrifice and the criterion of justice: it is *injustice* (not death) that constitutes ugliness in the Cuban imaginary. In fact, death is hereby tantamount to the beautiful insofar as it is a *sacrificial* death. For, according to Vitier's exegesis, there is no ethics (or aesthetic) more astonishing or enthralling than the "vocation of sacrifice" that is "*mambí* epicness" (*epicidad mambisa*), no act more sublime than for a Cuban to bequeath her or his life in the service of justice.[72] The awe and terror that such a vocation can (aesthetically) conjure is not, however, just related to a life surrendered; so, too, is it predicated on lives taken. As much as Vitier would like to affiliate the mambí with a prophet and his death with martyrdom, that is, death and the heroic as epic entails an ethics that partakes in violence: it is a willingness to surrender *and* to seize life. In this regard the epic possesses an affinity for a *necro-aesthetics,* an aesthetics that fetishizes death and violence. As Cuba's national hero José Martí put it: "To die is to live, is to sow."[73] The elision that operates here is one that presupposes a violence that is not murder inasmuch as sacrifice and that resignifies death not as the end, but as a beginning—not destruction, but creation and renewal. The critic must, accordingly, reckon with this necrophilic ambivalence and parse out whether the epic text fetishizes the violence and death of the mythical hero or obeys the liberation and "will-to-live" of the people.

The Mambí and the Mythopoetics of Cuba Libre

This inquiry elects, thus, to read the cumulative text that is the mambí epic as a *mythical, catachrestical,* and *obediential* text. It reads that text for the "perpetual alibi" (Barthes) it can constitute in the historical present and for the ritualistic piety with which it holds the future hostage to a petrified past (Bakhtin). Yet so, too, does it tease out and reckon with the "utopian impulses" (Jameson) that enliven and vitiate that aesthetic remembrance of things past (Marcuse). That it has been routinely emplotted (White) as an epic of the dispossessed makes it, moreover, a "special" case. For it appropriates the grandeur and sublimity associated with the words "epic" and "revolution" and applies them to subaltern subjects and histories. The referential equivocations (Spivak) that are consequent to such appropriations create, accordingly, opportunities to tell new stories with new emancipatory plots (Arendt). And the fact that these new stories are meant to dignify and empower the "social bloc of the oppressed" recommends an aesthetic that depicts obediential power (Dussel) as the beautiful. As a narrative intimately tethered to war and the martial hero, however, there is a proclivity of the epic to fetishize violence and death in lieu of beautifying life and liberation. Consequently, the decolonial epic is a story as fraught with anachronistic pieties and necrophilic pleasures as it is with imminent provocations and radical hope.

These criteria and theses make for a rather unique, if not peculiar, book. The scholarly literature on Cuba's wars for independence is ample and excellent, and this study could not have been written without it. It owes a special debt to the work of Ada Ferrer on the rhetoric of race and nation in the wars; Teresa Prados-Torreira on the mambisa and her transgressions of gender norms; Ambrosio Fornet, Diana Iznaga, and Blancamar León Rosabal on the various motifs found in the war's "testimonial" literature (*literatura de campaña*); and Jorge Ibarra on the anti-imperialist and internationalist dictums of mambí "ideology."[74] But unlike these works, this study reads closely for the mambí in twentieth-century artifacts and iterations. This is not to say that critics and scholars have overlooked the wars' salience in post-1898 Cuba. Marial Iglesias Utset has documented how mambí symbols were institutionalized in the politically fraught years of 1898–1902; Lillian Guerra how José Martí and martyrdom were enshrined and symbolically utilized in the late republican years; and Antonio Kapcia and Louis Pérez Jr. how the rebellious past has been "encoded" as a duty, even if "suicidal," for subsequent generations.[75] But none of these studies surveys the mambí's story and aesthetics as a *mythopoetic* text, nor do they critically theorize it vis-à-vis epic emplotment and obediential aesthetics.

The Epic of Cuba Libre is indebted, too, to studies on revolutions in the Americas, especially those that look to collective memory and the literary imagination. Kindred studies include Doris Sommer on Latin America's "foundational fictions" in romantic novels; Thomas Benjamin on the Mexican Revolution's "warring pasts" and mythology; Marlene Daut on the tropology, Victor Figueroa on the "decolonial options," and Philip J. Kaisary on the "radical recuperations" of the Haitian Revolution in literary and artistic texts throughout the Antilles and Black Atlantic; and Shalini Puri on the "urgent memory" and Laurie Lambert on the "feminist revisions" of the Grenada Revolution in postrevolutionary texts and artifacts.[76] David Scott's mythopoetic probes of the Haitian and Grenadian Revolutions in our "post-romantic" times are especially noteworthy.[77] Like Scott's attentiveness to tragedy, this study explores the epic as a nuanced *mythos,* not merely a colloquial word used to denote a literary genre or a large-scale event. But more akin to Puri's study, I draw on a larger corpus of cultural artifacts (not exclusively literary) and, unlike so many of these studies, I reckon with wars and a revolution for which "tragedy" is not the only or most viable mode of emplotment. For the epic has not lost relevance to our contemporary world or, especially, the Global South. Scholars in postcolonial theory and criticism like Jonathon Repinecz and Sneharika Roy have creatively traced its metamorphosed salience in West Africa and India, as do I in the case of Cuba.[78] All told, thus, *The Epic of Cuba Libre* strives to contribute a new vocabulary and critical theses to the fields of myth and archetypal criticism, the poetics of history, subaltern studies, decolonial aesthetics, and revolutionary politics—not just Cuban studies.

To these ends, the book is structured thematically and recursively. Each of its five substantive chapters draws on an array of cultural artifacts to analyze the mambí as heroic archetype and the story of Cuba Libre as epic narrative, but each focuses on different instantiations of that archetype and narrative: the mambí as *Afrocubano,* as mambisa, as populist trickster, as guerrilla saboteur, and as martyr, respectively. In this way, the chapters explore racial equality and Black consciousness, gender normativity and women's empowerment, populism and the comical, the ethics and aesthetics of (epic) violence, the sacred and the catastrophic. And since *each* chapter starts from the wars themselves on to the republican and revolutionary eras and, lastly, to the 1990s "Special Period," the book reads overall recursively more so than chronologically.

Chapter 1, "The Epic Marooned," asks what becomes of the epic when its hero is not a noble or demigod, but a racially stigmatized (and enslaved) other. When Cuba's wars for independence broke out in 1868, the Liberation Army's likeliest (and most expendable) recruits were enslaved Afro-Cubans. This historic and strategic coincidence fueled what became an epic tale of racial redemption, one in which (it was said) benevolent whites and valorous Blacks fought and died together for the Patria (homeland) and expiated the sins of slavery and racism. Thereafter, the epic of Cuba Libre became that revered mythical text in which racial democracy was depicted as a consummated fact, whatever the reality of the historical present. But the emancipatory promise of racial justice it embodied and the catachrestical referent that was the Black or mulatto epic hero (not least Antonio Maceo) enlivened expectations and dissent, as, most emphatically, with the Independent Party of Color and in Black veteran Ricardo Batrell's memoir and jeremiad *Para la historia* (1912). With the Revolution of 1959, such expectations and dissent coalesced in unprecedented reforms to remediate racial inequities and a new obediential aesthetic in which not only "olive green" but also blackness was synonymous with vanguard politics and the beautiful, as evidenced in the "imperfect cinema" of Sergio Giral and the "testimonial novel" of Miguel Barnet and Esteban Montejo. Yet what racial equity had been secured between the 1960s and 1980s unraveled in the 1990s as Cuba fended for itself in the absence of a Soviet alliance and with renewed American hostilities. Few options there were except to rebuild an economy reliant on tourism (and the US dollar). Under these circumstances and as centennial years, there emerged a Black consciousness movement, expressed most notably in hip-hop music, that looked to the mambí epic as a resource for revolutionary critique and the beautification of blackness.

Chapter 2, "*¡Empínate!,*" asks what becomes of the epic when its hero is not a virile man but a woman. The mambisa's heroism was subsumed within a logic of sacrifice, except that she was to sacrifice not herself but her sons. The mambisa was understood, thus, to be first and foremost a mother, and the consummate—indeed mythical—mambisa was Mariana Grajales, whose husband and nine of her eleven sons died in the wars for independence. The wars did create possibilities for women to assume roles that defied gender norms and, thereby, to narrate new stories with new emancipatory plots, but republican-era Cuba memorialized the maternal and philanthropic mambisa in ways that reinforced, rather than subverted, patriarchal prejudices and "feminine" ascriptions. With the revolutionary war of the 1950s, women assumed empowered roles and depicted their rebellious acts as homages to their mambisa ancestors. Women's equality was affirmed in the Revolution's rhetoric and policies, and the mambisa rearticulated as a *militant* heroine. That said, so much of this era's rhetoric and iconography subsumed the mambisa (and the Cuban woman) within a logic of epic mimicry: she was "heroic" insofar as she, too, wielded a machete and willingly died for the Patria. Nor were women's affiliations with and expectations to perform domestic and caring labor so easily undone. Indeed, such labor could not be valued by epic emplotment as were martial or stately duties: the (feminized) former did not possess the drama, grandeur, or dignity that the (masculinized) latter so classically evoked. Despite these (and other) difficulties, Cuban women continued to organize and agitate for each other and to write themselves and their foremothers into the nation's epic as archetypes of rebel dignity and militant hope. With the mambisa we question, thus, the extent to which epic emplotment can accommodate an obediential aesthetic relative to a radical feminist agenda.

Chapter 3, "The Epic Travestied," explores the extent to which the comical can inflect, if not "travesty," the epic. It looks in particular to the immensely popular comic and animated series *Elpidio Valdés* (1974–2003), a series about a fictional mambí and the wars for independence. What stands out about the series, I argue, is its reliance on vernacular humor and jovial antics in ways that render it a far cry from the panegyric texts and sober tones that characterize the epic genre. I read the series as a more democratized and comically inflected epic that cleverly puts forth an alternative to the genre's tired solemnity and bourgeois chivalry. By contrast, it offers an epic hero more akin to a populist trickster than to a Spartan warrior (Maceo), saintly martyr (Martí), or "heroic guerrilla" (Che Guevara). With its idiomatic vernacular, carnivalesque ethos, multiracial solidarity, and *guajiro* (peasant) affinities, it is exemplary of an obediential aesthetic. In fact, the series' truest protagonist is not Elpidio inasmuch as "the people," whose humorous ways invite viewers to laugh not only at their foes but also at their fallible selves.

Chapter 4, "*¡Al machete!,*" reckons with the question of aestheticized violence. The classical epic is, after all, inconceivable without exceptional violence and the hero's ornate, divinely sanctioned weapon. On that count, the mambí is inconceivable without his machete. But in the hands of the subaltern, this catachrestical symbol, with historic ties to slavery and agricultural toil, becomes a populist (and, no doubt, phallic) symbol of liberation and prowess. To this end, no other symbol and no other act was as mythologized as was (and is) the mambí machete charge. The truth, however, was that the Liberation Army was at its most dangerous when not fighting in battles: the strategies of choice were to torch the colony's valuable sugar estates and to let mosquitoes (i.e., yellow fever) wreak havoc on their Iberian foes. The truth, in other words, is that the mambí was more akin to a guerrilla saboteur than to a Spartan warrior. But rare is the narrative or artifact not seduced by the bewilderment and awe that is the machete charge, and rarer still an aesthetic that did not accordingly fetishize epic violence and the martial hero.

Chapter 5, "The Epic (De)Sacralized," asks how the epic can account for deaths not convincingly narrated as "heroic" or "sacrificial." For while the quintessentially epic death is a death in combat, one was far likelier to die in a "camp of reconcentration" than on the battlefield in Cuba's wars for independence: for every mambí soldier who died in combat as many as twenty *reconcentrados* (mostly children under six years of age) died in the camps. From 1896 to1897, Spain "reconcentrated" Cuba's rural inhabitants into improvised camps where they were strategically let to die by the tens of thousands. The way in which the wars were narrated did not, however, deviate from the glorifying emplotment that was the "epic" and "revolution." The abject suffering of the reconcentrados, as mostly women and children, served to ennoble the (manly, virile, and chivalric) cause of the mambises and vilify the Patria's foes. So far from the classically heroic was the reconcentrado that rare were the postwar occasions when her grief and loss were narrated or mourned at all. It was not until the centennial 1990s that the reconcentrado was revived as a heroic "resister" and "patriot." This was meant to dignify contemporary Cubans, who, embargoed and starving, were called on to emulate their ancestors' "revolutionary intransigence." The catastrophic emplotment that the reconcentrado embodied was not, as such, called on to rethink epic emplotment and sacrifice, let alone the Revolution's own history with forced labor camps (1965–68). But closer scrutiny reveals that the reconcentrado could be read as a figure who bespeaks a will-to-live and an ethical injunction to care for life as it most precarious.

The book closes, accordingly, by asking whether the mambí has outlived his utility and whether there are worthier "moral equivalents" for twenty-first-century Cuba's (and the planet's) emancipatory futures. I do not argue against the epic or myth per se. For the struggle that lays ahead for life and a livable planet shall no doubt prove epic, and at no time in humanity's history has an anti-capitalist myth been more necessary. To that end, Cubans could "novelize" their epic and avow the kinds of heroism they (and the world) most need now. Instead of the machete-endowed mambí or bearded guerrilla, they could look to the organic farmer and internationalist doctor as the new revolutionary "vanguard" of Cuba in the twenty-first century, and this can be alloyed to the mambí's historic affinities to the rural *guajiro* and to Black heroines like Rosa la Bayamesa, the soldier and healer versed in "green medicine." Such affinities and referents could constitute the basis of new stories and a new iconography that bespeaks emancipatory plots more wedded to life, plentitude, and care than to death, sacrifice, and violence. For such edifying and empowering stories are the kind we most need in these decisive and dangerous times.

1 The Epic Marooned

Blackness and the Desire Called Cuba Libre

Poor us if we continue with this sepulchral silence!
—Ricardo Batrell & Alejandro Neninger (1907)

ARGUABLY NO other attribute is as archetypal to the epic as is the virile hero and his prowess. Gilgamesh subdued lions and stone men, Beowulf conquered the monster Grendel, and Sundiata tore a baobab tree from its roots as a child. Indeed, the epic hero is rarely a mere mortal and is never less than regal. Gilgamesh was son to the goddess Ninsun; Rama the son of Vishnu; Achilles the son of King Peleus and the sea nymph Thetis; Beowulf becomes king of the Geats; and Sundiata, son to a chieftain and a sorcerer mother, becomes emperor of Mali.

In Cuba, Antonio Maceo comes closest to the classical epic hero. His twenty-six wounds and over six hundred battles (nearly all victorious) all but defy the merely mortal. Not coincidentally is he known as the "Bronze Titan," an epithet that cast him as sturdy as a resilient metal and as otherworldly as Greek deities renowned for their colossal stature. Yet his heroic title did not refer to nobility inasmuch as his skin color. And this was no idle referent. For the Bronze Titan was mulatto at a time when racial slavery was legal (until 1886) and anti-Black racism normatively entrenched. The *mambises* were mostly men of color and, at least initially, the formerly enslaved. But rather than sully the national epic, this fact endowed it with a sense of poetic and populist justice. Maceo and the mambises came to symbolize a "moral republic" in which citizens were judged by merit and character—not by caste or color—and the wars narrated as a seductively redemptive tale in which the sins of slavery and racism were atoned for.

In the postwar "republican" years, racial justice was treated, accordingly, as an issue one need only commemorate. Yearly odes to the Bronze Titan and chronicles and memoirs of the wars lauded Cuba as a racial democracy or else did not substantively address the "race question" at all. Afro-Cubans were not pleased, that said, with the postwar "republic," as evidenced by the formation of the Partido Independiente de Color (PIC), the Independent Party of Color. Led by Black and mulatto *mambí* veterans, the PIC advocated for Afro-Cubans' rights and framed Cuba Libre as a hope not yet realized. One of its members, Ricardo Batrell, wrote the only known chronicle-cum-memoir of the War for Independence authored by a Black soldier, an account that inflected the *mambí* epic with Black valor and prophetic critique. That Cubans were not ready to heed the PIC's or Batrell's words was, however, best evidenced by the massacre of 1912, whereby Afro-Cubans' hopes for racial justice were tragically silenced.

The "Afrocubanismo" movement of the 1920s and 1930s and the Revolution of 1933 did enliven such hopes. Afro-Cuban symbols, religion, dialects, and music were incorporated into the island's culture and arts, and the Patria identified as a "mulatto nation." Yet this movement was more about white bourgeois festivity than racial justice, and the Revolution of 1933 largely stifled. It was not until the Revolution of 1959 that racial justice was substantively addressed. Under the auspices of the "bearded ones" (*barbudos*), various reforms and color-blind policies were called on to enact a socialist republic in which racism was, allegedly at least, eradicated. To be a revolutionary—and, later, a communist—meant to be anti-racist. The story of Cuba Libre was not inconsequential to any of this. A series of artistic and literary innovations projected *Cuba Rebelde* (Rebel Cuba) as indebted to the mambí epic and, more exactly, Black resilience and insurgency. The mambí was no longer a slave liberated by benevolent masters inasmuch as heir to the emancipatory desires and rebel spirit of the *cimarrón* (maroon). In works such as the heterodox Marxism of Walterio Carbonell, the "imperfect cinema" of Sergio Giral, and the "testimonial novel" of Miguel Barnet and Esteban Montejo, blackness was recast as the revolutionary vanguard and Africanness as a decolonial aesthetic. And such cultural politics echoed in Cuba's internationalist politics—not least its "African epic" in Angola and its cachet as headquarters to the Organization of Solidarity with the People of Asia, Africa, and Latin America (OSPAAAL), popularly known as the Tricontinental.[1]

With the fall of the Soviet Union (1989–91), however, socialist Cuba found itself adrift in a world where history had come to an end, so to speak. No longer able to capitalize on Soviet subsidies and subject to renewed US hostility, Cuba entered its "Special Period in Times of Peace"—a period marked not only by hunger, scarcity, and disenchantment but also racialized inequality. In these fraught years, patriotic pleas resounded hollower than ever. Against this, Afro-Cuban artists and intellectuals curated their own narratives and looked to the mambí (not the barbudo) as an archetype of emancipatory desire and Black dignity and to hip-hop (not *nueva trova*) as an aesthetic to voice Black consciousness and critique.

Thy Brother's Keeper

No one knows the etymology of the word *mambí*—at least not conclusively so.[2] What is known with certainty is that in the mouths of Spanish loyalists and soldiers *mambí* was a racial epithet, a term meant to evoke and jeer at the blackness of the Cuban rebel soldiers. Its closest equivalent was not thereby "insurgent" or "bandit" inasmuch as "African savage." And this was no trivial accusation in a colony so nearby to Haiti and the Haitian Revolution (1791–1804). In the Atlantic world, the Haitian Revolution was narrated in apocalyptic (not epic) terms. The sheer name "Haiti" sufficed to conjure up the slaughter of white men and defilement of white women by godless Africans.[3] Spaniards were, thus, keen to use a racially laden rhetoric of "another Haiti" to discredit the Cuban Republic in Arms. They spoke of a "black conspiracy" and a "race war," of "negro hordes" and "runaway slaves" driven by vile impulses. And such rhetoric did not fall on deaf ears, especially in a colony where slavery was still legal and roughly one-half the population "colored."

Yet in the midst of these wars, what was once a derogatory term (*mambí*) meant to arouse racial animosity became synonymous in Cuban vernacular with racial equality and fraternity. It was the Liberation Army, after all, that most compellingly embodied it. Its soldiers were not racially segregated—at least not by mandate—and as many as 60 percent of its noncommissioned officers (e.g., sergeants) and 40 percent of its commissioned officers (e.g., captains, colonels) were men of color.[4] In fact, by the 1890s Brigadier General Antonio Maceo, a mulatto, and his brother, Major General José Maceo, enjoyed a multiracial loyalty and esteem across the island and in exile communities that, as Ada Ferrer has said, "in the United States would have been rare in local contexts and unthinkable at the national level."[5] It was by virtue of these wars that Afro-Cubans came to be identified not as slaves or colonial subjects but as *libertos* (freemen), *ciudadanos* (citizens), and *mambises*. And it was this metamorphosis—historically unprecedented and, to an extent, socially unthinkable—that endowed the wars with a moral grandeur that only words such as "sublime" and "epic" could convey.

As the story goes: October 10, 1868, marks the first "transcendent" event in the epic of Cuba Libre. That day, at his sugar estate La Demajagua, Carlos Manuel de Céspedes declared Cuba free. This he did to an audience of his own slaves, who were likewise declared free. The next day he and fellow rebels led an assault on the local town, Yara, where the first casualties fell in what came to be known as the Ten Years' War. From its earliest days, thus, Black liberation and racial fraternity were inextricably bound to the collective desire called *Cuba Libre*. This was the case not only in word but also in deed. Within days of Yara, Céspedes and his forces seized the town of Bayamo and reconstituted its town council, appointing white creoles, Spaniards, and—for the first time in the nation's history—two men of color: José García, a bricklayer, and Manuel Muñoz, a musician.[6] Indeed, in due course men of color came to count among the Republic in Arms' most highly regarded advocates, and the Liberation Army in particular was touted as the embryo of a racially democratic Cuba to come. This gave way to a romantically emplotted narrative in which war and collective sacrifice expiated the sins of slavery and racism. If Cuba was not yet liberated from the yoke of colonialism, Cubans at least had rid themselves of racial prejudice and, in its stead, embraced patriotic camaraderie.

Yet only fitfully and falteringly was this ever so. In its earliest years, the Republic in Arms' leaders issued cautious decrees for slavery's abolition—"gradual and indemnified"—and the Liberation Army was closer to an "apprenticeship" system (*patrocinado*) than to a racially democratic institution. Freed slaves (libertos) were reassigned to new "masters" (*amos*) and expected to fight without pay.[7] And while this policy ended officially in 1870, libertos continued to be de facto menial laborers and subjected to punitive measures akin to slavery (e.g., stocks, flogging).[8]

That said, it was no small irony that Cuba Libre's most beloved and loyal soldiers proved to be men of color. If the Ten Years' War was initiated by the Grito de Yara (1868), it ended with the equally "sublime" Protest of Baraguá (1878). In other words, if it was initiated by Céspedes, it was carried to its most radical conclusions by Maceo. The 1878 truce known as the Treaty of Zajón was rejected by Antonio Maceo and his cadre of mostly Black and mulatto officers (e.g., Flor Crombet, Guillermo Moncada, Quintín Banderas). That treaty, as Maceo saw it, offered only palliatives.[9] He and his soldiers would not lay down their arms until the "indispensable provisions of independence and the abolition of slavery" were honored.[10] Spain conceded neither. So Maceo kept his word and renewed hostilities, an act that has lived on in nationalist lore and historiography as the Protest of Baraguá.

In doing so, Maceo, the colonial subject and man of color, had faced off with the Spanish crown and its Governor General. He also defied the white aristocratic delegates of the Republic at Arms. Cubans could, thereby, look to the mulatto commander and his multiracial forces as the hallmark of patriotic valor and anti-racist integrity. Yet so, too, could that commander and his forces constitute a liability. Although Maceo would be "absolved" by history, he and his fellow officers were controversial in their day. Many white Cubans, especially landowners, were not eager to fund or fight in a revolution headed, militarily at least, by officers of color. And talk of a "black conspiracy" and "race war" only heightened in the wake of Baraguá. To wit, when war was renewed in 1879, Commander Calixto García forbid Antonio Maceo to hold military office. Granted, it was a strategically informed choice. García had hoped to dispel talk of "another Haiti." But it was a costly choice: the Liberation Army fought (and lost) without its most beloved and formidable field general.

What was clear by the 1880s and early 1890s, thus, was that if Cubans wanted to wage an effective war they had to reorganize themselves discursively and ideologically. That is to say, they had to tout and engender multiracial unity as much as allay fears of a "race war." One strategy was to portray the Black soldier as a heroic yet subordinate and innocuous patriot. Commander Máximo Gómez's "El Viejo Eduá, o mi último asistente" (1892) was exemplary to this end. An elegiac account of his most trusted and admirable of assistants in the Ten Years' War, "El Viejo Eduá" tells the story of the elderly Eduardo—Eduá for short. Eduá, a slave on a coffee farm, was "taken" by the revolution and assigned to the general. Gómez tells us that he was a natural leader (to other liberto assistants) and a most proficient aid. He goes as far as to comment on Eduá's "agile movements" and the "care and tidiness" with which he performed the most mundane tasks (e.g., making coffee). But above all, he is loyal. Eduá declares himself ready to leave aside his own wife and children to serve under Gómez even after the war's end.[11]

Not all accounts were of elderly and docile Cubans of color. One of the "episodes" in Manuel de la Cruz's popular *Episodios de la revolución cubana* (1892) tells of Fidel Céspedes, a Black soldier nearly as wide and tall as a "royal palm" and endowed with the "vigor of a bull." Céspedes was "fierce in battle," always at the lead of charges, and feared by the enemy. A deserter, however, led the enemy to Céspedes, who enacted his last epic stand. Céspedes cut off the head of his horse—"You won't enjoy him!"—and, with machete in hand, dared his adversaries to fight him one at a time. They dared not. Instead, they shot him.[12] With Fidel Céspedes the mambí as

Black soldier was thus rendered sheer bodily prowess and violent capacity. Neither his ethical sensibility nor his political desires were relevant, let alone narrated. What mattered was his robust body and the ferocity with which he served the Patria. That his surname is that of the nation's "Father" (i.e., Carlos Manuel de Céspedes) was no petty detail either. Symbolically at least, it situated him as son and subaltern to a respectable white leader.

The capable and loyal Black soldier under white auspices was nothing shy of a motif in this literature. Other well publicized anecdotes included that of Captain Edmundo Agüero and his (nameless) "mulatto assistant." Agüero's troops were captured and offered amnesty, provided they pledge their loyalty to Spain. Agüero and his assistant refused. "You're a young man and don't have to bear the responsibilities and duties that I must," the "heroic master" said to his assistant. But his "redeemed and dignified servant" replied, "No Captain, your fate is my fate; we shall die together."[13] Ramón Roa's "The Blacks of the Revolution" (1890) recounted a similar dynamic with the story of José Antonio Legón. A former slave, Legón fought in the war with "astounding agility" and "audacity." A Spanish commander offered him amnesty and bounties to defect, but José Antonio replied: "When my master—who raised me and who was good—was dying, he told me: 'José Antonio, never stop being Cuban', and the poor man left this world for another. Now I comply by being Cuban until the end[. . .] You may kill me if you wish." A few months later, he died in combat.[14] The reader (or *lectura,* listener[15]) was left thus with the image not only of an exemplary death but also an exemplary Afro-Cuban: he who abides by his white master's will—even in the latter's earthly absence! Valiant and skilled yet always under the auspices of respectable whites—how could one justifiably fear a "race war"?

The specter of a "race war" haunted the rebels' legitimacy and their army's efficacy. Black commander Guillermo Moncada was said to "kill every white man who fell into hands and to keep women (white and otherwise) in 'harems.'"[16] Quintín Banderas's "black infantry" was said to wear nose rings and mercilessly plunder any village on its warpath.[17] Such accusations were not taken lightly by Cuba Libre's intellectuals, Black and white alike. Black journalist and civil rights leader Juan Gualberto Gómez wrote a rigorous rebuttal to the specter of "another Haiti." He noted five key differences: (1) Haiti's Black Africans hailed from warlike tribes in Senegal and Dahomey, whereas Cuba's were drawn from the "gentler" dwellers of the Congo; (2) the slaves who revolted in Haiti were nearly all African born (*bosal*), whereas Cuba's Blacks were mostly Cuban born; (3) the ratio of persons of color to whites in Haiti was 24:1, whereas it stood at 1:2 in

Cuba; (4) Spanish slavery was (allegedly) milder than the French variety, making Cubans of color less resentful; and (5) in Haiti it was the metropolis that abolished slavery against the will of local masters, whereas in Cuba it was the local masters who "freed" their slaves against the will of the imperial metropolis.[18] Gómez thereby rendered Cubans of color relatively harmless and morally indebted—to their former slaveholders no less.

Arguably, no other voice was as crucial in these years as was Cuba Libre's intellectual leader José Martí. When the Ten Years' War broke out, Martí was a mere adolescent, son to a Canary Islander mother and Valencian father. Yet already his ardor for Cuba Libre was evident. In the early months of the war he wrote his play *Abdala*. Albeit a relatively clichéd "national epic," the play was, as Roberto González Echevarría has said, allegorically provocative.[19] A Nubian warrior, Abdala, is summoned to rescue his homeland from foreign invaders. Against his mother's wishes, he answers Nubia's call. Abdala stirs his warriors with patriotic speeches and runs off to battle. In the final act, a wounded Abdala is carried back from battle, where he utters his last words: "Nubia is victorious! I die happy: death/Little does it matter, for I was able to save her . . . /Oh, how sweet it is to die when one dies/Struggling audaciously to defend the patria!"[20] That Martí foregrounded a Black protagonist and an ancient African kingdom was no idle choice. At odds with the rhetoric of "another Haiti," it allegorically (and *catachrestically*) conferred nobility and valor onto the mostly Black and mulatto rebels in Cuba's far east.

Years later, the exiled poet and patriot had become Cuba Libre's most influential orator and organizer, with a sense for the strategic value of unity. His 1892 essay "My Race" referred to race as a "sin against humanity," one that has sullied our ability to judge men in terms of their "affinity of character" rather than their "affinity of color." Such affinity of character was evidenced in the Ten Years' War, he said, where the valorous and the "self-abnegating" fought and died side by side, regardless of color.[21] Martí then addressed the People of Cuba in the widely circulated "Manifesto of Montecristi" (1895). He "indignantly" denied that the revolution was tantamount to a "race war." If there was any hatred to be dealt with it was the white's projected fear of Black Cubans: "Only those who hate the black see hatred in the black." Vouching for the "intelligence and virtue" of the Black Cuban, the Manifesto reassured its reader that it was upon his "shoulders" that the Republic entrusted its safety.[22] Yet never did the Manifesto entrust to Cubans of color the Republic's policies or governance. One could only infer that their lot was to die (and kill) heroically for the Patria.

Worse still were those accounts that portrayed Cubans of color as indebted to whites. In the interim war years, fierce polemics ensued to this end. Manuel Sanguily, colonel and veteran of the Ten Years' War, said of the Black Cuban: "His slave's shackles were broken by the bones of two generations of Cubans, innocent before History and deserving of the love and gratitude of the redeemed." But not all Cubans of color took kindly to such paternalistic ovations. In 1893, the premier periodical of the Cuban Black press, *La Igualdad,* published the article "Por justicia y patriotismo." It asked rhetorically: "Did men of color not figure in the Revolution? Did they not lend eminent services? Did they not distinguish themselves as much as the whites? Did they not shed their blood with as much abnegation? Were they not as perseverant? Were they not the last to surrender?"[23] Sanguily retorted: "Even if there had been thousands of men of color alongside the whites in the Revolution, the origin, preparation, initiative, program, and direction of the Revolution, that is the Revolution in its character, essence, and aspirations, was exclusively the work of whites."[24] What Sanguily failed to stipulate was that this was due to racist prejudice and discrimination. Save as war fodder, Afro-Cubans were not called on to envision, much less adjudicate, the initiatives and institutions for a Cuba Libre.

These racially inflected antagonisms were never truly reconciled in the War for Independence (1895–98). In fact, it is hard not to conclude that these civilian elites were eager to rid themselves of commanders of color and the populist social justice they incarnated.[25] The Republic in Arms was in the hands of wealthy and upper-middle-class whites: its president, vice president, ambassador to the United States, nearly all its assembly members, and the secretaries of war, the treasury, the interior, and foreign relations. It was this cadre of "revolutionaries" who recklessly endangered the lives of Brigadier General Antonio Maceo and Mayor General José Maceo. It was they who stacked the Liberation Army's officer corps with wealthy white Cubans. And it was they who reached out to Americans to militarily intervene on the island, an intervention that came in 1898 and would bewilder the epic of Cuba Libre for years to come.

Whiteness and Posterity

As of 1898, no hero was more venerable to Cubans than was the mambí. But this could hardly be said of Americans, for whom the mambí was a lazy ingrate or an addendum to their "splendid little war."[26] The war was now known as the "Spanish-American War," as if Cubans had no say or relevance. And this was not altogether untrue. Once American soldiers were on Cuban soil, the mambises were pulled from combat and sent to the rear. They were neither delegates to armistice negotiations nor signatories to the Treaty of Paris, which ceded Cuba (and Puerto Rico, Guam, and the Philippines) to the United States. And when the Spanish flag was lowered at Havana's El Morro on January 1, 1899, Cubans were mere bystanders as the US Stars and Stripes rose in lieu of Cuba's tricolor "lone star."[27]

A more accurate account would point out that Americans won the war so handedly precisely because their Spanish foe had been bled dry by years of war against tenacious mambises in Cuba and *katipuneros* in the Philippines.[28] Yellow fever, scorched sugar estates, and the expenses to deploy and garrison well over two hundred thousand soldiers had taken their toll on Spain. But Americans chose to explain their war (and Cuba's ills) in terms of Anglo-Saxon superiority. Cubans, it was said, were plagued with "Negroid" laziness, superstition, and promiscuity as well as "Latinate" fatalism and fanaticism.[29] When asked by journalists whether Cubans were fit for self-government, US general William Shafter colorfully remarked, "Why, those people are no more fit for self-government than gunpowder is for hell." His colleague general Samuel Young was no less unequivocal: "They are no more capable of self-government than the savages of Africa."[30]

What Americans most feared was that the mambises were indeed mostly of African descent and, all the more ominously, armed. It was no accident that the occupying forces wasted little time to disarm and disband the Liberation Army. Soldiers were offered a meager bounty for their rifles and, later, a certificate of service (i.e., discharge papers). Very few were reenlisted into the new army, rural guard, or police force. Employment was now dependent on criteria such as literacy, being vetted by "well-known citizens," and the ability to bankroll one's own uniform, horse, and equipment—strictures that imperiled Afro-Cubans' odds for employment. The new forces did, admittedly, enlist some Afro-Cubans, and units were racially integrated—a choice that went against US recommendations. Yet Black and mulatto soldiers were largely restricted to the lower echelons, and the new army a hollow shell of its emancipatory precursor.[31]

Instead, the state apparatus in postwar Cuba stayed in the hands of white Cubans and, ironically enough, Spaniards. The United States reinstated many of the former colony's civil servants, and once empowered, the new Republic actively sought out to "whiten" the island. To this end, no fewer than 750,000 Spaniards migrated to the island between 1902 and 1931. Cuba's elite social strata had hoped to avow their "Latinness" as a nationalistic reply to their "Anglo" wards. Yet to do so was, simultaneously, to disavow Cuba's blackness. As elsewhere in the Americas, the Black subject in Cuba was a socially stigmatized subject that aroused anxiety, if not terror, in whites. Aside from the fear of "another Haiti" or Black conspiracy, white Cubans and Spanish immigrants were no less fearful that Afro-Cuban religions such as Palo Monte and Santería (Lucumí) or cultural practices such as *comparsas* (processions) would sully their "civilized" ways of life. Of comparsas, Liberal Party leader Ramón Vasconcelos said: "Go to the wilderness, where you can unleash your rapture and obscenity without offending the sight and refinement of those who want to live in a civilized society, not in an African village[. . . .] As long as the drum exists, there will be barbarians."[32]

Nevertheless, the myth of racial democracy lived on in postwar Cuba, and no other narrative was as instrumental as the mambí epic. The Ten Years' War continued to be invoked as that redemptive (white) act that ended slavery and "liberated" Cuba from racism. None other than José Martí had said: "It was the revolution that returned the black race to humanity, and that made the dreadful fact [of slavery] disappear . . . She was the mother, she was the saint, she was the one that seized the master's whip, she was the one that lifted the black man from his ignominy and embraced him—she, the Cuban revolution."[33] No other evidence was more conclusive than the Liberation Army itself, which lawmakers and historians extolled as an institution in which "equality proven by virtues and talents" became the new normative order.[34] Such "adorations" did not, however, reflect postwar Cuban reality. Black intellectual and Cuba Libre organizer Rafael Serra voiced a salient grievance when he said: "Unfortunate are Cuban blacks if all they will get as a just remuneration for their sacrifices for the independence and freedom of Cuba is to listen to the [national] Bayamés anthem and to the fictitious adoration devoted to the memory of our illustrious martyrs. No, my brothers, we deserve justice, and we should no longer continue to encourage a humiliating and ridiculous patriotism."[35]

And discourage they did. With so many illustrious veterans and martyrs to their credit and the rhetoric of a Cuba "with all and for the good of all," Afro-Cubans had bolstered their esteem and expectations for life in the postwar Republic. Yet their services rendered to the Patria were met with no antidiscriminatory laws or reparations, few officeholders, high unemployment, and their lands sold off to American corporations. That Afro-Cubans were discontent was best evidenced by the formation of the Partido Independiente de Color (the Independent Party of Color, or PIC).

Founded in 1908 and led by mambí veterans Pedro Ivonnet (who fought with Antonio Maceo) and Evaristo Estenoz (aide to General Quitín Banderas), the PIC advocated for Afro-Cuban rights and a progressive agenda that included land redistribution, an eight-hour workday, and universal higher education. They registered thousands of members throughout the island, especially in historically Black Oriente.[36] Yet "what was sensible politically," as Alejandro de la Fuente has noted, "was unacceptable ideologically."[37] Their choice to identify with and advocate for Cubans of color was sacrilege to the myth of a racial democracy. The established parties and the Cuban press conjured anew the specter of a Black conspiracy and, in 1910, outlawed the PIC on the grounds that it was "racist" and its leaders seditious. When in 1912 its leaders organized an armed protest to relegalize the PIC, the Cuban army and vigilante mobs brutally repressed and killed no fewer than two thousand Afro-Cubans in Oriente.[38] The fact that the massacre was authorized and led by many white mambí veterans was bitter testament to how far Cubans had come.[39]

A Prophetic Cry

The tragedy on which (white) nationalist Cubans fixated was not, however, 1912 inasmuch as 1898 and the Platt Amendment. In the wake of 1898, Cubans looked to their history, as mambí general José Miró Argenter said, through a "veil of melancholy."[40] Hundreds of thousands had died in the independence wars only to see the Patria handed from one imperial sovereign to the next. Cuba's nominal independence (declared May 20, 1902) did little to dispel this sentiment. The new republic's Constitution was, after all, haunted by the so-called Platt Amendment. Named after US senator Orville Platt, the amendment stipulated that the United States could intervene in Cuban affairs at its discretion. And intervene they did. The island was again occupied by US armed forces from 1906 to 1909.

Hardly was it any wonder, thus, that Cubans were eager to inscribe their nationhood within the symbolic, if not material, economy. Cubans were called on to commemorate their most hallowed martyrs (i.e., Céspedes, Maceo, Martí), and October 10 (Grito de Yara) and February 24 (Grito de Baire) were declared national holidays. Streets, parks, schools, clinics, community centers, placards, and monuments were dedicated to national and locally beloved war heroes.[41] And within due course a series of war diaries, memoirs, chronicles, and, later, scholarly histories were published.[42] Those written by mambí martyrs and veterans were particularly coveted. As irreproducible texts that bear witness to a history of mythical proportions, they enjoyed a singular, if not sacral, quality in Cuban letters as *literatua de campaña,* which can be roughly translated as "literature of the wars for independence" or, more freely, "testimonial narratives." These were no trifling texts or speech acts. To recall those who wagered their lives for Cuba Libre could be read, however elliptically, as an indictment of those who betrayed that collective desire and a cry to emulate the heroic mambí. Only rarely, however, was a testimonial memoir used to reckon with the unredeemed project of racial justice. Even rarer was a testimonial written by a rank-and-file Black soldier. Nearly all such works were authored by white officers who either did not speak substantively about racial issues or reiterated the myth of racial democracy.[43]

But such was not the case with Ricardo Batrell's *Para la historia* (1912). Batrell joined the mambí army in 1895 and fought throughout the entire war. He was not quite sixteen years of age and hailed from sugar-rich Matanzas, a province that accounted for nearly half of the island's sugar output. At war's outset, he and his kin were illiterate manual laborers and field hands, like so many other seasonally employed (Black) cane cutters. After the war, he was employed as a police officer and would pursue a politically active career. He took part in the revolt of 1906, was protégé to Juan Gualberto Gómez of the Liberal Party, and later was an active member of the PIC. This latter affiliation would land him in jail twice, in the highly volatile years 1910 (when the PIC was banned) and 1912 (the massacre). We know very little about his life thereafter.[44]

Batrell also taught himself to read and write, thanks to which we have the rare testimonial that is *Para la historia.* The testimonial is driven by four themes: Black valor, racial prejudice, racial democracy, and providential justice. Batrell tells us that his regiment was (by circumstances) nearly all Black and is said to have fought and defeated more Spanish troops than any other mambí regiment in Matanzas. He "authenticates" this statement with an epilogue that lists the fifty-one battles in which he fought, and throughout the text the reader encounters a fair share of machete charges and what Batrell called the "great feast of Cuba Libre." But the reader is also reminded that such valor was not always recognized or properly rewarded. Batrell took care to list each of the honorable officers who fell prey to their racist brethren: Cajizote, Simeón Sánchez, Ceballo, El Tuerto Mato, Severindo Ricardo, "etc." If a Black officer did not have a white superior to vouch for him, he could very well end up demoted or executed. Wrongly accused of conspiracy, Cajizote had to flee the mambí army and surrender to the Spanish—a "disgrace." Other injustices included acts that needlessly endangered Batrell and his regiment, such as assigning him as a scout or depriving his unit of munitions for "no other reason . . . except for racial prejudice."[45]

The text, nevertheless, reassures the reader that Cuba Libre was once a reality, not a vacuous slogan. In this regard, no other story was more poignant than that of Colonel Dantin and his "black assistant" Ciriaco. An ambush left Colonel Dantin wounded. The sturdy Ciriaco carried his commander off but, in the act, was mortally wounded by enemy fire. Colonel Dantin mustered enough strength to pull Ciriaco out of harm's way, but it was too late: the "self-sacrificing" Ciriaco bled to death. Dantin survived. It is at this point in the text that Batrell interjects and addresses his audience directly: "Isn't it true, reader, that this scene inspires us to believe that humanity was perfected in such a display of democracy?" In so doing Batrell renders Cuba Libre synonymous with racial democracy, but he does so in ways that subvert the Ten Years' War narrative of benevolent whites who "liberated" the Black slaves. Here it is the Black soldier who is honored as the "devoted and heroic savior" and whose "memory will never die."[46]

Indeed, one could read *Para la historia* as an encomium to the Black mambí, albeit with odes to racial fraternity: "Black and white embraced each other, and so together they celebrated victory; and together they fell under the enemy's steel."[47] But as Mark Sanders has recommended, the text is most compellingly read as a jeremiad.[48] *Para la historia* does not render racial democracy a consummated fact. Rather, it laments its absence in postwar Cuba: the "soul is saddened when the cause of freedom is politicized the way it is today by a large number of those who didn't purify their souls in the Revolution." The "heroism and valor of those with dark skin" has either been forgotten or tepidly honored. Yet for Batrell such injustices shall not go unpunished. His text is filled with stories of immoral acts that end in calamity for the offender. And it is in this regard that it reads more akin to a biblical jeremiad than a mere memoir or chronicle. Take, for instance, the case of the slain goat. Against a mother's pleas, Batrell's fellow soldiers ate a poor rural family's "invaluable" goat. The morally flawless Batrell refused: "Señora, you have my promise that I will not eat any of that animal, and I deeply regret that my comrades have not listened to me." Batrell's comrades ridiculed him, but it was they who rued the day. Two of the soldiers died within days, their bodies covered in "filthy worms." Two others were killed in combat, one of them hacked to death by machetes. And the commanding officer would later surrender to the Spanish, living out the rest of his days with the "sad stigma the penitent of that era bore: *Presentado* [one who surrendered]."[49] This and other such events are not random anecdotes. They are crucial to the text's moral force. Batrell's epilogue included a list of battles fought and those who served (and died) honorably. It also recounted the fates of dishonorable characters. The notoriously cruel general Avelino Rosa, we are told, was dragged to death from the tail of a horse. Events of this kind "prove to humans that there is a higher power."[50] *Para la historia* is not as such a romantically emplotted epic inasmuch as a prophetically emplotted jeremiad. And all the more hauntingly so, since it was published the same year as the PIC massacre.

Batrell's was not the only lament. Mestizo troubadour Sindo Garay's "Clave a Maceo" was a lyrical commentary on the sad state of affairs that was postwar Cuba. Its chorus reads: "If Maceo were to come back to life/and contemplate his Patria anew/surely shame would kill him."[51] Known by the sobriquet the Bronze Titan, Antonio Maceo was taken to be the embodiment not only of the epic warrior but also racial democracy. And this quite literally so: he was mulatto, racial fraternity incarnate. Yet the early republic and its epic memory were entrusted to a state keen to "whiten" the island and an intelligentsia keen to avow its "Latinness." In this context, Maceo could just as readily constitute a racial enigma that aroused anxiety more so than harmony. At no other point was this more emphatically the case than in late 1899 when three (white) scientists examined Maceo's exhumed cadaver. In their published report, *El cráneo de Maceo* (1900), the scientists laid out their meticulous "osteometrics" and concluded that Maceo was a "truly superior man." His characteristically Black limb proportions met with a cranial capacity associated with whites.[52] In other words, the study "scientifically" corroborated not so much Maceo's superiority inasmuch as a well-established racist credo, namely that blackness equates brawn and whiteness intellect. As case in point: no one was as curious about the anatomical peculiarities of José Martí's exhumed cadaver, precisely because the cranial capacity of the "Apostle" was never in doubt.

It was not at all unusual to affirm Maceo's blackness only in the end to disavow it. In her commemorative speech of December 7, 1936, congressional member María Gómez Carbonell said of the Bronze Titan: "The *Illiad* would have been more beautiful if it had as its model men like Maceo; bronze on the outside and inside, the purest of marble, without a sole black vein."[53] Indeed, rarely was the mambí not subsumed within Hellenic referents (e.g., the Homeric epic, Spartans) and even rarer was

Antonio Maceo Monument in Havana. (CC, photograph by Randolf Croft, 2010)

whiteness not a symbol of purity, intellect, or grace. In 1905, José Martí was memorialized in immaculate white marble. The Havana central park monument cast the Cuban "Maestro" as biologically pure, not a sole black vein to speak of. In 1916, Antonio Maceo was memorialized in a dark pewter monument near Havana's seaside promenade known as the Malecón. Here an epic grandeur of brawn and soldierly valor stand out: Maceo with machete and astride a horse that rears. But the angelic muses and citizenry that populate the monument's base are decidedly Greco-Roman, an aesthetic that did not convey the *mestizaje* or *mulatez* (mulattoness) of the Cuban polity—let alone extol the blackness of the mambises.

A Grotesque Phantasm

However unexpectedly, Cubans came to more freely identify as a "mulatto" nation in the 1920s and 1930s. Nicolás Guillén's "Ballad of Two Grandfathers" (1934) was exemplary to this end. It opens:

Shadows which only I see,
My two grandfathers escort me.
A bone-tipped spear,
A drum of hide and wood:
My black grandfather.
A ruff on a broad neck,
A warrior's gray armament:
My white grandfather.[54]

It is not a harmonious relation that Guillén poetically invokes. Africa and grandfather Taita Facundo are indexes of those who have suffered abductions and enslavement: "So many ships, so many ships! / So many Blacks, so many Blacks? So much resplendent cane!" Whereas Don Federico, with his "warrior's gray armament," symbolizes the conquistador and colonialism. They are what Cuba (and the mulatto Guillén) viscerally embodies:

I bring them together.
Federico!
Facundo! They embrace.
They sigh. They
raise their sturdy heads;
both of equal size,
beneath the high stars;
both of equal size,
black and white yearning,
both of equal size
they cry out, dream, weep, and sing
They dream, weep, and sing,
They cry and sing.
They sing![55]

For Cubans to identify as "mulatto," their Africanness could no longer be disavowed. And so it was in the 1920s and 1930s. In this era African-derived religions, dialects, symbols, rhythms, and dance were popularly culled and consumed. Yet rarely were such appropriations as dignifying as Guillén's. As Robin Moore has argued, many "vanguard" white artists merely reproduced folkloric and stereotypical portrayals of Africanness (i.e., as sensual, primitive), whereas others cashed in on Afro-Cuban music's commercial viability to middle-class Cubans and American tourists.[56] That said, for Cuba's Africanness to be so openly validated was not socially or politically inconsequential. Blackness could come to signify oppositional cultures and consciousness. This was the case with the Cuban Communist Party (PCC), which collaborated with and advocated for the island's unemployed and its exploited sugar workers, both of which were mostly Afro-Cuban and West Indian immigrants. The fact that critics depicted the PCC as a "Negro party" speaks volumes.[57] To its credit, moreover, it was not a racially paternalistic hierarchy. The PCC's secretary general (for twenty-eight years) was the mulatto Blas Roca and the head of the island's most formidable labor federation was Black PCC militant Lázaro Peña. After the viciously repressed PIC, the militant and multiracial PCC was the republic's closest heir to the Liberation Army. Elites and liberals feared its anti-racist, anti-imperialist, and populist politics, which called for a new Cuba in which Afro-Cubans would be empowered materially and politically, not just culturally or artistically.[58]

That search for a "new Cuba" coalesced in the revolutionary situation that was the year 1933, when President Gerardo Machado was ousted by a "sergeant's revolt," radicalized students, and a generalized strike. A depressed economy and Machado's increasingly repressive politics had taken their toll, as had the Mexican and Russian Revolutions buoyed expectations. What came of it was the storied "one hundred days of government" under University of Havana professor Dr. Ramón Grau San Martín. A precarious coalition authorized women's right to vote, the eight-hour workday, and a minimum wage; instituted a new Ministry of Labor, and abolished the notorious Platt Amendment. Others, especially the communists, had more radical hopes to nationalize key industries and institute affirmative action laws. But the liberal Grau and his radical allies were ousted by a US-friendly coalition led by Fulgencio Batista, who was promoted from sergeant to colonel and, later, to president in the wake of 1933. The racially ambiguous Batista did cause some unease. Rumors were conjured anew of a Black conspiracy, but this was sheer hyperbole, if not racist hysteria. One index of whether racial justice was on the agenda in the new "Cuba for Cubans" was the fact that of the seventy-six delegates sent to the constitutional assembly of 1939, only five were Cubans of color (three of them communists). Not surprisingly did the Constitution of 1940 only tepidly avow a color-blind equality, which is to say it dared not include antidiscriminatory clauses, as the PCC delegates had insisted.[59]

Granted, it was easier than ever to evoke the mambí epic as, at last, consummated. With the Platt Amendment abolished (1933) and a decidedly populist Constitution ratified (1940), Cubans could indulge in the fantasy of independence at last conquered and collective welfare soon to come. But the years that ensued proved otherwise. Cuba's economy was no less dependent on US capital, and its new Constitution a farce. Neither land reform nor health care, education nor racial equality were pursued with any real vigor. Batista's coup in 1952 only aggravated this scandal: Congress was dissolved, the Constitution suspended, elections cancelled, the press censored, and rebels tortured. As poet Cintio Vitier put it in 1958: "It is obvious that within a very few years of the founding of the Republic, what remained of the political inspiration of the founders . . . was hardly anything more than a grotesque phantasm. Today, not even that."[60]

A Bearded Script

The years 1952–58 were not, however, years in which a "veil of melancholy" reigned. They were years, as Lillian Guerra has pointed out, in which martyrdom and messianic justice abounded and in which the mambí epic was as lively a referent as ever. It would be in the words and deeds of Fidel Castro and his Movimiento 26 de Julio that it echoed most emphatically. When asked to answer for their attack on the Moncada barracks in 1953, a twenty-seven-year-old Castro said it was an act faithful to the Titan Maceo and "intellectually authored" by the Apostle Martí.[61] History had "absolved" the mambises, and so, too, would it absolve his Movimiento Revolucionario 26 de Julio (MR 26-7).

Castro and his comrades deftly inscribed themselves in the mambí epic and its symbolic economy. They waged their war from the historically rebellious Oriente and named their newsletter *El Cubano Libre,* after Antonio Maceo's 1895 newsletter: "Today *El Cubano Libre* . . . is the voice of those of us . . . who struggle to reclaim the liberty that forms the legacy that the *mambises* bequeathed to us."[62] Arguably no other act was as symbolically dense as was their historic reenactment of Antonio Maceo's "Invasion," as Che Guevara's and Camilo Cienfuegos's columns marched westward to Havana with torched sugarcane in their wake and straw hats on their heads. The resemblances were so uncanny that when the *barbudos* (bearded ones) marched into Havana they were welcomed as reincarnated mambises. *Times of Havana* columnist Carlos Todd referred to them as "living embodiments of the famed *mambises* . . . a reincarnation of the men led by Maceo, Máximo Gómez, and Calixto García, bearded, long-haired, bristling with bandoliers and rifles and carbines."[63]

Whatever their clever mimicry or symbolic affiliations, the barbudos did not *phenotypically* resemble the mambises: Fidel Castro, Raul Castro,

Camilo Cienfuegos, Che Guevara, Huber Matos, Vilma Espín, Haydée Santamaría, and other key leaders all were white.[64] And this did not altogether cohere with the nationalist epic and its archetypal heroes. That said, at the time blackness and Afro-Cubans were not synonymous with revolutionary politics. They were more closely associated with the dictator Fulgencio Batista. The racially ambiguous Batista was known to court Cuba's societies of color and the Black electorate. So, too, were his armed forces well stocked with Black and mulatto sergeants and junior officers.[65] But Batista's reign did little to alter the fact that the prisoners, slum dwellers, and unemployed of Cuba were disproportionately Black, and the island's university graduates, landowners, business elites, and national assembly members mostly white.

All the same, if their "olive green aesthetic" and phenotypically white cadre did not unerringly resemble the Liberation Army of yesteryear, it was not lost on these bearded rebels that the collective desire called Cuba Libre was as much about racial justice as it was national sovereignty. Nor was it lost on them that they had Black comrades in their midst. Fidel Castro's Rebel Army was an estimated one-third Afro-Cuban. But these soldiers, presumably "heroes," were not so warmly welcomed by Havana's urban white elites. Such elites would rue the day. The island's finest beaches, hotels, clubs, central parks, and schools had been effectively reserved for them. But within short order the Revolution waged a crusade against segregated institutions and recreational sites. Citizens and elites were expected to defer to the letter and spirit of the new revolutionary times (and laws). All such cultural centers and leisure sites were declared universally accessible. Cubans were to realize that dream of racial democracy that the liberation wars had bequeathed. As Fidel Castro said in his Santiago de Cuba speech of January 2, 1959: "This time the revolution is for real."[66]

The Revolution also sought to rectify Afro-Cubans' lack of access to jobs and social services. This it did via social investments and color-blind policies that brought employment, better wages, health care, education, housing, and the arts to Cuba's poorest sectors. That these reforms conceded a relative dignity to Afro-Cubans was conveyed in Guillén's 1964 poem "Tengo" (I Have):

> I have, let's see:
> that being Black
> I can be stopped by no one at
> the door of a dancing hall or bar.

Or even at the desk of a hotel
have someone yell at me there are no rooms
. . . .

I have, let's see:
that I have learned to read,
to count,
I have that I have learned to write,
and to think,
and to laugh.
I have that now I have
a place to work
and earn
what I have to eat.

I have, let's see:
I have what was coming to me.[67]

So, too, was it conveyed in the anxiety or resentment that white Cubans vocalized, whether with their mouths or their feet. It was no idle detail, after all, that those who fled to the United States were predominantly white (upper-middle-class) Cubans. The Revolution strategically exploited this fact to recast racism as synonymous with capitalism and "Yankee imperialism." And vice versa: to be revolutionary—and, later, communist—was to be anti-racist. Cubans of color were deemed a decisive class to court (and cautiously empower) and Fidel Castro cast as their ally and kin. "Fidel," as he was lovingly known, was affiliated with Afro-Cuban symbols and religious beliefs. He was known as "El Caballo" (the Horse)—a symbol of Chango (deity of war)—and the red and black colors of MR 26-7 read as his loyalties and debts to the trickster Elegua (deity of roads).[68] Most spectacular of all was when a white dove perched on his shoulder at a victory rally in Havana (January 8, 1959). This was taken as a sign that Castro was a divinely ordained leader and devotee of Obatala, father of all *orishas* (deities).[69]

That Fidel Castro and the Cuban Revolution were friends to Africa and the African diaspora of the Americas was an image symbolically and substantively cultivated. With the decolonial wars in Asia and Africa and the civil rights movement in the United States, race (and blackness especially) had a vitality and volatility that could not be ignored politically. This the Revolution knew well and fully exploited. In its newsreels, press headlines, and speeches, the revolutionary government depicted the United

States as a haven for racists. If white Cubans found asylum in the United States, what awaited Black Cubans were police brutality, KKK terror, and Jim Crow humiliations.[70] And vice versa. African Americans could expect hospitality and solidarity in Cuba.

Indeed, so sure of its anti-racist credentials was the Revolution that it actively courted African Americans to tour the island and see for themselves the project that was revolutionary Cuba. Celebrities such as boxer Joe Lewis, singer Harry Belafonte, actor Sidney Poitier, and radicals such as Stokely Carmichael, Robert Williams, Eldridge Cleaver, Angela Davis, Elaine Brown, and Assata Shakur all visited the island as guests of honor or as asylum seekers.[71] Not all were taken by what they saw. Carmichael, Williams, and Cleaver would later recant their favorable impressions of socialist Cuba, while Davis looked to it as an auspicious experiment that had made strides where only a few years earlier racial injustices were endemic.[72] Nor was the Revolution not without its own Black critics. Juan René Betancourt, Carlos Moore, and others were critical of the paternalistic ways in which a mostly white revolutionary cadre dealt with Afro-Cubans and the "race question."[73] Afro-Cubans were not well represented in the higher echelons of power, and subtler forms of racism persisted in the workplace, family, and educational curriculum. What organized power Afro-Cubans once had, the government had dissolved. The Black press and societies of color were jettisoned as bourgeois institutions out of touch with socialist comradery.[74] And while mass organizations for youth, women, and workers were instituted, no such officially sanctioned bodies materialized for Afro-Cubans.

That said, as headquarters to OSPAAL (Organization of Solidarity with the People of Asia, Africa, and Latin America) and cast as "vanguard" of Third World liberation, socialist Cuba was a far cry from the Hispanophilic state of the early republican years. Even less so was it a carryover of the late republican fetish with the "American way of life."[75] Rather, socialist Cuba improvised new institutions and fostered a renewed revolutionary ethos for racial camaraderie not rivaled since the wars for independence.

The Imperfect Past

Of all its new institutions, none was as internationally acclaimed as was the Revolution's Film Institute (ICAIC) and its "imperfect cinema." ICAIC set out to create a national cinema that did not mimic Hollywood formulas or abide by the dictates of mere fantasy and amusement—let alone lucrative ends. Armed with inferior technology and less formally trained staff, its "imperfections" were celebrated as a more authentic art, one ideologically attuned to the popular classes and revolutionary possibilities.[76]

What this amounted to was a cinema that looked not only to the socialist future but also to the historic lessons and moral credibility of the mambí past. This was especially evident in or near the year 1968, centennial of the Grito de Yara. Cuban historiography and the arts creatively elaborated on the motif of *cien años de lucha* (one hundred years of struggle), and to this end ICAIC released a series of documentaries and films relevant to the independence wars: Jorge Fraga's *La odisea de General José* (1968), Humberto Solás's *Lucía* (1968), Alejandro Saderman's *Hombres de Mal Tiempo* (1968), Manuel Octavio Gómez's *La primera carga al machete* (1969), Bernabé Hernández's *1868–1898* (1970), and José Massip's *Páginas del diario de José Martí* (1971).[77] In many of these works Cuba Libre is portrayed as a populist project in which Afro-Cubans were not mere bystanders or beneficiaries. In fact, Afro-Cubans and blackness often came to signify emancipatory desire and a history of resilience and rebelliousness.[78]

The richest account of the intimacy between blackness and Cuba Rebelde came with Sergio Giral's so-called slave trilogy, which consists of the films *El otro Francisco* (1974), *Rancheador* (1977), and *Maluala* (1979). The trilogy can be read as a cinematic commentary on Walterio Carbonell's seminal *Crítica: Cómo surgió la cultura nacional* (1961). Carbonell argued that Cuba owed its revolutionary culture to the enslaved Afro-Cubans far more so than to the creole landowners and bourgeois intellectuals celebrated in the nation's historiography (i.e., Felix Varela, José Saco, José de la Luz y Caballero). In order to decolonize its history and identity, Cubans had to look beyond the narrative of "humanist" slave owners and "progressive" creole elites. Such narratives eclipsed the history of pre-1868 Black resistance, which included mass slave revolts and conspiracies such as the 1812 Aponte Rebellion and 1844 Escalara Conspiracy.[79] The decisive antagonism in Cuban history was master and slave—not bourgeoisie and proletariat—and its revolutionary "vanguard" the enslaved Afro-Cubans who rebelled.[80]

But the Revolution, cautioned Carbonell, was still wedded to these "aristocratic" and Eurocentric prejudices. It had yet to dwell on and earnestly embrace its African debts. Carbonell's "unorthodox" Marxism did cost him dearly, with time served in labor camps and a psychiatric ward and his book taken off shelves.[81] But it did resonate, and was artistically honored, in the works of other Cuban intellectuals, not least the Black filmmaker Sergio Giral. In Giral's trilogy, blackness and Cuba Rebelde are synonymous, and slave rebellions are antecedents to the liberation wars, with the cimarrón (maroon) and the *palenque* (maroon community) discursively framed as predecessors to the mambí and Cuba Libre. In his works, Afro-Cuban cultural practices are neither savage nor "exotic" or "folkloric." Instead, they are narrated and visualized in ways that confer dignity, cunning, and complexity to Afro-Cubans and Afro-Cuban culture.

El otro Francisco inventively deconstructs the abolitionist novel *Fransico: El ingenio o las delicias del campo,* by Anselmo Suarez y Romero.[82] Set in the late 1830s, the novel's premise is that of a tragic romance between the house slaves Francisco and Dorotea, who have a child together and wish to marry. What stands in their way is the young master Ricardo, who lusts for the mulatta Dorotea and lashes his jealous fury out on Francisco. Francisco is sent to the plantation and the cane fields, where he is beaten and worked to near death. Out of desperation for her beloved Francisco, Dorotea gives herself to Ricardo, a disgrace that drives Francisco to hang himself. The film version, however, scrutinizes the credibility of Suarez's account. A didactic narrator and alternative scenarios tease out the Afro-Cuban resistance silenced in the abolitionist text. Romance and the pathos of victimhood are displaced for a larger historical drama of Black resistance. The viewer learns that enslaved Africans sabotaged expensive machinery, fled for the *monte* (mountains), used herbs to induce miscarriages, and openly rebelled. They also looked to their faith, music, rituals, and dance as ways to exorcise their grief and foster their hopes. In one of the film's most memorable scenes, the slaves are gathered at nightfall around a fire for a ritual sacrifice that invites Ogun, warrior orisha of metal works, to possess Andre Lucumí. In *bosal* (African-inflected) vernacular, Ogun tells the tale of Haiti, where Blacks are free and where the machete that was once used to cut sugarcane was turned against the master. All agree it is time to "purify" the plantation and flee for the mountains.

It is no easy path to tread, however. Those who initially flee are caught. The defiant Crispín is hunted down, brought back, and publicly castrated. An elder woman leads a collective chant and prayer for his soul to find its way back to Guinea, the name for their ancestral (western) Africa—and, not incidentally, the name of the palenque to which Crispín had fled. According to Crispín, in Guinea Blacks are masters of their own lives. They plant what they please, share equally what they have, and trade their surplus with the rural peasantry. In this regard, the film endows

Afro-Cubans not only with a rebellious spirit but also a visionary utopia and egalitarian values. They know, however, that insofar as the plantation exists—as proxy for imperial power and white supremacy—the Black utopia of Guinea will not peaceably stand. Hence the slaves-cum-maroons torch the sugarcane, destroy the mill, and hunt down and kill the overseers with their machetes. All these cinematic cues situate the maroons and Guinea as, allegorically, the mambises and Cuba Libre. Not incidentally does the film's closing caption read: "Several years would have to pass and many horrors come about before the revolutionary vanguard would breakdown the color barrier. Céspedes, Agramonte, Martí, Maceo, Gómez, and many other patriots joined blacks and whites together and merged all the forces in the fight for the liberation and independence of the island in their fight for our nation." That Maceo is the only Black revolutionary named does not exactly cohere with a film whose "vanguard" is exclusively Black. But it does not render Afro-Cubans any less intelligible as forefathers and foremothers of Cuba Rebelde. To wit, the film does not offer any whites with whom to identify as heralds of Cuba Libre. Whites are either sadistic masters and overseers, hypocritical Christians, or paternalistic abolitionists.

Giral's *Rancheador* focuses on the cruelty and obsessions of Francisco Estévez, a *rancheador* (mercenary hired to hunt down fugitive slaves). Estévez is after Melchora, the most feared of maroon leaders. She is a mysterious priestess who the viewer never sees, at least not in human form. She is said to have the ability to shape-shift, and we only see her, implicitly, as an allusive *majá* (boa constrictor) or as doves in flight. All those who have hunted her down have been swallowed by the mountains over which she has clairvoyant dominion. Estévez has no scruples and will do whatever it takes to hunt her and maroons down, even if that means terrorize and murder white and mestizo *guajiros* (peasants). This he does with the military and commercial elite's blessings, for what is really at stake is the land the guajiros occupy and the Black bodies whose labor shall render it profitable.

In this regard, *Rancheador* visually postulates a multiracial solidarity between exploited and persecuted classes. Guajiros trade rifles for the wild honey gathered by cimarrones, and the latter use those arms to raid plantations and free their enslaved kin. That said, the film always situates revolutionary initiative in the hands of Afro-Cubans—or, more exactly, maroons—whether the elusive Melchora or the defiant Mataperro (literally, Dog-killer). That dogs were used to hunt fugitive slaves speaks volumes to his namesake. Mataperro is captured and forced to lead Estévez to Melchora. But the clever Mataperro leads Estévez into an ambush, where the vicious rancheador is struck down by Mataperro's machete.

With *Maluala* the viewer bears witness to Afro-Cuban cultural integrity and organizational capacities. The film features a network of palenques, each with their own chieftains. Maluala is the largest, and its leader, Gallo, is a bearded and stout man. The film's drama focuses on the indecisiveness of fellow maroon chieftain Coba, who is not sure whether to trust the Spaniards' offer for freedom, for maroon chieftains are granted their freedom only insofar as they agree to serve the Crown. And as Cabo comes to find out, this means to hunt down fellow maroons and allow one's kin to "work off" their debts in slave-like conditions. At stake throughout the film is honor, astuteness, and loyalty. There are, after all, those who betray their kin or naively trust the colonial authorities. This leads to a disastrous assault on the palenques. But not all is lost. Cabo dies an honorable leader; the three traitors meet a disagreeable end; and most importantly: Maluala never falls.

The deference that *Maluala* cinematically extends to Afro-Cuban beliefs, symbols, and capacities is remarkable. Shamans, ritual sacrifices, prayers, dance, divinely blessed amulets, and a liturgical vernacular are all reverently invoked to mourn the dead, consult the gods for ethical clarity, and to raise morale for (defensive) battle. Catholic priests, chapels, banners, and rites are, by contrast, cinematically situated as handmaidens to empire. The charitable priest who tries to broker the maroons' surrender proves ethnocentric and naive—and fatally so. Nor do the "freedom" and "civilization" he or the Spanish governor laud coincide with the maroons' desires or capacities. They do not wish to be "free to work" for others or to be baptized and attend Mass. They are already organized in socially harmonious and productive units. They have women and men leaders, humble yet adequate homes, sufficient food, artisanal laborers, cultural vitality, trade partners, and land. What is at stake is their sovereignty and autonomy. And this they will defend with their lives.

Epic Testimony

The Black subject as (historic) symbol of Cuba Rebelde was also touted in Cuban letters. By the close of 1961, the Revolution had eliminated illiteracy on the island, and by the mid-to-late 1960s its editorial houses and Book Institute (ICL) offered readers the works of internationally acclaimed writers such as Jean-Paul Sartre, Julio Cortázar, and Gabriel García Marquez and Cuban authors such as Nicolás Guillén and Alejo

Carpentier.[83] It also released historic texts and humbler "nonliterary" voices with whom ordinary Cubans could identify. Accordingly, the first in a series named Literatura de Campaña was Máximo Gómez's *El viejo Eduá: Crónicas de guerra,* released in 1965. The slim text included various short essays written by the former commander of the Liberation Army, most notably the account of his elder and loyal Black assistant Eduá from the Ten Years' War. But as series editor Ambrosio Fornet recalled, it was difficult to elicit the interests of contemporary readers in works deemed relevant only to historians.[84]

This was not the case with *Biografía de un cimarrón* (1966)—a sensationally popular text that inaugurated a genre, namely the "testimonial novel."[85] Edited by Miguel Barnet, *Biografía* reads as if the oral history of Esteban Montejo, an elder Black Cuban who was born into slavery, lived as a maroon, fought in the independence wars, and was 103 years old when Barnet came to know and interview him (in 1963). This made for a unique voice and text. The scale of Montejo's life and the momentous events to which he bore witness rendered it an "epic testimony," as Roberto González Echevarría has said.[86] Yet Montejo was a far cry from the typical hero of epic chroniclers and official historians. Granted, there was already a history of prose, poetry, and ballads to the anonymous or rank-and-file soldiers of the independence wars. Máximo Gómez's very own "El viejo Eduá" and "Mi escolta" (My Entourage) were exemplary to this end. But such works were always *about* the soldier or the deceased. Never were they in his own voice or perspective. *Biografía,* by contrast, is told with the intimacy and vernacular of a storyteller who hails from the popular classes. Not only its narrator (Montejo) but also its style of address are those of the "people without history." The testimonial novel is not, thereby, a species of literature meant to entertain or merely amuse the reader with exotic tales or folklore. It is a text that critically examines social stereotypes and situates the subaltern classes as history makers. It does so, said Barnet, with an ear for the "idiosyncratic essence" of their (oral) discourse and an eye for the ways in which their lives bear witness to larger historical processes. The white and middle-class editor and interlocutor (Barnet) is, accordingly, a "caring and ready" servant to those who history has silenced.[87]

Montejo's life is recounted in three chronologically ordered sections: "Slavery," "Abolition of Slavery," and "The War of Independence." Born into slavery (circa 1860), Montejo did not get to know his parents. He was raised by godparents and, at that, only to early adolescence, when he fled for the woods. He recounts for the reader the stocks, infirmary, barracks, and exacting labor of slavery. But he also substantively delves into Afro-Cuban cultural beliefs and practices. These range from jocular pastimes and festivities to the altars, amulets, and medical knowledge of shamans and African elders. There is an attentiveness to the ethnic heterogeneity of Afro-Cubans as well. They are Congos, Lucumís, Mandigos, and Carabalíes, each with their own virtues and vices. Afro-Cubans are as such an ensemble of jokesters, storytellers, healers, workers, and warriors—not a generic mass of "slaves" or "Blacks." And their story is told in a way that is not realist inasmuch as, pace Alejo Carpentier, "magically real."[88] Montejo does not speak lightly of ghosts, hexes, souls, or the afterlife. His prose and perspective are a far cry, that is, from that of the historical materialist. As William Luis has noted, myth and religion are privileged in this testimonial over written literature and history.[89]

After a year and half of solitude in the woods, Montejo returned to civilian life and plantation labor. Slavery had been abolished (1886), and Montejo and his kin could move about more freely. They enjoyed their cockfights, gambling, bars, fiestas, and women. But not all was well. Cuba was a "tinderbox." Black Cubans were still very much exploited, banditry endemic, the Rural Guard "hellish," and talk of a new war consumed everyone. When war at last broke out (1895), Afro-Cubans flocked to the mambí ranks: "We blacks protested, too. It was an old protest, years old." As Montejo tells us, their motives were driven by desires for racial justice as much as anti-colonialism: "Not a one wanted to see himself in shackles. . . . That was why they went to war." It is noteworthy, however, that mambises are not portrayed as chivalric or Spartan heroes. Throughout the text the mambí army is an unruly ensemble: fierce *machateros* (machete-wielders), arsonists, bandits, patriots, and, yes, "degenerates"—white and Black alike. As Montejo says: the revolution was a "fine mess everybody fell into." Into that fine mess fell the Americans, too. With "trickery" and the collusion of racist Cubans, they "grabb[ed] the best piece of pie for themselves" and left Afro-Cubans empty handed. "When the [Liberation] army was disbanded, the black revolutionaries were unable to remain in [Havana]. They returned to the country, to the cane field, tobacco fields, to whatever, except to the offices. . . . [I] returned to the countryside without a peso in my pocket [and back to] my same old job [at the sugar mill]. It seemed like I was back in the past all over again."[90]

With its subaltern narrator and its oral style, *Biografía* offers the reader a humbler alternative to the otherworldly heroics of Antonio Maceo or the baroque oratory of José Martí. Montejo comes to embody the history of an oppressed people and their rebel spirit as cimarrones and mambises.

His life is "epic testimony" to the (Black) Cuban desire to be free and to the "trickery" and "scoundrels" who endanger that liberty. Granted, the editorial power of the text always already laid in the hands of Barnet. The text is not, after all, an autobiography. And it is not easy to explain the conspicuous silence on the republican or revolutionary years. One wonders what Montejo would have had to say about the racist massacre of 1912 or the anti-racist rhetoric and reforms of the Revolution.[91] *Biografía* is most gainfully read, thus, as a text that projects a collective voice, one that yokes together generations as well as social classes. The epic past is in dialogue with the revolutionary present as is the young white middle-class writer with the elder Black working-class mambí. As a textual strategy, thus, the testimonial novel enabled Barnet (and the white Cuban reader) to identify with blackness, and this was neither unusual nor undesirable. The decolonial ethos and aesthetics of revolutionary Cuba and the Tricontinental rendered blackness not as a skin color inasmuch as subaltern positionality and an emancipatory sensibility. Blackness thereby bespoke one's subalternity vis-à-vis the capitalist world-system as much as one's allegiances to liberation struggles—what Anne Garland Mahler has referred to as "metonymic color politics."[92]

The African Epic

Fidel Castro was no stranger to such metonymic color politics or the sentiment that blackness was synonymous with the revolutionary vanguard of the Third World. At a 1975 mass rally in Havana, he famously declared: "We are a Latin-African nation . . . African blood flows through our veins. [*applause*] Many of our ancestors came as slaves from Africa to this land. As slaves they struggled a great deal. They fought as members of the Liberation Army of Cuba. We're brothers and sisters of the people of Africa and we're ready to fight on their behalf!"[93] This was no mere rhetorical flourish. As early as 1963, Cuban tanks and artillery helped fend off Moroccan forces in newly independent Algeria, and two years later Che Guevara and Victor Dreke trained and fought with guerrillas in the eastern Congo (later known as Zaire). In the ensuing years Cuba would send internationalist combatants and civilians to aid and abet liberation movements in Western Sahara, Congo-Brazzaville, Eritrea, Ethiopia, Guinea-Bissau, Zanzibar, Mozambique, and, most dramatically, Angola. Between the years 1975 and 1991 the small island of Cuba sent no fewer than 375,000 soldiers and 50,000 civilians to Angola, with a mission to assist the MPLA against aggressors from within (UNITA and FLNA) and abroad (Zaire and the South African armed forces). This protracted "civil war" culminated in the so-called Battle of Cuito Cuanavale (1987–88), when Cuban and Angolan armed forces decisively held back a UNITA and South African offensive.[94] As Nelson Mandela later said, Cuito Cuanavale "destroyed the myth of the invincibility of the white oppressor."[95]

In the war's wake, peace accords were signed and Cuba's internationalist credibility buoyed. "What other country," asked Mandela, "can point to a record of greater selflessness than Cuba has displayed in its relations with Africa?"[96] Indeed, Cuba could take its share of credit for Angola's sovereignty, Namibia's independence, Mandela's release, and the fall of apartheid in South Africa. Little wonder, thus, that Cubans refer to this chapter of their history as the "epic of Angola."[97] The lengthy years, major battles, and historic consequences all recommend it. That the epic of Angola was symbolically alloyed to the epic of Cuba Libre was no less noteworthy. The first mass deployments to Angola were named Operation Carlota, after an African "heroine" who led two slave rebellions in 1843. The war was discursively framed as such as a reverse "middle passage," whereby Cuba's African descendants redeemed their enslaved ancestors and colonized homeland. The majority of the soldiers sent to Angola were Afro-Cubans, a strategically wise choice that eased Angolan anxieties and facilitated camaraderie with Angolan soldiers. For critics like Carlos Moore this was a "heavy price paid [by Afro-Cubans] abroad . . . with low dividends in return at home."[98] Arguably, however, the moral and social dividends of having sounded the death knell of Portuguese colonialism and anti-Black apartheid in South Africa were not so meager. Nor was it all that trivial to receive military honors and be cast as a revolutionary heir to Antonio Maceo, the most *epic* of all mambises. The fallen were returned to the island and buried on December 7, 1989, the anniversary of Maceo's death and a national holiday.[99] At the El Cacahual memorial site, Head of the Revolutionary Armed Forces Raul Castro avowed that Maceo, "invincible leader of the Baraguá Protest, within whose veins flowed the unredeemed blood of Africa," would be proud.[100]

Maceo was, no doubt, a politically expedient choice in these years. He was well known as a masterful tactician and fierce fighter, the stoutly built Bronze Titan renowned for his Protest at Baraguá in 1878, when he refused to lay down his arms lest Cuba be declared independent and slavery abolished. What Maceo most forcefully symbolized was intransigence. And this was no token "revolutionary virtue" in the 1980s. At the Third Party Congress of 1986, Fidel Castro announced the Campaign of Rectification of Errors and Negative Tendencies. Its mission was to counteract "errors" such as the market-friendly reforms of the early 1980s and negative tendencies such as bureaucracy, corruption, and an emergent materialistic ethos. So-called minibrigades, moral incentives, and volunteer labor were revitalized to build or renovate houses, clinics, and schools; small enterprises reincorporated into the state; ministries purged of ineffective or opportunistic bureaucrats; grassroots politics institutionally enlivened; and Cuba's internationalist ethos revived, not least by Cuito Cuanavale.[101]

Hence, in the midst of these years Maceo's intransigence and the rallying trope of Baraguá were called on to buoy Cuban morale. The 1986 film *Baraguá,* directed by José Massip, can be read as precisely such a tactic. A far cry from ICAIC's earlier "imperfect cinema" days, the rather dull and didactic film reiterates racial justice and Black loyalty.[102] The enemies of Cuba Libre are all racists. They are either Spanish officers who refer to Cubans as "savages" or Cubans who surrender to (and spy for) Spain. Cuba's heroes are, by contrast, mostly Black and mulatto. The Maceo brothers—Antonio, José, and Rafael—and their Black soldiers are all virile and astute. They lead, too. It is no idle detail that for half the film the classically epic Titan is convalescent, which enables a portrayal of a man and officer who thinks, strategizes, and counsels—not just wields a machete and straddles a horse. Loyal and anti-racist white mambises do appear, nearly all of them bearded. The film's contemporary relevance as such was not likely lost on the viewer. For that same year Fidel Castro admitted that one of the errors to "rectify" were the race and sex inequalities in governmental power, which lead to an affirmative action policy that facilitated more Afro-Cubans and women to hold office in the National Assembly and the PCC's Central Committee and Politburo.[103]

That said, what mattered most was the resolve and tenacity that Maceo and Baraguá symbolized. In 1991, a monument in Maceo's honor, known as Revolution Plaza, was inaugurated in Santiago de Cuba. The plaza features an enormous equestrian Maceo (carved from granite) and equally enormous iron machete blades thrust from the earth.[104] Maceo's horse is in full stride as the Titan looks back and, with a free hand, calls forth for others to follow his lead. He is headed westward, indicative of the historic "invasion" of 1895 and the historically rebellious Oriente. The monument's scale, sturdy material, and martial motif all classically evoke epic emplotment and sentiment, as do the eternal flame and the Titan's quoted words: "Anyone who attempts to conquer Cuba shall reap only its blood-soaked soil, if he does not perish in the struggle first." And never was such mambí resolve timelier. For that same year the Soviet Union dissolved, and socialist Cuba's perilous descent was all but assured.

Plaza de la Revolución Mayor General Antonio Maceo Grajales in Santiago de Cuba. (Author's photograph)

Centennial Obsessions

Officially known as the "Special Period in Times of Peace," the 1990s engendered crises both existential and symbolic. With the loss of Soviet subsidies and renewed US hostility (i.e., the Torricelli and Helms-Burton Acts), Cubans entered a period of unprecedented scarcity and hunger.[105] Rations for coffee, rice, bread, and beans had never been more meager; meat and spices were either scarce or nonexistent; and an illegal market for foods emerged as prices soared. Energy, too, was rationed as oxen, bicycles, wood fires, and candles came to replace tractors, automobiles, gas stoves, and electric bulbs, respectively. Even items as prosaic as soap and matches became coveted commodities, as material life for Cubans no longer resembled the twentieth inasmuch as the nineteenth century.[106] Such stark and relatively sudden privations went hand in hand with disenchantment, cynicism, and embitterment. This was most evident in 1994, when as many as thirty thousand Cuban *balseros* (rafters) took to the sea in hopes that the US Coast Guard (and State Department) would come to the rescue.[107]

The PCC did not, of course, stand idly by in these most distraught years. The economy was dollarized, state farms handed over to cooperatives, and farmer's markets and small businesses in hospitality legalized. The economy was also opened to foreign (especially European) investors so as to renew and expand the island's tourist economy. Such reforms were neither in vain nor altogether felicitous. Food was no longer so scarce by the late 1990s, schools and hospitals were never shuttered, new trade partners were courted, and the state did not succumb to drug cartels or mass incarceration schemes.[108] Some Cubans were in fact considerably better off. Those with access to US dollars (versus Cuban pesos) could live well. But the only real access to dollars was via remittances or jobs in the tourist sector, neither of which were favorable to Afro-Cubans. The vast majority of Cubans who live abroad identify as white, and it is they who send remittances to their (white) kin on the island. These dollars serve as the basis not only to cover daily expenses but also to finance small businesses. Moreover, save for jobs in folklore, music, and dance, Afro-Cubans are routinely passed over in the tourist sector for more "qualified" employees—which almost invariably means lighter skinned.[109]

Indeed, one of the most scandalous effects of the Special Period was the reemergence of economic inequality. One indicator is income. Prior to 1989, the salary of the lowest compared to the highest-paid employees in Cuba amounted to a ratio of 1:5. In 1995 that ratio had catapulted to 1:289 and, by 2001, was 1:12,500.[110] That this inequality had (and has) such a decidedly racial profile was (and is) a sore subject for the revolutionary cadre and citizens alike. The Revolution's accomplishments in racial justice were bona fide. By the early 1980s, racial differentials in educational level, life expectancy, employment, nutrition, access to health care, and professional occupations were virtually nonexistent—a feat that could hardly be said of Brazil or the United States at the time (let alone now).[111] But that relative equality had largely fallen to the wayside in the wake of the Special Period. Afro-Cubans still enjoyed universal access to health care and schools, but their overrepresentation in prisons, Havana's slums, and the illicitly employed was (and is) indisputable—and controversial. Cuba's minimally socialist state and color-blind policies led some to believe that Afro-Cubans have no one to blame but themselves. Yet, as many scholars and critics have noted, the Revolution was never so "color-blind." As Esteban Morales and others have noted, anti-Black racism persisted in coworker relations, television programs, everyday speech, and educational curricula. Afro-Cubans were habitually depicted as criminals, lazy, or sexually licentious in Cuban television and rarely in lead roles, and their history and culture were not substantively addressed in schools—save for the occasional tributes to Antonio Maceo or Juan Gualberto Gómez. Pejorative expressions such as *pelo malo* (kinky hair), *ñata* (wide nose), and *bemba* (thick lips) were, moreover, not any less archaic.[112]

How to strategically finesse the racialized disparities that emerged in post–Soviet era Cuba was (and is) a controversial matter. It was not lost on Cuba's cadre that the 1990s were years rife with *epic* history: the centennials to the Grito de Barie, Martí's death, Maceo's death, and the US intervention were culled for their symbolic power. But to speak of racial democracy or to rally the cry of an "eternal Baraguá" fell on disillusioned ears, especially those that could not recall the relatively stable 1980s—let alone the exuberant 1960s.[113] Younger Cubans of color bore witness to the discrepancy between rhetoric and reality with hip-hop music.[114] That they did so in a musical genre so firmly affiliated with Black consciousness (and the Black diaspora of the Americas) was no trivial matter. The Revolution's musical genre of choice was the *nueva trova,* a musical style known for its socially conscious yet poetic lyrics and folksy, even melancholic melody. Wildly popular throughout the leftist Americas of the 1970s, nueva trova (also known as *nueva canción*) was oriented around the acoustic guitar and the phenotypically white or mestizo singer-songwriter: Violeta Parra and Víctor Jara of Chile, Mercedes Sosa of Argentina, Roy Brown of Puerto Rico, and Cuba's internationally renowned Silvio Rodriguez. By contrast, hip-hop is known for its stylized baselines and viscerally delivered lyrics, lyrics that often decry anti-Black racism and engender Black consciousness. Hip-hop as such also defied the tourist economy's fondness for the more festive and romantically oriented *son, bolero,* or *danza*—as evidenced by the revival of the Buena Vista Social Club.[115] With an underground and oppositional cachet, the newly emergent hip-hop in Cuba cited Black nationalist icons such as Marcus Garvey and Malcolm X and flaunted the revolutionary credentials of blackness. An exemplary work was Obsesión's "Mambí" (2000), whose opening chorus reads:

> Here I am saying
> OBSESIÓN MAMBÍ in battle
> Don't wait for luck
> If Quintín Banderas never gave up
> Then why should I?
> Let's fight!

'Cause the *manigua* is screaming: I'm me
And it's for me whom the bell tolls.
Don't lie.
The Morro knows I run to battle and run with the *bayameses,*
Cuba's proud of me!
I don't fear a hero's death.
So chill, to be a rebel and black is still trouble
Rebambarambara![116]

What is noteworthy here is that Obsesión duo Alexey and Magia chose to cite Quintín Banderas (not Antonio Maceo) as their heroic referent. Banderas fought in all three independence wars and was one of the Liberation Army's most seasoned generals. He was, nevertheless, subjected to many disgraces. He and his troops were notoriously mocked (and feared) as "African savages," and Banderas was court-martialed (1897) and, later, assassinated (1906) at the orders of President Estrada Palma. Far less venerated and decidedly blacker, Banderas is not the lionized or mulatto Maceo. Obsesión's choice is quite provocative, thus. The mambí is not hereby multiracial but Black, yet all the same patriotic. She or he runs with the Bayameses and, as the national anthem says, fears not a heroic death. Nor is the mambí a strictly historical referent. Obsesión—and, by extension, the interpellated listener—identifies *as* a contemporary mambí. And what this amounts to, lyrically, is not a tired nationalistic plea but a rebellious call for racial justice—a call corporeally and culturally inscribed:

immersed in this blackness I ask,
Who are you,
who calls into question my legitimacy?
Who are you, who questions my
decency,
integrity and appearance?
Who are you, who doubts my
capabilities
And denies the virtues that are part
of
my flesh and bones?
. . . .
I am rapping to the beat of my
kinky hair,
my wide nose, my thick lips, my

family tree, my history, my customs,
my religion and my way of thinking.
I know the court is watching me,
but
I also watch back with fixed gaze.[117]

Afro-Cubans continued thereby to look to their mambí patrimony in order to creatively elaborate their and Cuba's revolutionary horizons. But the case of Obsesión is particularly noteworthy because one of its duo, Magia, is a woman, and rarely are women foregrounded in hip-hop. More to the point, rarely are women foregrounded in national epics—except as erotic objects, hysteric mothers, or dutiful wives. That Magia credits her revolutionary fervor to her mother, Caridad, renders the lyrics all the more salient.[118] For even when the mambí epic is heroically narrated as a *Black* epic, its litany of heroes and muses is all men—as attested to by this chapter: Antonio Maceo, José Maceo, Quintín Banderas, Guillermo Moncada, Evaristo Estenoz, Pedro Ivonnet, Ricardo Batrell, Walterio Carbonell, Sergio Giral, and Esteban Montejo. The next chapter, accordingly, looks to women's empowerment and rights and the ways in which the *cubana* as mambisa has critically enriched the epic known as Cuba Libre.

2 *¡Empínate!*

Of Motherhood, Mimicry, and the Mambisa

> The revolutionary epic was much too profound, dramatic and beautiful for me not to have immediately made it my own.
>
> —Excilia Saldaña (1982)

WOMEN ARE not customarily, if ever, the heroic locus of epics. This is not to say that they are inconsequential or powerless. The women of ancient epics included goddesses, queens, sorceresses, and, occasionally, soldiers who facilitated or could frustrate heroic deeds. The goddess Ninsun counseled her son Gilgamesh; Isthar conjured the Bull of Heaven and seduced kings; Athena conspired for the Greeks and Aphrodite the Trojans; Dido, Queen of Carthage, cursed Rome; Sundiata's mother, the "Buffalo Woman," had occult powers; and the Amazonians were legendary warriors. That said, the women of epics are usually known as the mothers, wives, and daughters of heroic men. They figure in the drama as those who mourn for the dead or as docile and chaste victims whose "honor" must be defended. Indeed, rare is the epic authored (or recited) by a woman.[1]

The epic of Cuba Libre has proved just as ambivalent when it comes to women. In the wars for independence, Cuban women were praised as "Spartan" mothers who stoically bore the deaths of their husbands and sons. This conferred a measure of moral gravitas onto the wars and the nationalist cause, but women as such were mere familial appendages to heroic men. The truth is that the mambí epic never amounted to a narrative in which *women*'s liberation was crucial—certainly not as crucial as Black liberation. Never did the words *mambí* or *mambisa* bespeak a critique of patriarchy—let alone a robust feminist agenda. But as historian Teresa Prados-Torreira has pointed out, women did take on roles that defied gendered ascriptions and, consequently, rearticulated their sense of entitlement and capabilities. No longer bound to prayer, embroidery, or domestic servitude, the wars offered women the opportunity to contribute as spies, propagandists, delegates, and even soldiers.[2]

All the same, the identity (and attendant labor) to which women were most tenaciously bound was as mothers. This was the case not only in the wars but throughout the republican years, years fraught with social ills such as prostitution, alcoholism, gambling, suicide, illiteracy, orphanages, and poverty—let alone the Platt Amendment and other such humiliations. But the "maternal" had a moral authority that could be socially and politically consequential. And women capitalized on this. In the 1920s, they joined the campaign to "regenerate" Cuba. The utopian ecstasy that Cuba Libre once held out could not be realized, women insisted, without the moral integrity that they as "feminine" and, especially, as mothers embodied. To this end Cuban women evoked mambisa heroines as philanthropic benefactors and respectable citizens; the *Virgen mambisa,* as chaste and compassionate mother who cares for and blesses her children (i.e., the Cuban people); and Mariana Grajales, as fecund mother who birthed titans. But only belatedly was a woman's right to vote (1933) and legal equality (1940) constitutionally recognized, and only episodically did the mambisa receive commemorative honors. The lives and deaths of men were what prevailed in the poetry, ballads, oral history, chronicles, monuments, and miscellanea that was the mambí epic.

With the Revolution, however, a more militant iconography and historiography emerged, as did new sympathies and opportunities for women's empowerment. Women advocated for and received access to health care, university education, equal pay for equal work, maternity leave, childcare centers, divorce, and reproductive rights. And in due course, they began to rank among the nation's doctors, engineers, athletes, and union and civic leaders. Consistent with this was the impetus to retell the nation's history with women as protagonists, as evidenced by the film *Lucía* (1968) and Nancy Morejón's poem "Black Woman." The mambisa was recalled as a rebel combatant whom the new socialist woman could emulate. But such processes were not without their contradictions. The revolutionary expectations placed on women were unfair insofar as they continued to do most, if not all, of the childrearing and domestic labor. Nor was it clear whether the revolutionary woman was celebrated sui generis—as embodying, that is, a *different* conception of the "heroic"—or as someone who merely mimicked the revolutionary man and his ascribed "epicness." It was not auspicious that women continued to be underrepresented in the Revolution's highest echelons of state power, whatever the celebratory invocations of the militant mambisa, and it was an outright scandal that for so many women the most economically viable job of the Special Period was sex work. Despite the difficulties, they continued to organize and agitate for each other, and to write themselves and their foremothers into the nation's epic as archetypes of rebel dignity and hope.

War, Women, and the Maternal

In April 1869, delegates from the Republic in Arms convened in the small town of Guáimaro for Cuba's first constitutional assembly. Its attendants no doubt knew this was a momentous event, one that would resound evermore in the nation's annals. But who could have predicted that the event's most lasting words would be those of a woman? Ana Betancourt, author of revolutionary pamphlets and coeditor of the rebel paper, *El Mambí,* took the podium and declared: "Citizens: The Cuban woman in the dark and peaceful corner of the home [has] waited patiently and resignedly for this beautiful hour, when a revolution would break her yoke and untie her wings." Fellow assembly members had decided to end slavery by cradle (colonialism) and color (racism), but they had not yet opted to end slavery by sex (patriarchy). "The time has come," she concluded, "to free women."[3]

The assembly did not, however, heed her words. The Guáimaro Constitution did not stipulate a woman's legal equality or right to vote and hold office. Nor, for that matter, did the constitutional assemblies of Baraguá (1878), Jimaguayú (1895), or Yara (1896). The chief powers of the Republic in Arms were vested in the confident hands of men, and neither the rhetoric nor ethos of Cuba Libre was unequivocally associated with women's equality and empowerment. This is not to say that women were inconsequential to the wars. They served as cooks, seamstresses, nurses, secretaries, and couriers—labor without which no army could thrive. And they served, too, as organizers, pamphleteers, spies, saboteurs, and soldiers. In fact, despite the era's prejudices, women were 37 percent of the delegates to the Cuban Revolutionary Party (PRC) and as many as twenty-five women were officers in the Liberation Army.[4]

Nevertheless, in the wars' epically emplotted discourse women were little more than devout appendages to heroic men. Whatever a woman's accomplishments as club organizer or as spy, that is, she was mostly celebrated as patriotic daughter, wife, or mother. To an extent, this was a strategically crucial role. As wives and mothers, Cuban women were uniquely positioned to recruit rebel forces and morally vet the independence cause. It was they who could shame or exalt their husbands and sons as cowardly or valiant. In an 1870 manifesto to the Cuban people, the "Father of the Nation" Carlos Manuel de Céspedes wrote: "With what profound scorn would a wife look upon a husband who refused to join the insurrection, would a mother view a pusillanimous son, would a girlfriend look at her fiancé. And with what pride would a woman in any of these three situations look upon a husband, a son, and lover, covered with the dust of combat and bearing the laurels of battle."[5] But this bound her (and him) to a gendered order whereby men embodied valor and virility and women a pious fecundity. It was men who bore arms and risked their lives, whereas women were to bear sons and offer them as sacrifices to the Patria.[6]

A "patriotic" mother was, thus, one who repressed any disquiet or grief should her beloved husband or son die. This was precisely the drama that characterized José Martí's *Abdala* (1868). The play is not, tellingly, crafted around scenes of injustices or, for that matter, epic battles—all of which are either presumed or take place off stage. Rather, it focuses on a mother's fears that she shall lose her son. When Espirta asks her son what his love for her amounts to, Abdala dryly replies, "Do you truly think there is anything more sublime than love for one's patria?" And that patriotic love (*pater,* father) is indistinguishable from a love of war and martial prowess. Nubians are "fierce tigers" and "ferocious panthers" mounted on "noble steeds" with spears at hand—allegorically, the mambí cavalry and their machetes. Abdala, their "chief," can barely temper his orgasmic enthusiasm to see "torrents of blood" flow through the African plains: "Oh! What strength and life such joy brings to my soul! How my valor grows! How the blood in my veins burns! How this invincible ardor stirs me! How I desire to be off to battle!" Even Abdala's sister, Elmira, scolds her mother for her tears and grief: "Do you not hear the sublime sound of the roar of battle? . . . With what joy I would swap out this humiliating dress for the lustrous armor of the warriors, for a noble steed, for a spear!"[7]

The gendered ascriptions in Martí's war fantasy are unmistakable. The two women in the play possess an identity that is relevant only insofar as it relates to Abdala: sister and mother to the "illustrious warrior." Their dramaturgical roles are to embody the women's (im)propriety in times of war: "A Nubian [i.e., Cuban] mother is not she who cries if her son soars to the patria's rescue!" says Elmira to her grieving mother.[8] Rather, as Elmira has done, she sees her brother, son, or husband off to war with a loving kiss and great pride—if not (phallic) envy. In so doing, she subordinates her love of family to that of love for one's Patria and her deeds as woman to that of his as man: *he* redeems the Patria, and *she* exalts him for it, not least if he dies in the act. "Battle laurels" and the "crown of martyr" are what await Abdala—never Espirta or Elmira.

A mother who beseeched her son *not* to fight in the wars or who openly bereaved her dead mambí son was no trivial affair. Her bereavement had the power to demoralize any would-be soldier and, however obliquely, to call into question the merit of the cause. It is hardly a coincidence, thus, that the most revered and iconic mambisa became Mariana Grajales Cuello. Best known as mother to Antonio Maceo, Mariana Grajales was in fact mother to eleven sons, nine who died in the wars for independence. But what stood out about Mariana was not just the *quantity* of her loss, but the *quality* with which she bore that loss. In 1894, Martí eulogized her in the leading Cuba Libre periodical, *Patria,* as honorary "Mother to all Cubans." In it, he recounted what would become an iconic scene in the mambí epic:

> It was the day that they brought Antonio Maceo in wounded: he had been shot in the chest. Carried on their shoulders, he was unable to focus, and pale with the color of death. All the women, and there were many, began to cry, some against the wall, others on their knees by the dying man, another in a corner, her face sunken in her arms. And his mother, with the scarf from her head, expelled the crying women from her hut, as if scarring away chickens: "Out, out of here you skirts! I won't stand for tears!"

Having already lost one son and with three others wounded, Martí explained, Mariana then turned to her youngest son, Marcos, and (allegedly) said: "And you, stand tall [*empínate*], because it's time for you to go to the field of battle."[9] The fact that Mariana acted in a way that so radically contradicted what one would expect of a (Cuban) mother did not trouble Martí inasmuch as leave him in awe: as against the inconsolable (and, as a corollary, unpatriotic) Espirta, stood the exemplary Mariana, whose only regret in life was that she did not have more sons!

Martí also publicized how Mariana reacted to the war's outbreak in 1868. This, too, would become legendary. According to María Cabrales—known, tellingly, as Antonio Maceo's wife—Mariana ran to her room, came out with a crucifix, and said, "Everyone on their knees, father and sons, before Christ [. . .] and let us swear to liberate the Patria or die for it."[10] Both the crucifix and Mariana's biblical namesake (as mother to Jesus) were symbolically dense referents that endowed her and the cause of Cuba Libre with a moral cachet not easily rivaled. So, too, did it sanctify an act that under other circumstances would be deemed unconscionable, not least for a *Cuban* mother vis-à-vis her *son.* It is Mariana and her sons, after all, who the mambí epic recalls and venerates. Rarely, if ever, are her daughters Dominga and Baldomera mentioned. For what else could they offer, except sons of their own?

Eros and the (Anti-)Mambisa

Whatever was said or presumed, mambisas endured hardships that rivaled or surpassed those of their male comrades. Bernarda Toro, wife to Generalísmo Máximo Gómez, birthed and reared eleven children, five of them in the Cuban "wilderness" (*manigua*) or mambí encampments. Rebel soldiers sought refuge in the inhospitable regions of the Oriente mountains and jungles. They made do with whatever was expedient for shelter (including caves), were exposed to inclement weather, and were habitually without adequate food and medicine. These were harsh conditions for adults, even more so for infants and children. Not surprisingly did Bernarda lose two of her infants. María Cabrales, wife to Brigadier General Antonio Maceo, was said to have birthed two children in the manigua, a son who died at seven days old and a daughter who died at three years.[11] Like many others, Bernarda and María served as nurses, cooks, seamstresses, and confidants throughout the wars and, when in exile, as fundraisers, organizers, and propagandists. All the while, there were children to care for and feed. Bernarda was one such woman. Yet she suffered her lot, at least publicly, with a stoic dignity that read as if out of a Homeric epic. When in 1896, the PRC offered her financial aid she famously replied, "Do not waste on us what should go to pay for gunpowder."[12]

It is noteworthy, thus, that the mambisa was not an eroticized—let alone intellectual—subject. She was virtuous mother or devout wife. But the rhetoric of Cuba Libre was not without (fictitious) women who, like Espirta, were *liabilities* to the epic. Francisco Sellén's *Hatuey* (1891) illustrates this point. A play ostensibly about the Taino chieftain Hatuey, *Hatuey* in reality renders the mambises as heirs to the indigenous peoples of the Antilles and, thereby, as rightful (and rebellious) heirs to the island of Cuba.[13] In it, Hatuey warns his kin of the cruel strangers who have arrived and who care only for gold. He beseeches them to fight for their liberty. In an echo of *Abdala* and the national anthem, "La Bayamesa," he declares: "lesser evil it is to die than to live enslaved."[14] He then joins forces with fellow chieftain Macorijes to wage a guerrilla war against the conquistadors. The fearless Macorijes is captured and tortured to death but keeps safe the whereabouts of Hatuey's forces. But Macorijes's sister, Atabaiba, is not so circumspect, let alone valiant. A Spaniard seduces her and convinces her to lead him to Hatuey's camp. The Taino warrior is then captured but at least dies his legendary death. Offered last rites and eternal happiness, should he renounce his indigenous gods, Hatuey turns to the Franciscan priest and asks if Christians (i.e., Spaniards) go to heaven. When the priest answers yes, Hatuey replies: "I do not wish then to go [. . .] for hell is favorable, without their presence/to a heaven filled with such wicked people."[15] Accused of heresy and treason, he is burned alive at the stake.

It is local Cuban lore that Hatuey was executed in Yara, the site of the Grito de Yara (1868) and, thereby, the onset of the nation's wars for independence. Sellén's play tethered together these mythologized events. In Hatuey's words: Yara is "earth that my ashes today enrich!"[16] But, to be clear, Hatuey's words and deeds were addressed to men. The play interpellates able-bodied men to mimic the warriors Macorijes and Hatuey. It is, after all, their camaraderie in arms and (homoerotic) loyalty that facilitate the drama, whereas women are either irrelevant or naive traitors. When she learns that her naivety has led to Hatuey's demise, Atabaiba begs for his forgiveness. "Cursed be the fruits of your breast!" he replies.[17] Afterward she is found dead in the river, having committed suicide.

A similar disgrace befalls women in Manuel de la Cruz's *Episodios de la revolución cubana* (1892). None of its twenty-one "episodes" features a woman as protagonist. Only as the temptress Rosa does a woman narratively count—and at that, as foil. Lt. Salazar has been shot in the leg and left in Rosa's care by her husband Emilio. Emilio is a dear friend to Salazar, an honorable soldier who, one infers, saved Emilio's life. But the dark-skinned and voluptuous Rosa, "flesh filled with grace and fire," proves too tantalizing for Salazar to resist. Her fawning and her melodious voice cry out to the convalescent Salazar, "I want you! . . . I'm yours!"[18] It is crucial herein that it is *she,* Rosa, who initiates the infidelity and that *he,* Salazar, is the one who expresses remorse. In this regard, De la Cruz's florid and sensual descriptions of Rosa are tantamount to an *alibi* for Salazar, and her silence after the deed synonymous with a remorseless adulterer. It is Salazar who atones for sin in what is the last honorable act he can muster, namely suicide. His letter to Emilio reads: "I have inflected the most odious of offenses that one can inflict on a friend, but a remnant of honor demands that I offer you this satisfaction: my cadaver."[19]

Hence, the literary construct that was the mambí epic ambivalently endowed women with power. Whether as loyal sister, inconsolable mother, naive accomplice, or seductress, it was she who could either buoy or corrupt men's morale and efficacy as soldiers. For, discursively at least, the mambí was a desexualized subject. Or, more exactly, he was a subject whose erotic passions were invested in Patria and in homosocial camaraderie. The actual mambí was another matter. It was routine for soldiers to be accompanied by their wives or by "consorts." The latter situation was tolerated insofar as it was discreet, but it could be subject to disciplinary actions if flaunted.[20] All told, however, the rule was conspicuous silence on such matters, especially when it came to high-profile leaders. None other than Antonio Maceo and Máximo Gómez fathered "illegitimate" children while married, respectively, to María Cabrales and Bernarda Toro. With its (moral) legitimacy at stake, the Republic in Arms depicted its soldiers as solely devoted to Patria or, at the very least, as heterosexual subjects in nuptial and monogamous relationships.

The requisites of war made it such that the carnal and "erotic" subject, broadly conceived, repress his or her own drives for life and pleasure and, in their stead, stoically embrace the austerities and hazards of war and death. Cuba Libre became, thereby, a rhetorical injunction for men to bear arms and women to aid and abet those men, whether as nurses and cooks or as confidants and moral witnesses. And while not a few were structurally or socially coerced to do so, Cuba Libre as a dramatized epic rendered such choices morally and "erotically" driven—driven, that is, by a *love* for Patria. Whichever the case, their options to enact that love were decidedly gendered. It was presumed and, at times, openly asserted that women should—or indeed, *could*—not perform the odious duty of a soldier, namely to kill and die for the Patria. The effect of this "chivalric patriarchy" was to foreclose to women the most revered roles. The mambisa who sees her son off to war or who nurses the infirmed is a mere prelude or subsidiary drama to the momentous battles and heroic deaths of epic history. Granted, more women than ever rendered their services to the Patria as delegates, organizers, spies, soldiers, and saboteurs in the War for Independence (1895–98). These roles defied the normatively "feminine" and would open up possibilities to rearticulate expectations and women's advocacy in the postwar years. They would nevertheless have to finesse a more or less official narrative in which the archetypal mambí was a virile and valorous man and the mambisa a patriotic mother.

Caridad and the Regenerate Mambisa

The "Republic of Cuba" was inaugurated May 20, 1902. Here was the "sublime hour" that three generations of Cubans had sacrificed and died for. But circumstances begged to differ. The United States had militarily intervened in 1898 and, thereafter, oversaw elections so riddled with "irregularities" that mambí general Bartolomé Masó withdrew his candidacy in protest. This left Tomás Estrada Palma, son to wealthy ranchers and US citizen, to run uncontested. Among his first acts as president, Estrada Palma dissolved the mostly Black and guajiro Liberation Army, in whose stead were empowered the white and urban elites of the Assembly of Representatives.

Other, less publicized scandals ensued as well. The vast majority of women who served the Republic in Arms did not receive pensions, since so few were officially enlisted or conferred a rank. Nor did widows qualify for their deceased husband's pensions. And despite their petitions to the contrary, no woman voted in the 1901 elections.[21] In short, their contributions to Cuba Libre were not valued, if at all acknowledged. This was a *tautological* scandal, of course, for it was sexist and patriarchal prejudices that barred women from the most lauded (and, incidentally, best compensated) positions in the Republic in Arms and relegated them to auxiliary (and non-pension-qualifying) roles. As a consequence, Cuban women did not have the "epic capital," so to speak, that men of the postwar republic had.

But advocate for their rights they did, and other modalities of capital they had. Theirs was an advocacy that exploited the reverence conferred on to the "feminine" and, especially, the "maternal." For although they were not looked to as armed rebels or intellectuals, women were cast as the nation's *moral* compass. Momentum to this end was found in the 1920s, which hosted the First National Women's Congress (1923).[22] In the opening speech, Pilar Morlón de Menéndez avowed: "We shall give our activities the plain title of 'Nationalism' [. . .] It will be the emblem of those who are pure, good, and true patriots. The Cuban Revolution [independence wars] has not ended with the sight of the Cuban flag raised on el Morro [Havana fort], no, because in the wake of political freedom we have now to conquer moral freedom and this will not be achieved without the corresponding virtues."[23] The Congress showcased a women's advocacy attuned to nationalist sentiment and its moralistic connotations. The epic enthusiasm that had characterized postwar expectations had been muted, if not mortified, by US interventions and the servile or corrupt Cubans who condoned it. Hence, as the era's most popular slogan read, there was a need "For the Regeneration of Cuba." That it was the slogan of the Veterans and Patriots Association was noteworthy. In the same year as the Women's Congress, the association campaigned for a transparent and accountable government.[24] Flushed with donations and endorsed by major civic and professional organizations, the veterans movement organized councils and delegates across the island and declared it would use whatever means necessary to regenerate Cuba.

Not surprisingly, its leaders were censored, imprisoned, or exiled, and its 1924 rebellion in Las Villas repressed, but the movement revitalized the epic sensibility that martial and chivalric men could redeem the Republic. For years, after all, "Cuba" had been rendered a woman in the nation's arts and letters. When she was not a tragi-erotic *mulata,* she was a fair-skinned woman in Phrygian cap the likes of France's Marianne or the United States' Columbia. During the wars, Cuban men were called on to rescue and redeem her, lest she be "enslaved" or "outraged." To do so was likewise to redeem their manhood, for colonialism was synonymous with emasculation. And so it was hardly a coincidence that the veterans movement organized against President Alfredo Zayas (1921–25), who had never fought in any independence battles and was regarded as a bookish civilian president. This was not the case for his predecessors, the major generals José Miguel Gómez (1909–13) and Mario García Menocal (1913–21), nor for his successor, Gerardo Machado (1925–33), who had worked his way up the mambí ranks to brigadier general and was elected in 1924 on a "Platform for Regeneration."[25]

The veterans movement of 1923 and Machado's electoral campaign of 1924 did, nevertheless, differ from the Republic in Arms in one crucial respect: they endorsed a woman's right to vote. The First Women's Congress of 1923 had signaled that women were politically organized and morally invested in Cuba's regeneration and could no longer be ignored. For they, too, had their own mambisas to salute and emulate. How and which mambisas were venerated was a crucial choice, for it bespoke the virtues and capabilities affiliated with—or ascribed to—women and womanhood. One such choice was to memorialize the mambisa as philanthropic patriot. Marta Abreu (1845–1909) was the perfect candidate. Heiress to an affluent family, Abreu proved to be one of Cuba Libre's most generous benefactors. From exile, she financed legal defenses, the periodical *La República Cubana,* and arms shipments to the island. She was also patroness to her hometown Santa Clara, where she (all but anonymously) underwrote public works and social services such as elementary schools, a children's hospital, a theater, a fire station, a police station, and a nursing home for the elderly.[26]

Abreu was the mambisa as charitable benefactor, modest and compassionate. Such respectable mambisas suited well the sensibilities of the women's movement, whose leadership was in the hands of white, university educated, financially secure, and relatively conservative women.[27] In their hands, the women's movement did not critique inasmuch as reiterate the normativity of a chaste and charitable womanhood. Such notions could of course be knowingly exploited to more radical social and political ends. But even radical voices like Ofelia Rodríguez Acosta and Mariblanca Sabas Alomá, the "Red Feminist," dared not disavow motherhood as a woman's signature power.[28]

It is noteworthy, to this end, that the most venerated of mothers in Cuba was the Virgen de la Caridad (Our Lady of Charity). A cult to the Virgen de la Caridad had existed in eastern Cuba since the 1600s. According to church-sanctioned testimony, a small statue of the Virgen appeared to three men off the shores of Barajagua and, later, was found in the mining town of el Cobre, where a sanctuary was built. Miracles were attributed to the Virgen, and her statue and sanctuary became Oriente's holiest site. None other than Céspedes, "Father of the Nation," brought his troops to the sanctuary and prayed that the Virgen intercede on behalf of Cuba Libre. It is said that throughout the independence wars mambí soldiers carried medallions and pendants with her image and chanted popular verses such as "Virgen de la Caridad, / patroness of Cubans/with machete at hand/we pray for liberty."[29] Not incidentally is she lovingly known as the Virgen mambisa.[30]

The Virgen was a *people's* icon, after all. In popular lore, she appeared to three men known as the "three Juans": Juan Blanco, Juan Indio, and Juan Moreno.[31] In other words, she appeared to a white, an indigenous, and a Black man. They are the humble and dispossessed of the multiracial nation. In nearly all versions of the story, Juan Blanco and Juan Indio are farmers or fishermen and Juan Moreno (i.e., Juan Black) a slave. That she is herself described or depicted as "morena" (dark), "trigueña" (wheat-colored), "mulata," or "mestiza" is equally significant.[32] Fitting it was, then, that mambí veterans orchestrated her designation as Cuba's patron saint. In September 1915, a multiracial contingent of former officers and two thousand soldiers rode on horseback to the sanctuary in nearby Cobre, where they submitted their petition that the Virgen be named the island's patron saint—a request that Pope Benedict XV granted in May 1916.[33]

That said, the Virgen was simultaneously an icon against which Cuban *women* were measured: the chaste, charitable, and compassionate mother, as her appellations (virgin, *caridad*) and effigies (with child in hand) recommend. Granted, *marianismo* could (and can) constitute an ambivalent norm, not least because the Virgen de la Caridad is syncretized with the voluptuous and sensual Regla deity Oshún. But the Virgen was (and is) typically esteemed as she who is pure and who nurtures. That she was called on to sanctify the cause of Cuba Libre reinforced, accordingly, the presumed roles for women in the independence wars: a mambisa was she who blessed her mambí husband and sons and who cared for her children and the infirmed.

Marianismo and the *Mambisa* Bronzed

The Virgen mambisa was not the only maternal and nationalist icon. The consummate mambisa continued to be Mariana Grajales. Her affinities with the Virgen de la Caridad were not, of course, irrelevant. Mariana was devotee to the Virgen, shared her namesake (María), and was mother to martyred sons—the most famous of whom was named in the Virgen's honor: José Antonio de la Caridad Maceo y Grajales. And despite her epic celebrity as mother who knowingly *sacrificed* her sons, she could symbolize caridad, too, not least for her renown as a nurse and healer in the Ten Years' War. But above all else she was lionized as fecund and patriotic mother. The same year as the First Women's Congress (1923), a Cuban delegation set sail for Kingston, Jamaica, to exhume and repatriate Mariana's remains to her hometown of Santiago de Cuba. The delegation rode aboard the revealingly named coastguard cruiser *Baire* and was welcomed at Santiago's port to the tune of the national anthem and exuberant crowds. Her remains were then displayed in an adorned closed casket in the city hall's chapel and, later, buried with military honors at the Santa Ifigenia cemetery, where the Apostle Martí's remains and mausoleum rest. Poets, dignitaries, veterans, choirs, orchestras, and floral arrangements all commemorated her as patriotic mother who birthed "titans." The epithets speak for themselves: "To the heroic mother of the Maceos," "To the sublime matron of the Maceos," "Mother of the Nation," "Mother to all Cubans."[34]

This read of the consummate mambisa as fecund and patriotic mother was echoed in 1931, when Mariana was honored with a monument in the nation's capital. Designed by Afro-Cuban sculptor Teodoro Ramos Blanco, the bronze monument evoked the "epic scene" for which Mariana is most renowned.[35] She stands and with one arm points, presumably, to the field of battle. Against her stands her youngest son (Marcos), who looks up at her. Her tender yet firm gaze and outstretched arm in effect reiterate her famous words: "And you, stand tall, because it's time for you to go to the field of battle." The son's muscular bare chest signals mambí

Mariana holds her wounded son, Antonio, and orders the other son, Marcos, to the field of battle. Relief on pedestal to the Mariana Grajales Monument in Havana. (Author's photograph)

virility, whereas the tall and youthful Mariana (mother to eleven sons) embodies a woman's fecundity. At the monument's marble base is the image of Mariana holding a wounded Antonio Maceo, with Marcos looking on. The monument in effect rendered Mariana both a mambisa and, allegorically, the Patria, she who calls on her mambí sons to bear arms and wager their lives. *Her* duty, as mambisa, is to patriotically foster those mambí sons, whatever the cost. Mariana and the mambisa are not, as such, referents in their own right. She is meaningful vis-à-vis heroic men, not least her son the Bronze Titan. To wit, the monument was dedicated on December 7, 1931—the anniversary of *his* fall in battle.[36]

Indeed, rare was the memorialized woman—belatedly and inequitably at that. The José Martí Havana park monument was dedicated in 1903 and Maceo's in 1916. Mariana's came much later in 1931. Moreover, the iconic men stand alone: they need not be qualified as venerable vis-à-vis a woman. Prior to Mariana's Havana monument, there stood on the island only two other prominent statues that featured a woman: *El Alma Mater* (1919) and *La Estatua de la República* (1929).[37] *Alma Mater* is set on the steps to the University of Havana. She is seated with arms outstretched and in a thin robe under which ample and pert breasts stand out, not too subtly eroticized as "generous mother." *Estatua de la República,* in the Capitolio rotunda, is a rendition of the Greek goddess Athena. Armed with shield and spear and at a remarkable fifty-seven feet tall, she evokes every bit the "epic." But in both cases the women are *symbolic* or *mythical* and aesthetically Hellenic. With Maraina's monument, Cubans at last had a historic mambisa and Afrocubana to venerate publicly. And although she may have been reductively memorialized as patriotic mother, she was a revered symbol around which women could rally for *their* civil and political rights.

And rally they did. The women's movement had made relative strides in the early republican years. Adultery laws had been reformed, no-fault divorce was legalized, and women had secured the right to administer their own property. By the time Mariana's monument was on display, a woman's juridical status was doubtlessly superior to what it was under Spanish civil and penal codes, which granted men near absolute rights over their wife and daughter(s).[38] But women's suffrage had yet to materialize, despite petitions and deliberations for it since as early as the 1869 Guiámaro assembly. Most women (and some men) considered it a right bequeathed by the mambí epic. Aida Pérez de Villaurrutia's article "Yara Calls" (1929), published in *La Mujer* on the anniversary of the Grito de Yara (October 10), lamented that whereas the "pretty little island" of Cuba had "emerged beautifully with so much charm" from the independence wars, Cuban women had yet to be liberated. To honor their right to vote, she concluded, would be a "gesture of great patriotism."[39] That gesture at last came in the wake of the 1933 revolution and the storied "100 days of government" under President Ramón Grau, who in 1934 declared a women's right to vote. Woman's legal equality was thereafter enshrined in the Constitution of 1940—signed, ceremoniously enough, on the anniversary of the Grito de Yara (October 10) and in the small town of Guáimaro, the site of the Republic in Arms' first constitution and where Ana Betancourt spoke her famous words. The mythical aura of Yara and the Guáimaro Constitution was meant to communicate that the project of Cuba Libre had at last been consummated. But it was woefully evident that women's de facto equality was absent that day: of the seventy-three signatories to the 1940 Constitution, only three were women.

Marianas and *Anitas*

The 1940s and 1950s were not auspicious years for women's empowerment. Cuban women were no better than 3 percent of Congress and 14 percent of the salaried workforce. At that, those in the paid workforce worked, by and large, in the textile and tobacco factories or as domestic servants. Others were employed as waitresses, hostesses, cabaret dancers, "escorts," or sex workers in the (illicit) tourist economy. Cuba had become renowned as the brothel of the United States, and Havana was beholden to American crime syndicates, whereas Santiago de Cuba catered to the whims of US naval personnel. Both bourgeois and imperial decadence were in blossom. Cuba's elites flaunted their wealth with luxurious mansions and extravagant social events; its middle classes watched Hollywood movies and drank Coca-Cola; while its peasanty and lumpen Black proletariats languished in underemployment, poor housing, malnourishment, illiteracy, and inadequate health care.[40] All told, a "nefarious situation"—to quote a young Fidel Castro.[41]

Punctuated by Batista's coup in 1952, such circumstances nevertheless proved a stimulant for organized dissent. None was as spectacular as the assault on the Moncada barracks on July 26, 1953. In its wake, Fidel Castro issued his "epic" four-hour legal defense in which he explained his comrades' intentions to realize the historical project of Cuba Libre. The speech became the MR 26-7's manifesto, titled "History Will Absolve Me," and Castro a new prophet. The speech-cum-manifesto was not, for all that, a "feminist" text. In fact, it was rather performatively patriarchal, not least in its historical citations: Martí is referred to no less than fifteen times and (Antonio) Maceo five, whereas Mariana Grajales and Ana Betancourt are never mentioned. Nor are there any substantive policies for women's empowerment. This was not, of course, idiosyncratic to Castro. It was typical of how the liberation wars had been popularly narrated and memorialized.

So, too, was it consistent with how the Revolution and its charismatic "bearded ones" (barbudos) would be epitomized. The most iconic names and faces of the MR 26-7 and the Revolution were all men: Fidel, Che, and Camilo (Cienfuegos). This belied, however, the crucial roles that women played in the anti-Batista rebellion and in the Revolution.[42] Especially as conspirators in the urban underground, they raised money, nursed the infirmed, quartered the persecuted, and smuggled messages. In so doing, they exploited stereotypes of women as innocuous and incompetent and were able to participate undetected by naive fathers and sexist police officers. So, too, did they occupy less "traditional" roles as propagandists who wrote leaflets, spies who foiled ambushes, saboteurs who planted bombs, and soldiers who tossed Molotov cocktails.[43] Rebel women of the 1950s, in short, acted as did their mambisa ancestors. Nowhere was this more unequivocally underscored than with the Mariana Grajales Platoon, formed in September 1958 with Fidel Castro's approval. This small "platoon" of thirteen women proved their worth in battles in the Sierra Maestra and became known as the *Marianas*. So adept were they that Castro assigned them as his personal escort and claimed that women were more disciplined soldiers than men.[44] He of course failed to stipulate (or be aware of the fact) that women felt less entitled to voice grievances or question Castro's authority—let alone expect a higher rank or accolades. Their worth as soldiers was, no doubt, measured against masculinist criteria. But the Marianas were not idolized as mothers or as traditionally "feminine," and their very existence—proudly announced on Radio Rebelde—was evidence that the revolutionary movement was sympathetic to women's equality and empowerment.

And sympathetic it was. A select number of women held prominent positions in MR 26-7 and, later, the Revolution. Celia Sánchez was one of the Revolution's most valuable and beloved leaders. She was MR 26-7's most important logistics and intelligence officer. She routinely discussed strategies with Fidel Castro and, after the war, was appointed secretary to the Council of State and served on both the Central Committee of the Cuban Communist Party and, later, (as of 1978) its Politboru.[45] Haydée Santamaría was one of only two women (out of 160 men) who partook in the Moncada barracks assault and was a Sierra veteran. After the revolutionary war, she was assigned as director of Casa de las Américas, which, under her leadership, became the premiere literary and cultural institution of the leftist Americas.[46] The other key "matron" to the Revolution was Vilma Espín. She, too, had fought in the Sierra and would hold a critical position in the wake of 1959, namely as general secretariat to the Federation of Cuban Women (FMC).

Founded in August 1960, the FMC was (and is) the Revolution's most crucial "nongovernmental organization" dedicated to women.[47] To be clear, it was not tasked—at least not explicitly—with the mission to decry sexism and advocate for women's "liberation" inasmuch as to "integrate" women into the revolutionary process. Granted, these were not mutually exclusive. The FMC's municipal, provincial, and national committees; its two magazines, *Mujeres* and *Romances* (later renamed *Muchacha*); and its grassroots programs enlisted women to better each other *and* the Revolution. *Federadas,* as they were called, were active volunteers and leaders in the literacy campaign of 1961, in their neighborhood Committees for the Defense of the Revolution (CDR), and in the national militia. But the programs closest to their hearts (and organizational mandates) were those designed to mutually aid and empower other women. In early 1961, the FMC raised funds for and launched its first childcare centers in Havana and, within due course, helped institutionalize a national childcare system.[48] Albeit never adequate in quantity (or predictable in quality), the Revolution's childcare centers sought to facilitate women's entry into the workforce and out of the home. This, it was believed, would accrue benefits to women and to the Revolution. Women could enjoy greater financial autonomy and a sense of satisfaction in producing goods and services for the nation. So, too, could they (and their preschool children) socialize and be exposed to socialist values and praxis.

If the federadas volunteered and advocated for Cuba's socialist future, they did so attuned to its mambisa past. In 1960 the Ana Betancourt Schools for Peasant Women were opened. Administered by the FMC, the Betancourt schools brought eleven thousand young peasant women to Havana to be trained as seamstresses. The National Hotel and the mansions of Vedado and Miramar—the former haunts of mafia kingpins, business elites, and senators—were now classrooms and abodes to *Anitas,* as they were called. Similar programs were instituted for sex workers and maids, whose livelihoods were jeopardized by the Revolution's campaigns against hedonistic tourism and the parasitic upper classes. The FMC did its part to reframe such labor as degrading and exploitative and opened night schools for these women. Those with families were given stipends, and federadas watched their children for them as they attended classes. Thousands went on to be employed as secretaries, nurses, teachers, daycare workers, technicians, and bureaucrats.[49]

It would, then, be no exaggeration to say that Ana Betancourt's hopes to "untie the wings" of Cuban women had, to a noteworthy extent, come to fruition. The Revolution had measurably enhanced women's lives, most especially lower-income women. Other than childcare centers, it instituted maternity leave, equal pay for equal work, affirmative action–like policies, health care, university education, and safe and far less stigmatized access to divorce, contraception, and abortion. These were rights, to be clear, that women fought for. In the words of former Mariana and, later, Brigadier General "Teté" Puebla, "Before the revolutionary victory, women were objects—mere bed decorations. After the revolution this changed. Women began to organize massively, working to change the conditions of their lives and to free themselves."[50] But this they did within revolutionary "parameters." That is to say, it was never the FMC's modus operandi to be oppositional to the revolutionary state apparatus, however conspicuously *machista* (sexist) and patriarchal its leaders and institutions could be. Like the "race question," feminist politics was deemed "divisive" and sexism declared the residue of imperialist and capitalist cultures. The happy corollary to this thesis was that neither white nor male revolutionaries—which is to say, the vast majority of those in power—would be liable to Black or feminist critiques and reforms. That the FMC was tasked with affairs related to children and the family reinforced, moreover, sexist prejudices that such labor was the province of women. And whatever the historical gravitas and feminist credibility of names such as Ana Betancourt and the Anitas, the "pretty" aristocratic Betancourt was an ambivalent symbol under which "marginalized" and "underdeveloped" women received not just vocational training but also lessons in etiquette, dress, and diction.[51]

Indeed, even for those ideologically disposed to it, the call to embody the so-called New Socialist Woman was not easily answered. FMC members—and Cuban women in general—were expected to work diligently, attend study circles, partake in voluntary labor programs, stoically endure scarcities, and be vigilant and militarily prepared at all hours. That such expectations had to be finessed alongside more "conventional" expectations to be beautiful (and sexually available) as well as to assume the domestic and child-rearing responsibilities of the household made women's lives a "heroic," if not absurd, feat. In Belkis Cuza Malé's sarcastic words:

> They are making a girl for the times
> with lots of limewash and few tolls,
> wires, false hairpieces,
> cotton breasts and a wooden chassis.
> Her face will have the innocence of Ophelia's
> and her hands, a ritual to Helen of Troy.
> She'll speak three languages
> and be skilled in the art of shot, bow and arrow.
> They are making a girl for the times,
> an expert in politics
> and almost in philosophy,
> someone who never stutters,
> and never needs spectacles,
> who fulfills the requirements of an air hostess,
> reads the press every day,
> and, of course, liberates her sex
> without putting a foot wrong with a man.[52]

Whether Marianas or Anitas, revolutionary women had a tall order ahead and a precarious path to tread.

The Epic and (Feminist) Dialectics

An ironic or farcical sensibility was not, however, the norm for the late 1960s. If anything, these were momentous times, times that called for a heroic sensibility. As centennial to the Grito de Yara, moreover, they were opportune times for Cubans to recall that theirs was an epic history. The year 1968 in particular was awash in retrospectives and artistic works that commemorated the mambí. Thankfully, it was not only men they celebrated. That year, for example, Ana Betancourt's remains were repatriated from Madrid, where they had laid since 1901, and buried with military honors in Havana's Colón Cemetery.[53] But the "event" that most provocatively explored women's liberation vis-à-vis the epic of Cuba Libre was, undoubtedly, the film *Lucía* (1968).

Directed by Humberto Solás, *Lucía* is not implausibly described as an "epic." Its historical scope, its duration (160 minutes), and the grandeur of its theme(s) all recommend it. A tryptic, its three episodes each feature a different woman named Lucía set in a different historical period: the war for independence (1895), Machado's fall (1933), and the socialist revolution (1960s). Each episode's plot is structured around a love story, and the stories, as a whole, tell the tale of Cuba Libre as a passionate—not to say, futile—pursuit. A different aesthetic and mood are employed in each episode, as is a qualitatively different Lucía (i.e., Cuba). In this regard, it is no coincidence that with each episode Lucía hails from a humbler socioeconomic class: creole aristocrat (1895), urban bourgeoisie (1933), and campesina worker (1960s). Nor is it coincidental that her aesthetic evolves from the Castilian and genteel beauty of Lucía 1895 to the unpretentious beauty of mulata Lucía 1960s.

In Lucía 1895, Cuba is in the midst of war when Lucía, a middle-aged "maiden" of the creole aristocracy, falls in love with a Spanish merchant, Rafael. Much of the episode belabors Lucía and Rafeal's sentimental betrothal, and this serves well to expose it as frivolous and obscene. We see a stark contrast with the maimed Spanish soldiers and, most especially, with Fernandina, the town's madwoman. With unkempt hair and tattered clothes, Fernandina roves the streets hysterically and reveals to the viewer, albeit obliquely, why Cubans are at war. We learn that Fernandina was once a nun, who while blessing the dead in a battle's wake (presumably in the Ten Years' War), was suddenly pounced on by rapacious Spanish soldiers—hence, her madness. We see it on screen in overexposed shots and extreme close-ups with a hand-held camera that cumulatively evoke, as Anne Marie Taylor put it, a "dream-like allegory, the rape of Cuba by Spain."[54] As woman, with mestiza features and darker skin, as well as a nun (dressed in all white), Ferdinanda bespeaks a racially mixed and morally pure Cuba sullied by imperialist Spain.

Lucía's romance ends abruptly when she learns that Rafael is married. The purportedly apolitical Rafael does convince Lucía to take him to her family's estate in the countryside, away from the prying eyes and rumors of urban and aristocratic Cuba. Yet once within sight of the estate, the Spanish cavalry suddenly appears and raids it, for it doubled as a headquarters to the rebel army. Lucía is thrown aside, and Rafael flees. The truth sets in: Rafael was a Spanish spy. Lucía then searches frantically for her brother, Felipe, only to find him dead. Driven by a fierce grief, Lucía returns to town, finds Rafael, and stabs him to death. This climactic scene could be read as vengeance, but the context recommends otherwise. Felipe was not only her brother but also a mambí, and Lucía herself had covertly aided and abetted the mambí cause. Moreover, she kills Rafael publicly and with a dagger. She "executes" him in the space of the colonial town square, with Rafael dressed in his military regalia (i.e., unambiguously coded as the colonizer), and in an act that uncannily resembles the mambises' machete strike. At scene's end, Fernandina comes to comfort Lucía, whose is now also dressed in black (mourning her brother and Cuba Libre's loss) and with a maddened look on her face. The baroque musical score, the aristocratic opulence, Lucía's and Rafael's passionate gestures all amount as such to a farce of European aesthetics and the literary romance. The episode proves, instead, to be a tragedy and Lucía its tragic hero.

In Lucía 1933, Lucía is a young middle-class woman who falls in love with Aldo. Aldo is a member of the underground revolutionary movement

Lucía of 1895 in search of Rafael and, by extension, her justice. *Lucía*, 1968.

to oust Machado. Lucía opts to join the movement as Aldo's lover and as a tobacco worker, renouncing the financial comforts and shallowness of her class status and gendered expectations, as embodied by her mother. All of this Lucía leaves behind as she assumes the austere and dangerous life of a revolutionary. We see this accentuated in Aldo's sparse single room apartment and the drab frock Lucía wears at work. We see it, too, in Aldo's armed assaults on police officers.

The revolt does succeed. Machado is ousted, but a bona fide revolution never materializes. Aldo is employed in the new government, but all he sees is opportunism or worse. In one of the episode's most memorable scenes, we see Aldo at a celebratory event. The setting is a palatial-like ballroom, and all the guests are the affluent and powerful of Cuba. Men in tuxedos, women bejeweled, all with wine glasses in their hands—the scene is one of drunken stupors and gluttony. Aldo stands aside, a witness (not participant) with a repulsed look on his face. After this, the distraught Aldo enlists in a renewed armed struggle with other dissidents, but this time he is killed. Lucía is left pregnant and alone. The episode ends with a close-up of her haunting and melancholic gaze. Peter Biskind has critically noted that in this episode Aldo is the one who initiates and rebels, while Lucía accompanies and mourns.[55] But such a read does not credit the fact that Aldo is a tender, faithful, and vulnerable man—even, at that, a virgin: "You are my first love; I'm not ashamed to say it, you're my first woman," he says to Lucía. So, too, is he slender and rather petite. He does not resemble the epic archetype of a mambí "titan"—let alone a bearded "stallion" (*El Caballo*), as Fidel Castro was known. And all the more crucially, women in this episode are not restricted to aristocratic gossip and juvenile romance. Herein we see them as exploited workers who organize a strike and face off with repressive police offers in a street protest. This is no small difference from the women in Lucía 1895.

With Lucía 1960s, we leave behind the colonial town and urban factory for the humble countryside. We simultaneously leave behind the melodrama of Lucía 1895 and melancholia of Lucía 1933 for the exuberance of Lucía 1960s. But not all is well. The enemy of Cuba Libre is now the machista man, not the imperial metropolis or the dictatorial state. Lucía wants to partake in the betterment of herself and her Patria, but her machista husband stands in her way. At the episode's open, she joins her *compañeras* on the truck, off to a day's work, to discuss animatedly her new boyfriend, Tómas, who, she says, does not want her to work outside the home once they are married. Tómas does in fact make every effort to reduce Lucía to a sexual plaything and domestic servant. After a party

Comrades of Lucía of 1960s restrain a hostile Tomás. It is revolutionary women who will bring down machismo. *Lucía,* 1968.

at the local community center, a party in which a drunken Tómas fights with a man who dared dance with Lucía, Tómas nails shut the windows to their small home, rendering it a prison and yelling at her: "I want you to obey me, you hear? That's what you're my wife for!"

Tómas's reign is, however, steadily undone by the Revolution. The local foreman sees to it that a *brigadista* is assigned to their home. Members of Cuba's "literacy brigades," brigadistas were young Cubans who volunteered to go to rural Cuba and teach peasants how to read and write. They were expected, moreover, to earn their keep and do their share of agricultural and manual labor. Always under the watchful eye of Tómas, the brigadista, a handsome young man from Havana, teaches Lucía to read and write—and not without a playful intimacy that makes Tómas irate and abusive. In the end Lucía leaves, breaking the news to Tómas, poetically enough, in a note she herself wrote: "I'm going. I am not a slave." Not all ends well, however. The supposedly "liberated" Lucía is depressed and Tómas a drunk. In the closing scene, Lucía finds Tómas on the beach, distraught and pleading for her love. But rather than reconcile they break out into yet another fight. A young girl (presumably the next Lucía) looks on from afar, laughs, and walks away.

There is much to say about the exuberantly executed (almost comical) drama and aesthetic of this last of the three episodes—from Joseito Fernández's humorous commentary sung to the tune of the classic "Guantanamera" (well suited to the campesino milieu) to the intimacy and delirium that the hand-held camerawork delivers from within the confines of Tómas and Lucía's small home. But what stands out are, paradoxically, certain absences. This episode is not, for instance, the tale of armed barbudos in the Sierra Maestra, which would have made for a plausible ending to a film that dealt with historical rebellions. Rather, the viewer is interpellated by a history still in the making. The Revolution is identified with cooperative and socially useful (not alienated) labor as well as racial equality and women's empowerment. Lucía is now the mulata actress Adela Legrá, and the community's leaders are the loving and boisterous couple Flavio and Angelina, both Afro-Cuban. *Machismo,* by contrast, is identified with domestic violence, chauvinism, alcoholism, and laziness. Tomás is usually drunk or kicked back and joking about at work, whereas we see the brigadista's sweated brow and voluntary labor in the fields as well as his diligent work as Lucía's tutor. Tomás is, moreover, a tall white man who enacts the cigar-gesticulating bravado of a Che or a Fidel—a quite provocative resemblance. The film foregoes the revolutionary violence of the first two episodes for women's cooperative labor and a critique of machismo in the last. The revolutionary man is neither the armed mambí of 1895 (Felipe) nor the armed rebel of 1933 (Aldo); he is, rather, the conscientious Flavio or the modest and industrious brigadista. Nor is the revolutionary woman the maddened or bereaved (white) Lucía of 1895 or 1933; she is the committed Angelina or the now-literate Lucía in the throes of a "dialectical struggle" for liberation. By film's end there is hope and levity, despite its serious subject matter. The epic, if fraught, is less tragic and more *participatory* and *subaltern* than ever.[56] Indeed, while the film lends credence to the thesis that revolutions are necessarily tragic, it nevertheless inflects that tragedy with an epic sentiment, the effect of which is a curiously "tragi-epic" moral to the story, namely that we can at least "fail better" each time.[57]

Historical Poetics and the Militant Mambisa

In Cuban letters, Nancy Morejón's "Mujer Negra" (Black Woman), first published in 1975, could be read as poetically akin to *Lucía.* It is not epic in the strictest sense of length and form, but the poem's historical scope and solemn themes evoke and creatively partake in it. Like *Lucía,* "Black Woman" does not reiterate the tale of heroic "founding fathers." Instead, it looks to and poetically venerates she who has been all but written out of the national epic—cast aside as the sexually promiscuous, the repugnant, or the irrelevant. And the poetic narrator is not a traumatized victim inasmuch as a historical vanguard. Each stanza interjects with a defiant deed: "I rebelled." "I walked." "I rose up." "I left for the hills." "I came down from the Sierra." Her odyssey reads as the odyssey of Cuba Libre. It moves from trauma and injustices to rebellion and revolution: from the Middle Passage ("I still smell the foam of the sea they made me cross") and slavery ("His Worship bought me in a public square") to the independence wars ("I rode with the troops of Maceo") and the Revolution ("to put an end to capital and usurers,/to generals and the bourgeoisie"). In the poem's first stanzas she is the abducted, the enslaved, the raped, and the exploited, but in due course she becomes cimarrón, mambisa, and *guerrillera.* By the poem's close, she "exists," and her existence is that of a collectivity no longer dispossessed: "Now I exist: only today do we own, do we create./Nothing is foreign to us./The land is ours./Ours the sea and the sky,/the magic and the dream [*quimera*]."[58]

That Morejón named Maceo (not Mariana Grajales) in her poetic ode to the resilient and rebellious Black woman may strike us as regrettable choice. Perhaps this was because the "Mother of the Nation" was understood as strictly that, a mother, and Morejón wanted to validate the Black woman as combatant. So, too, did the Revolution, with its "olive green" aesthetic and internationalist ethos. This was an era, after all, in which armed Vietnamese and Sandinista women were celebrated as feminist icons and Cuban women volunteered for internationalist missions, to include Angola, where they served not just in clerical or logistical capacities but also in combat arms.[59] Little wonder, thus, that the mambisa would be recalled as a valiant soldier.[60]

This motif of a militant heroine was echoed in the books *La mujer en el 68* (1978) and *La mujer en el 95* (1982). *La mujer en el 68* opens with accounts of Mariana Grajales, María Cabrales, and Ana Betancourt but dedicates at least half its text to lesser-known mambisas and the heroic deeds of anonymous Cuban women. Most of the anecdotes are of epic last stands and famous last words. Juana de la Torre was held captive and placed in front of the Spanish lines so as to deter a mambí assault. But Juana would not have it. Her last words, "Let the mambí canons fire!"[61] Mercedes de Varona was captured but refused her captors' terms of surrender. She stood before a firing squad and shouted: "We will die blessing the bullet that kills us, should the patria be saved. Fire! Fire! Viva Cuba Libre!" The book's author, Armando Caballero, tells us that approximately two women were executed every day between 1868 and 1873. Nearly twice as many ended up in prison, where they either died or were sent off to Cueta, Spain's African penal colony. The overall stress in this text is not, thus, on women who stoically bore their sons' and husbands' deaths; it is, rather, on Cuban women who embodied "revolutionary intransigence" and heroically faced *their own deaths.*[62]

This logic was reiterated in *La mujer en el 95.* Women are celebrated as fundraisers, propagandists, and couriers, but the bulk of the text is devoted to women as *combatants,* which included over twenty women who obtained the rank of captain or higher in the Liberation Army. These included women so exceptional that they, too, were endowed with epithets: Magdalena Peñarredona, "la Delegada" (the delegate); Luz Noriega, "La Reina de Cuba" (the queen of Cuba); and, most popularly of all, Rosa "la Bayamesa." Rosa la Bayamesa was, in a sense, the embodiment of Morejón's "Black Woman." Born a slave in Bayamo, Cuba's first "liberated" city, Rosa Castellanos joined the mambí ranks at the age of thirty-four in 1868. Renowned for her knowledge of medicinal herbs, she was appointed captain of the Medical Corps. She was also renowned as a soldier who fought in (and survived) all three independence wars—a "true virtuoso" with the machete, as the book puts it.[63] And this is to say nothing of all those who fought "brandishing the fearsome machete" or tending to the ill and the infirmed: "So many are those lost to anonymity!"[64]

That the women of *La mujer en el 68* and *La mujer en el 95* are not identified as mothers or wives inasmuch as militant mambisas was symptomatic of the new times. But closer scrutiny reveals that the books are fairly superficial. They read more like propagandistic pamphlets than nuanced histories. Whatever her uniqueness, each woman's story reiterates the same ethos of patriotic loyalty and sacrifice, and never is there a robust feminist agenda voiced. Their stories do not substantively modify what constitutes the "heroic" or the "epic." In many respects they merely celebrate women who could *mimic* or *follow the orders* of heroic men. It was men, after all, who decided on the strategy and laws enacted by the Republic in Arms. Other than the occasional delegate or captain, women were almost always their subordinates. As case in point, it is no small irony that these books were authored by a man, and their last words are the quotes of world-historic men—Vladimir Lenin and José Martí, respectively.[65]

Such contradictions persisted. The PCC confessed its disquiet in its "Thesis: On the Full Exercise of Women's Equality" (1975). The FMC and Cuban women are touted as revolutionaries who have contributed "their labor, their initiative, and their enthusiasm" to Cuba's socialist achievements.[66] But women's equality, it confessed, was not (yet) a reality in the home, the workplace, or the state. Eighty-five percent of women surveyed said that child-rearing and housework were a decisive "limiting factor" to their fuller participation in revolutionary activities and the salaried workforce. The cumulative effect of this was that women did not make up better than 25 percent of the salaried workforce and 13 percent of the PCC (and only 5.5 percent of its national leadership).[67]

By the 1980s, the FMC could nevertheless boast about its and the Revolution's accomplishments. Its membership was at an all-time high;

an unprecedented number of Cuban women were now physicians, scientists, engineers, lawyers, and professors; the PCC's membership had climbed to 21 percent women; and women were close to one-third of the National Assembly of People's Power. A closer look, that said, revealed some "errors and negative tendencies." Honors for national service and cultural excellence continued to be awarded disproportionately to men, and women remained underrepresented in influential bodies such as the Council of State and the PCC's Secretariat.[68] The FMC was of course relevant and influential. As *the* women's representative body on the island, even the Revolution's undisputed patriarch knew well enough not to miss its congresses. But this meant that the FMC pled its case to Fidel Castro once every five years and that Castro was not bound to their recommendations. At the Third PCC Congress of 1986, he publicly lamented the lack of women's equality and insisted that sexism was a "residual" social ill that the Revolution had to "rectify." But the world's affairs had other "negative tendencies" in store for Cuba, and these would not bode well for Cuban women, especially young women of color.

'98 and the Promiscuous Mambisa

The crisis that beset Cubans in the early-to-mid 1990s was unprecedented. Hunger and blackouts went hand in hand with disenchantment and cynicism, forcing the Revolution to make capitalist concessions that were as necessary as they were regrettable. The shift to a tourist economy yielded much-needed foreign currency, for instance, but also income and racial inequalities not seen since prerevolutionary days. Moreover, while the ensemble of tropical beauty and revolutionary panache were attractive to many tourists, what drew the most tourists were Cuban women, especially the exotic mulata. All of which is to say that the period's circumstances fostered *jineterismo* (prostitution), a socially scorned "livelihood" that jeopardized the Revolution's moral credibility.[69]

That these post–Soviet years were centennial years was, in a sense, a happy coincidence, a coincidence the revolutionary cadre did not squander. For if Marxist-Leninist ideology was no longer as viable, the Revolution could always retrench itself in the mythical past. As Cintio Vitier clarified: "Our alliance with Soviet socialism was never more than just that—an alliance. Where the Soviets had hoped to find an ideological voice, the community of Céspedes, Maceo, and Martí was waiting for them. It was more than an ideology; it was a true vocation for justice and freedom."[70] Little wonder, thus, that the era's speeches, billboards, honors, museums, textbooks, and other such paraphernalia abounded in "lessons" that the mambí epic had to offer the besieged present.

Cuba's cinema was enlisted, too, as evidenced by a film titled none other than *Mambí* (1998). The film tells the fictional story of Goyo, a Canary Islander *quinto* (conscript) whose life changes irrevocably by virtue of his tour in war-torn Cuba. In Havana, Goyo meets and falls in love with Ofelia, a beautiful mulata and adopted daughter to his Cuban uncle. Little does Goyo know, however, that his uncle and Ofelia are underground rebels. Off to the war front, Goyo finds himself at odds with the war and his superiors. He eventually deserts the Spanish army but is caught by the mambises. To his surprise, Goyo is reunited with Ofelia, who vouches for him and is herself, it turns out, a mambisa. Whether to prove his loyalty to the cause or his love for Ofelia, Goyo then partakes in a mission to deliver dynamite for sabotage operations. But the mission goes awry, and Goyo and Ofelia must flee to the wilderness. It is here that, under a clichéd waterfall and sentimental music, they "consummate" their love. And it is hereafter that Goyo emerges a bona fide mambí: on horseback and with machete in hand. By the film's close, in fact, Goyo decides to stay in Cuba after the war: "My home is here now," he says to his friend, Sevillano, in the Havana port, with a pregnant Ofelia at his side.

But the film is less a love story about Goyo and Ofelia than a story about Goyo's metamorphosis into an honorary Cuban—that is to say, *the* Cuban. As the drama unfolds, Goyo progressively takes on an uncanny resemblance to José Martí. By the film's closing sequence, he looks as if a reincarnated Martí: statesmen-like attire, receding hairline, and chevron-style mustache. There are other cues throughout the film that render him an honorary Cuban, if not Martí: Goyo is an islander, recites poetry to Ofelia, and is imprisoned by the Spanish, as was a young Martí. But what is at stake here is a timely issue. That Goyo is a Spaniard and Ofelia Afrocubana is no coincidence. For in the 1990s the most notorious

Ofelia, the mambisa, with fellow mambí officers. *Mambí*, 1998.

demographic to visit the island as tourists were middle-aged Spanish and Italian men who flaunted their "purchasing power," which is to say, their ability to "consume" exotic women of color. The women who sold themselves were socially stigmatized, for hardly could it be said that they cohered with the empowered socialist woman.

Mambí as such points to real social contradictions and, like a mythical text, offers unrealistic solutions, namely that Ofelia is a mambisa (not a jinetera); that Goyo marries (instead of hires out) Ofelia; and that he stays to live with her and their children in Cuba (rather than have her flee to Europe with him). Goyo is the respectable Spaniard and honorary Cuban. He is sensitive and scrupulous about violence, vomiting at the sight of his fellows' corpses and refusing to torture or execute a mambí prisoner of war. He does not kill anyone until he stabs the Spanish officer who tried to rape Ofelia, and thereafter he is shown in a montage series of machete charges against armed Spanish soldiers. The film thereby plays out a familiar logic and aesthetic vis-à-vis the mambí epic. The mambises are portrayed as a valorous and multiracial constituency of men at arms. Once Goyo defects to the Cuban Liberation Army, his new commander is the stoic and war-wise Colonel Nazario, a mulatto. But the film also surprises audiences with a nuanced and humanized portrayal of Spaniards. Other than Goyo's former regiment commander, Captain Gonzalo, Spanish soldiers are an honorable and humble lot who would rather be at home with their loved ones: Goyo and his friend, Sevillano, were miners in the Canary Islands, and his sergeant was a sheepherder in Salamanca. This, too, reflected contemporary affairs. For the film, albeit stocked with Cuban actors and credited to ICAIC, was coproduced with Spain and directed by the Canary Islanders filmmakers Teodoro and Santiago Ríos.

Spaniards, in fact, are cast as the lesser enemy of Cuba Libre. Her truest enemies are "bad" Cubans and the United States. The "bad" Cubans are the *latinfundistas,* those whose loyalties are to their own wealth rather than the Patria. In the film, mambí colonel Nazario is invited to meet with a faction of wealthy (white) landowners at one of their plantation estates. Dressed handsomely and with a banquet of food at their table, they break the news that General Weyler has been dismissed and toast with wine that '98 brings "peace and prosperity"—to which they add, with a snicker, "and higher sugar prices." Nazario, dressed in mambí fatigues, toasts to "independence." The men plea that now is the time for "dialogue" and "negotiation," but Nazario replies, "In what language? The language of Spain or that of Cubans?" Riled, he stands, pulls out his pistol and says, "Let me tell you what my men will say. If you propose autonomy reforms . . . Fire [*Fuego*]! If you propose provincialism . . . Fuego! No one here is going to put down his machete!" Nazario punctuates each "fuego" with a gunshot to the sky. But the meeting is a ruse. Soldiers surround the estate. Nazario quickly mounts his horse and charges into the foggy night (i.e., his death) yelling, "¡Viva Cuba Libre!" Nazario thereby consummates the mambí epic with a heroic death at arms and interpellates the contemporary viewer with a call to "revolutionary intransigence." An allegory of a contemporary Cuba burdened with inequalities, the scene codes as traitors those who choose individualistic wealth and bourgeois amenities over Patria and socialist solidarity.

The United States does not appear in the film until the closing scenes. As Goyo bids farewell to his Spanish friends in the Havana port, a US Marine brusquely interrupts them and, in southern drawl, barks at Goyo, "Whatta ya doin' here? Git back in line." That the soldier is on horseback accentuates the power differential, a visual cue to the proverbial David (Cuba) against Goliath (United States) scenario. Goyo does not slay the giant, so to speak, but he does grab hold of the horse's rein and tempers it in quiet defiance. A tense stare down ensues, which does not end until Goyo is called away by his lovely and noticeably pregnant wife Ofelia. There is as such no resolution, only an antagonistic encounter that is meant to be prophetic. For the marine not only symbolizes the occupation of 1898–1903 but also the "Yankee" imperialism that endures a century later in 1998. The scene's (and film's) salience for Cuban *women* is no less historically prophetic. Ofelia, the only woman of any dramatic relevance in the entire film, begins as object of desire and ends as object of domesticity: beautiful, vulnerable, and sexually available, by film's close she is little more than expectant mother and wife to the defiant, heroic man.

Mariana and the Matria

The film *Mambí* was not, of course, the only work to revisit the mythic past in this period, nor was it the last word on the mambisa. Mariana Grajales continued to be *the* epic referent for Cuban women, and not all accounts of her reduced her to a stoic or "Spartan" mother. *Mariana, raíz del alma cubana* (1998), by Ayds Cupull and Froilán González, offered its readers an uncharacteristically nuanced discussion of Mariana's life and life lessons. In it, she is depicted as her children's first and most consequential *moral* educator. The stress herein is on an *ethical* Mariana who teaches her children discipline, honor, hard work, and honesty as well as anti-colonialism and anti-racism.[71] Another noteworthy exception was the Afro-Cuban poet Georgina Herrera's 2005 play, *El penúltimo sueño de Mariana* (Mariana's penultimate dream). The play is set in the last days of Mariana's life. The octogenarian Mariana is frail and in the care of her daughter Dominga. She is tormented by dreams (or are they memories? visitations?) of loss and death, the deaths of at least seven of her sons (José and Antonio would die later in 1896). She is confused or haunted and, unlike her popular portrayals, tearful. She hears the voices of her dead sons and asks for them. Indeed, time itself is no longer linear inasmuch as *mythical* and Mariana, we learn, not a mother inasmuch as daughter and prophetess.

Her penultimate dream takes her back to the night she learned that the war for Cuba Libre had broken out (1868). But the play's scenarios and dreams actually predate 1868. In fact, Mariana is rendered the spiritual heir to Fermina Lucumí, an African-born woman who led a historic 1843 slave revolt. In one of Mariana's dreams-cum-visions, it is the Yoruba goddess Yemayá who sees to it that the "force" of Fermina's spirit will live on in a "fortunate" other, namely Mariana. Fermina and Mariana are as such "proud daughters" of Yemayá, goddess of the oceans and, hereby, spiritual *matron* to rebel Afrocubanas.[72] The "Mother of all Cubans" is as such rendered *daughter* to an African deity. Or more exactly, the epic of Cuba Libre is rendered matrilineal. That Oshún (syncretized with the Virgen de Caridad) is not the chosen deity is, no doubt, crucial. Oshún is goddess of rivers, fresh and "sweet" water (*agua dulce*), whereas Yemayá invokes the bitterness of salt and the oceans, which is to say, the injustice and trauma of the Middle Passage and bondage. But the ocean is also that which ties Cuba to other islands, to the Black Atlantic and the African diaspora of the Americas.

"Mariana's penultimate dream" reads, accordingly, as an echo of Morejón's "Black Woman." It rewrites Afrocubanas into the nation's epic as heirs to spiritual depth and revolutionary ferment. One need only look to Fermina, who leads a revolt (machete in hand) and is defiant till her last quintessential stand. Facing a firing squad, she cries out: "But Fermina Lucumí does not die in shackles; she dies free! (spits)."[73] This epic scene is as the national anthem would have it. Fermina takes up arms and lives not in "shame" or "opprobrious submission." Nor does she die. She lives on in Mariana. Hence, the literary device of dreams and the spiritual legacy of the Lucumí peoples enables Herrera to rearticulate Mariana's uneventful death in Jamaica as kindred to Fermina's unequivocally epic death on Cuban soil. That the heroic is hereby affiliated with Black women also rearticulates the Patria (*pater*, father) as Matria (*mater*, mother)—a catachrestical revolt, in other words. But to what effect? Does Herrera's drama simply reiterate the mambí sublime with little other than Afro-Cuban symbols and armed women? And what will be the fate of Mariana's daughter Dominga and the ethics *she* represents as her mother's caretaker? Is such an ethics hopelessly wedded to the "feminine"? Or does it embody an ethos that the epic overlooks, if not forecloses?

In any case, an inquiry and aesthetics that elaborated a *Matria* and what differences it could embody were still a far cry from the norm. As Fidel Castro put it at the outset of the Special Period: "We know who our teachers were and we know who pointed the way. And none of those who showed us the way abandoned their position. Céspedes never abandoned his position. Agramonte never abandoned his post. Neither did Máximo Gómez, nor Maceo nor Martí."[74] That Mariana Grajales, Bernarda Toro, María Cabrales, and Ana Betancourt should have been included in such a list few Cubans would deny—Castro included. But the fact that their names did not as readily come to mind in nearly all of Castro's extemporaneous and "epic" speeches is just as undeniable. This was not his fault (or burden) alone. It was a symptom of a deeper mythopoetic prejudice that, at century's close, had yet to be rectified.

3 The Epic Travestied

Choteo and the Mambí as Populist Trickster

¡Eso habría que verlo, compay!

—Elpidio Valdés

THE COMICAL and the *epic* are not exactly literary comrades—at least not conventionally so. Classics like *Gilgamesh, Ramayana, Iliad, Aeneid, Beowulf, Sundiata*, and *Song of Cid* are not known to elicit laughter, nor do they revel in irony or the vulgar. Indeed, the comical may well be understood as inimical to the epic. With subjects as sober and as lofty as war, sacrifice, and nation, the epic arouses and dwells in solemnity and grandeur. Hardly, that is, does it call for or easily accommodate humor.

The epic of Cuba Libre echoes precisely this generic proclivity. It tells the tale of archetypal heroes and momentous events that the interpellated are expected to admire, if not stoically emulate. For rarely, if ever, do such epic narratives and their memorials yield jovial pleasure—let alone laughter—inasmuch as reverence and awe. The ritualistic tributes to the Bronze Titan Maceo and the Apostle Martí call on citizens to emulate their military prowess, moral rectitude, and love of Patria. The interpellated, in short, are called on to enact their own Protest at Baraguá or Fall at Dos Ríos.

Yet the epic is not altogether immune to the comical, whether as mockery or otherwise. The ancient Greek *Battle of the Frogs and Mice* (*Batrachomyomachia*) employed the poetic metrics and heroic motifs of Homer's *Iliad* to comical effect, whereby grandeur was rendered laughably trivial. Parodies, satire, and the burlesque are all renowned for their capacity to travesty and scandalize the serious and the sublime. With their levity and folly—if not outright vulgarity—they can render the lofty lowly and the venerable vile. And this is what makes the comical not only enjoyable but also politically salient.

Cuba, too, has enjoyed its quota of the comical. Its "buffoonery theater" (*teatro bufo*) and an idiosyncratic sense of humor known as *choteo* are no strangers to the enjoyable and the populist. Choteo and the jocular familiarity with which Cubans treat each other can be read as an egalitarian ethos in which all subjects are liable to ridicule and nothing is taken too seriously. Choteo can be understood thereby as a "salutary" humor that sullies, desacralizes, or otherwise "lowers" that which is unjustifiably venerated or esteemed. Yet so, too, can it be "toxic," as Cuban essayist Jorge Mañach famously put it.[1] For it could amount to a species of melancholic humor that knows not how to distinguish the venerable from the unvenerable. Choteo as such may perilously foster a belief that humans cannot better themselves or their world—a belief very much at odds with epic emplotment.

How the comical has come to inflect, if not "travesty," the epic of Cuba Libre is the subject of this chapter. Nowhere is this more richly the case than with the animated film series *Elpidio Valdés* (1974–2003). Largely set in the War of Independence (1895–98), the series chronicles the "adventures" of the fictional cavalry officer Elpidio Valdés and his merry mambises as they cleverly and courageously fight for Cuba Libre. Although a far cry from parody or satire, it does rely heavily on vernacular humor and jovial antics in ways that have rendered it irresistibly popular. Rare is the Cuban, whether young or senior, who does not speak fondly of Elpidio. This makes the series quite distinct from the panegyric sober oratory, hymns, manifestoes, and monuments that so routinely characterize the mambí epic. And this may well explain why *Elpidio Valdés* is so beloved and popular. It offers a portrayal of revolutionary war and nationalist loyalty as a jocular and festive affair. So, too, is it cast as a "genealogical past" that bespeaks a "prophetic future."[2] It interpellates Cuban youth as heirs to the mambí epic and conveys its relevance to the contemporary socialist epic. Yet its valorization of—and calls for—virtues such as vigilance, loyalty, and martial preparedness are neither dull nor didactic, which is why the series could simply be read as a more efficacious state propaganda: more efficacious precisely because so enjoyable.

But another read is possible. *Elpidio Valdés* could also be read as a "salutary" choteo that critiques and, accordingly, *enriches* the mambí—and revolutionary—epic. On this read, its portrayal of a far less "titanic" or "apostolic" mambí constitutes a less aristocratic alternative to the classical epic hero and the genre's hackneyed—or altogether impossible—chivalry and solemnity. With the series, Cuba's youth can revel in an epic hero more akin to a trickster than to a Spartan warrior (Maceo), saintly martyr (Martí), or "heroic guerrilla" (Che Guevara). In fact, one could argue that the series' true hero is a collective and populist subject (*el pueblo cubano*) whose humorous ways invite viewers to laugh not only at their foes but also at their fallible selves. In this regard, the ridiculing laughter and "carnivalesque" attributes of *Elpidio Valdés* can be read as tactics that productively exploit the comical's capacity, as Vladimir Propp and Mikhail Bakhtin theorized, to lower and scandalize the lofty.[3] Or, as Terry Eagleton has put it, they are tactics that bespeak the "plebian wisdom" of folk humor: we can only expect so much of our fallible selves and each other.[4]

Buffoonery and the Theatrically Political

In the mid- to late nineteenth century, what would soon be recognized as a uniquely *Cuban* species of humor was culturally instituted with the advent of teatro bufo, "buffoonery theater." Its closest kin was the Spanish *zarzuela,* a drama punctuated by musical and dance scenes as well as popular sayings and comedic lyrics. Bufo was at least as lively a spectacle as the zarzuela, and it, too, was characterized by short humorous acts enlivened with music. But with bufo, Cubans rejoiced in their own vernacular and, however vicariously, voiced their dissent.

Set firmly on Cuban soil and to the tunes of *décimas* and *guarachas,* bufos were renowned for their vulgar jokes, improvisational frolics, and a "social aesthetic" that countered the Hispanophilic zarzuela and the ostentatious Italian opera. Bufos were merciless and riotously so. They parodied the romances, operas, and melodramas of Havana's elite playhouses and popularized a "trinity" that came to symbolize the Cuban people: *el gallego, el negrito,* and *la mulata.* The gallego, colloquial for "Spaniard," was usually depicted as a rotund and gregarious shopkeeper whose naivety about Cuban affairs and human vices was laughable. That said, the genre's comedic forte was the buffoonery of blackness. In its earliest stages, the "thick-lipped Negro" (*el negro bembón*) was the bufo's most popular character. Played by a white actor in blackface, the negro bembón was a clown-like fool whose exaggerated Spanish pidgin (*bozal*) and mischievousness were a crowd pleaser—insofar as it was a mostly white audience in a racist colony. Later came the *negro catedrático,* the mock "Black professor," whose dandy attire and faux learnedness were considered laughably ridiculous—for rare was the (white) Cuban who took seriously a Black intellect. Such characters routinely shared the stage with the mulata, a young, fair-skinned Afrocubana who was sensual accessory or erotic foil to the comical act.[5]

Bufo could be read, thus, as a comedic drama that theatrically staged the racial anxieties of its era. It emerged and was popularly embraced at a time (i.e., 1860s) when Cuba was substantially Black. No fewer than half the island's inhabitants were of African descent, and the majority of them enslaved. With the abolitionist clamor of the era and an already substantial number of free Cubans of color on the urban scene, especially in Santiago de Cuba, bufo bound Afro-Cubans to demeaning stereotypes and policed the island's social hierarchy. Yet so, too, as Jill Lane argued, did it portray and popularize Cubanness (*cubanía*) as intimately, if ambivalently, indebted to blackness.[6] Nor was its humor politically inconsequential. Critics deemed bufo a trivial "anti-literary" and "immoral" amusement suited for the popular classes. What mattered to bufo theater was, though, neither the literary text nor artistic virtuosity inasmuch as the interpreters' rapport with their audience and the lyrics with their times. What mattered was its improvisational, interactive, and vernacular humor, one that reveled in local dialect, rhythms, and populist sensibilities. As such, bufo constituted a travesty of bourgeois respectability as well as peninsular prejudices and colonial authority.[7]

Not surprisingly, thus, was bufo deemed not only vulgar and immoral but also "subversive." Francisco "Pancho" Fernández's Bufos Habaneros at the Teatro Villanueva were staged in the early months of the Ten Years' War and conveyed, however elliptically, an *independentista* sentiment. It was suspected that the Villanueva and its bufos diverted their funds to the mambí cause. Nearly every visual and dramatic cue corroborated it. On January 23, 1869, the Villanueva was decked in red, white, and blue ribbons, with only the US and Cuban flags on display and women wearing their hair down—a symbol of independentista solidarity. When a performer cried out "¡Viva la tierra que produce la caña!" (Long live the land that produces sugarcane!), the audience erupted with cries of "¡Viva Cuba Libre!" and "¡Viva Céspedes!" But just as quickly, Spanish volunteers opened fire on the public and laid siege to Havana for four days.[8]

Bufo was censored for the remainder of the war, its writers and actors largely exiled to Mexico. It returned to the Cuban stage in the 1880s and early 1890s but was not as politically consequential. According to critic Rine Leal, it had "decayed" to mere jokes and musical amusement.[9] Perhaps this was because writers and actors remembered the 1869 massacre at Villanueva or perhaps the farcical was no longer as satisfactory. A new generation of Cubans, especially young men, were called on to tread in their mambí fathers' and grandfathers' likeness. This was a time, in other words, not for buffoonery or guarachas but for sacrifice and heroic hymns: a time for epicness.

Melancholic Choteo and El Pueblo Cubano

It would have been obscene to comically emplot the War of Independence (1895–98). That war engulfed the entire island and claimed the lives of as much as one-fifth of its residents. And this is to speak only of the dead. Nearly all of the island's villages, towns, roads, bridges, livestock, and rural estates had been rendered desolate. Those who had survived were mostly left penniless, jobless, displaced, and mourning lost loved ones.[10] That the United States militarily intervened and, thereafter, came the Platt Amendment was no balm either. Cubans who had once reveled in anticolonialist farce (i.e., bufo) and the mambí epic now languished in the tragedy of a "neocolony."

Yet humor and the comical were not altogether jettisoned in the republican years. Choteo, of which bufo was a theatrical species, lived on in everyday life. Jorge Mañach's *Indagación del choteo* (1928) characterized choteo as the levity (*ligereza*) and irreverence (*irrespetuosidad*) with which Cubans treat not only each other but also sacred or taboo subjects. At a crematorium in Paris, one of Mañach's Cuban colleagues joked, "I'd like it raw [*Démelo de vuelta y vuelta*]," as a cadaver was introduced in the incinerator.[11] For Mañach, this irreverent remark was symptomatic of a "toxic" choteo that befell Cubans of the republican years. Cubans were no longer as seduced by epic invocations of the sublime and Patria. What was once held sacred—or believed possible—was now dismissed with crass and caustic humor.

Choteo as such vocalized the "intimate sadness" of a "decidedly melancholic people," observed Mañach.[12] And if it did so, it was not for unsound reasons. As Sigmund Freud theorized it, melancholia is best understood as a fixation on a beloved yet lost object. It is a failure, more exactly, of the bereaved to find a suitable surrogate and reinvest all of the "cathectic" energy that once was bound to the now departed object.[13] The loss that plagued Cubans of the early republican years was the loss of Cuba Libre and all that the mambí epic had come to signify in the collective consciousness—whether it was sovereignty, Black dignity, women's rights, or collective prosperity. Cuba was to be a "moral republic," as the Apostle Martí had said, "with all and for the good of all." It was not, thereby, the trauma of the wars inasmuch as their anticlimactic and tragic denouement that plagued the Cuban "psyche." *Cuba Libre* was now *Cuba irredenta* (unredeemed Cuba) and its subservience to the United States a national disgrace. Choteo as such was symptomatic of a melancholic fixation on a desire for justice. This meant that its "egalitarian" capacity to ridicule anyone or anything could in fact desacralize that which deserved no such reverent attachment.[14] And in these early republican years, there was much that deserved little or no respect. Monopolies, clientelist politics, electoral fraud, underemployment, and organized crime had taken their toll.

The most popular articulation of choteo and the political in these years was not, however, in theater but in the weekly satire *La Política Cómica* (1905–34) and the graphic character Liborio. Created by cartoonist and editor Ricardo de la Torriente (1869–1934), Liborio was the era's unofficially acknowledged icon of the Cuban people. In his earliest renditions he was simply known as "Pueblo cubano" or "el pueblo."[15] Hardly was it a coincidence as such that Liborio was a guajiro (rural peasant). The slender build, sombrero, sideburns, mustache, and rural milieu all evoked Cuba's small farmers and artisanal classes. Liborio as guajiro was a symbol of honorable and productive labor as well as ties to the land. Albeit loosely, moreover, Liborio resembled the rural mambí aesthetic of straw hat and linen clothes, and his name resembled the word *libre* (free)—or rather: *Cuba Libre.*

What made Liborio so enjoyable and memorable an icon, however, were the ways in which that iconography conjured and was enriched by humor and a nationalist sentiment. He was renowned for the sarcasm and irony that his slender body and expressive face projected and his playful verses voiced. Every cartoon was accompanied by poetic quartets or *décimas* that voiced Liborio's comedic appraisal of timely issues—none as timely or as tenacious as US interventions in Cuban affairs. Indeed, Liborio was nearly synonymous with—and most remembered for—anti-interventionist sentiment. Not infrequently would the cartoons feature Liborio in dialogue with the United States, whether portrayed as Uncle Sam or as a caricatured US president. A November 22, 1908, edition had Uncle Sam say: "A toast to the good health of Cuba, my friend Liborio." Liborio replied, "And a toast to the great American Nation, which has *helped* us twice, and may it not have to do so a third time." The "help" that Liborio ironically refers to are the US military occupations of 1898–1902 and a *contemporaneous* one (in force since 1906). De la Torriente (and the reader) could not know when it would officially end (1909), nor did they have any assurances that it would not occur yet again.[16] In a

1908 edition, a caricatured President (elect) William Taft is featured with a scroll that reads "Platt Amendment" (*Ley Platt*), as Liborio stands over the island near Guantánamo, where a US flag waves. Mr. Taft says, "Liborio, do you know who I am?" His reply, "Yes, master: the new overseer."[17]

The slavery trope of master (*amo*) and overseer (*mayoral*) belies, however, the extent to which Liborio did *not* suitably represent the pueblo cubano. Liborio had a decidedly Iberian profile in the midst of a phenotypically and culturally "mulatto nation." That his popularity coincided with the early republic's policy to "whiten" the island was not, thereby, accidental. Nor should it come as any wonder that Torriente (white, male, and wealthy) had no sympathy for Black, feminist, or labor advocates. His cartoons routinely lampooned Afro-Cuban civil rights leader Juan Gualberto Gómez and dismissed the Independent Party of Color's politics as "racist noise" (*bulla racista*) and *eo ipso* "antipatriotic."[18] The feminist movement's advocacy for the rights to vote, divorce, and own property was likewise ridiculed as a "chimera" and "fantasy"—when not a menace to the patriarchal "happy home."[19]

In other words, Liborio graphically interpellated the island's white and mestizo male artisans, workers, and small farmers. He humorously pandered to the majority electorate and did so in ways that ridiculed Black and feminist advocacy. In doing so, he also domesticated populist grievances and rancor. He may have been a guajiro who sarcastically voiced an anti-interventionist sentiment, but he was not mistaken for a socialist proletariat or internationalist communist. Torriente's cartoons dismissed labor radicals as "anarchists" and "Bolsheviks" and cast aside their advocacy for living wages, pensions, sick leave, and the rights to unionize and strike as the whims of lazy or socially degenerate Cubans. As a case in point, Torriente issued the biblically ironic "Liborio's Commandments": "The guajiro's commandments must be ten, namely: First: Love work above all else. Second: Never stop being a good Cuban. Third: Sanctify the plow. Fourth: Honor and sow local products. Fifth: Kill the tobacco weevil. Sixth: Do not be lazy [*No majasear*]. Seventh: Do not take thy neighbor's vegetables or livestock. Eighth: Rise early and yoke the ox at sunrise. Ninth: Leave be in her hut your compadre's wife. Tenth: Do not covet foreign sweet potatoes."[20] Nor, incidentally, should we mistake Liborio for a mambí. Whatever his guajiro credentials or nationalist sympathies, he was only ever a lone, unarmed Cuban whose melancholic demeanor and sarcastic remarks could hardly be said to embody or arouse an epic sensibility. He and *La Política Cómica* were venues in which Cuba's popular classes could air their frustrations as (relatively) disempowered.

But never did Loborio unequivocally symbolize a collective and organized resistance, much less a Revolution.

Messianic Youth and the Quixotic

By the 1950s, neither bufo nor Liborio could, evidently, gratify Cubans' frustrations with the corruption and vice that had come to plague Cuba. Their 1933 "revolution" did not last longer than one hundred days, and their 1940 Constitution had not been meaningfully enforced. Fulgencio Batista took power in 1952 and could hardly be said to stimulate hope. The epic memory of the "liberators" of 1868 and 1895 was, nevertheless, alive and well. In these rebellious years (1953–58), the comical ceded to a milieu in which martyrdom and messianic justice abounded. Icons like the tragi-erotic mulata and the sarcastic guajiro were set aside for the "olive green" guerrilla.[21] For the barbudo symbolized a renewed mambí epic and his victory a hope that Cuba Libre's day had at last arrived.

But it was clear that hopes for a republic "with all and for the good of all" could not count on manna to fall, as if biblically, from the sky. For the Revolution to prosper, its cadre and citizenry had to reckon with an economy and political culture riddled with dependency, clientelism, mafioso vice, and a well-bred anti-communist sentiment. So, too, would it have to fend off counterrevolutionary ruses such as sabotage, propaganda, terrorism, and embargoes—subsidized, no less, by the wealthiest and most militarily powerful state in the world. Under such circumstances, what else could suffice if not a heroic will? And what else could Cubans anticipate if not a struggle of epic proportions?

Ernesto "Che" Guevara's "Socialism and Man in Cuba" (1965) argued that for the Revolution to thrive it would have to draw on both sound policy and a "quota of sacrifice."[22] This meant, no doubt, a more diversified and efficiently managed economy, but it also meant an altogether new consciousness and values—or, as it was said, a New Socialist Man and Woman.[23] The new economy would depend on a new worker, just as the new polity would depend on a new citizen, one driven by moral incentives and a willingness to sacrifice for the collective good. This, of course, was no easy task. In its earliest years, the Revolution had no choice but to rely on Cubans who had been born and raised in a neocolony where consumerism and meritocracy—let alone machismo and anti-Black racism—were fostered. With ironic irreverence, Guevara referred to this as the "original sin" that plagued Cuba and the Revolution.[24] Cuba's citizenry had been swayed by Hollywood fantasies and the American way of life, and its intellectuals indebted to Europhilic criteria and a bourgeois cult of artistic genius. The Revolution would have to rely, consequently, on a "vanguard" that could emulate for the "masses" exemplary conduct such as volunteer labor, austere living, vigilance, military preparedness, and the study of Marxist social sciences.[25] But this was only for the short term. For the longer term, the Revolution would have to invest in education and the arts—which is to say, invest in the youth, those who would not be burdened with "original sin."

The Revolution's national education system set out to do precisely that, with its curricular emphases on "work-study," the applied sciences, and Marxist historiography.[26] This was supplemented by the Union of Cuban Pioneers (UPC), an organization akin to the Boy Scouts but endowed with the mission to inculcate in Cuba's children and adolescents a socialist and internationalist ethos.[27] The youth's role models were, to this end, Che Guevara and José Martí. In 1968 the UPC adopted the slogan "¡Seremos como el Che!" (We will be like Che!) and in 1977 was renamed the José Martí Organization of Pioneers. For Martí, too, had an eye for how crucial the ideological and moral formation of the youth was if there was to be a republic "with all and for the good of all." Martí created, edited, and authored the monthly magazine *Edad de oro* (The Golden Age) for youth readers. It ran for only four months (July to October 1889) and was published in New York, but Martí's literary executor, Gonzalo de Quesada, republished the four editions as a book in 1905 for Cuban readers. It has been in print and taught in Cuban schools ever since.[28]

Whether it was the Heroic Guerrilla or the "eloquent and sincere" Apostle, thus, Cubans were held accountable to a sober and somber iconography and credo. But the Revolution was not without its (tragi-)comical sensibility, especially in the arts. The first book the Revolution made available for Cuban readers was Cervantes's *Don Quixote,* with four hundred thousand copies sold at a mere 25 cents each in 1961. Quixote was a salient allegory for Cubans in revolutionary times. *Don Quixote* (1611) is renowned, after all, as a mock epic in novel form. In it the heroic and romantic chivalry of feudal Christendom (e.g., el Cid) are rendered laughably anachronistic to a disenchanted "modern" world. Such a ridiculously out-of-joint ethos resonated, for Cubans, with their "quixotic" quest to build a world of equality and social camaraderie amid formidable odds. None other than Che Guevara invoked the quixotic in the opening lines of his April 1, 1965, farewell letter to his parents: "Once again I feel beneath my heels the ribs of Rocinante [i.e., Quixote's horse]. Once more, I'm on the road with my shield on my arm." These words are creatively cited on the Havana monument *El Quijote de América* by sculptor Sergio Martínez Sopeña. Erected in 1980, a metallic and wiry Quixote brandishes his sword while astride a Rocinante who boldly rears. Their naked and emaciated bodies accentuate the improbability or inefficacy of their power, while their posture evokes a heroic will.

Che's farewell letter and the *Quijote de América* monument are, admittedly, more heroically tragic than they are comical. But the sense that the Revolution could not be only ever a stoic and sacrificial affair was not lost on Cubans. Guevara was known to tout Cuba's Revolution as one with tropical flair and festivity (*con pachanga*), as distinct from the dreary and dogmatic connotations that Soviet socialism evoked. In fact, he explicitly rejected socialist realism as an aesthetic policy for the Revolution.[29] But it was not entirely clear how to reconcile the revolutionary utility of the arts with beauty, pleasure, and artistic freedom. The worry that the arts would be instrumentalized as dull and didactic was real and justified.[30]

Cuban filmmaker Tomás Gutiérrez Alea theorized that revolutionary arts have to embody a dialectic of "rupture" (Brecht) and "rapture" (Eisenstein).[31] They have to enlist both intellect and affect such that the viewer becomes emotionally invested in an emancipatory project yet simultaneously cultivates a capacity for self-reflexivity and constructive criticism. Alea's masterful works did precisely that, and they often did so via social comedy. *The Twelve Chairs* (1962), *Death of a Bureaucrat* (1966), and *The Last Supper* (1976) are exemplary of films that elicit critical reflection as much as sympathetic laughter.[32] But Alea's films were for adults, whereas the Revolution's most strategically vital stratum was the youth. It would fall on the shoulders of another filmmaker to create a series that could efficaciously speak to Cuba's youth. It would fall on the shoulders, that is, of Juan Padrón and his series *Elpidio Valdés.*

The Mambí Trickster and Ridiculing Laughter

Elpidio Valdés first appeared in a 1970 edition of the UPC's *Revista Pionero,* a youth periodical known for its colorful comics and its emphasis on the nation's anti-imperialist heroes and martyrs. Between 1974 and 1980 twelve *Elpidio Valdés* cartoon shorts were created, and in 1979 *Elpidio Valdés* became the first animated film in Cuban history, adorned with awards at the Havana and Moscow film festivals. Throughout the 1980s and early 1990s, Elpidio's jovial antics and mambí adventures were featured in the monthly *Zunzún,* known for its fairytale-like comics and their moral lessons; in the film sequel, *Elpidio Valdés contra dólar y cañón*

(1983), which was awarded the Latin American New Cinema Festival's Premio Coral; and in nine additional cartoon shorts created between 1988 and 1992.[33] All of which is to say that within relatively short order Elpidio had become the most well-known and beloved mambí in the Cuban popular imaginary.

When asked about the popularity of *Elpidio Valdés,* creator Juan Padrón affirmed: "We do not make films for profit, but for Cuba. That is why they speak in Cuban and touch on Cuban themes."[34] Minister of Culture Abel Prieto added: "I consider that Cuban culture must thank Elpidio Valdés for its decolonizing ability, becoming an alternative character to Disney."[35] Yet neither Padrón's nor Prieto's reply compellingly answers how and why it is that *Elpidio Valdés* came to so efficaciously interpellate Cubans. Nearly all comics, animated series, and dramatic films created under the auspices of the Revolution abide by the criteria they stipulate (e.g., not-for-profit, in Cuban vernacular, anti-imperialist ethos) but rarely, if ever, has any rivaled the popularity of *Elpidio Valdés.* Closer scrutiny reveals that *Elpidio Valdés* has proved so popular because it touches not merely on "Cuban themes" but on *the* Cuban theme—namely, the national epic—yet does so in unorthodox ways. Rather than offer its viewers a titanic or apostolic mambí or a predictably didactic and somber epic, that is, the series cleverly depicts the mambí as an "everyday Cuban" and the wars for independence as a lively and comical drama. Its truest efficacy as such is that the series enables the popular and the comical *to enrich* the epic, for never does the series disavow the emancipatory project of a Cuba Libre.

From the films, we learn that Elpidio is the quintessential Cuban and mambí. As a guajiro from the countryside (*el campo*), he hails from and

Elpidio astride Palmiche. Albeit comical, the series and its hero never disavow the "epic." *Elpidio Valdés,* 1979.

embodies the nation's "purest stock" (*la pura cepa*). Like Liborio, his guajiro credentials cue in agricultural labor and the land and, thereby, humility, productivity, and rootedness. But unlike Liborio, Elpidio is *mestizo*. His racial ambiguity echoes Padrón's choice to name Elpidio after—or as culturally kin to—Cecilia Valdés, the tragi-erotic mulata of Cirilio Villaverde's nineteenth-century novel *Cecilia Valdés,* the most critically acclaimed of Cuban novels. So, too, does it echo the novel's critique of slavery and colonialism. But what most radically distinguishes Elpidio from both Liborio and Cecilia is that he is a rebel soldier—born and raised in mambí camps, son to a cavalry officer and mambisa mother. This ranks Elpidio as more authentically Cuban and mambí than even the Apostle and the Heroic Guerrilla. Martí was born to Spanish parents and hailed from the urban middle class, whereas Guevara was Argentine and of upper middle-class descent. Both, moreover, were phenotypically white.

That said, the series' truest protagonist is the *collectivity* known as the Cuban People. One noteworthy fact is that the series does not include any of the liberation wars' most celebrated martyrs and heroes. Martí, Maceo, and Máximo Gómez are never visually depicted or narratively consequential in any of the cartoons or films. Instead, the series features an entirely fictitious cast of mambises that generically constitute the "ordinary heroes" with which contemporary viewers can identify. To this end the mambises of *Elpidio Valdés* are a People's Army, with a diverse array of hues and phenotypes and always in camaraderie. Elpidio's closest confidant (Major Marcial) and his commander (General Pérez) are, to wit, Afro-Cubans. Nor are the mambises urban or urbane. They are a relatively humble lot who speak a decidedly Cuban dialect and are closely associated with the campo and the peasantry, and it is not beyond the series to portray them as dressed in tattered slacks and, at times, barefoot. Women, too, are (relatively) empowered subjects. Elpidio's love, María Silvia, is a mambisa and captain in the army. She regularly takes initiative, is clever and defiant, and can wield a machete or pistol as skillfully as any male mambí. So, too, is her "sidekick," the prepubescent and sassy Eutelia. Cuba Libre is an intergenerational affair, after all, and the series' youth are no mere bystanders to the revolutionary project. Eutelia and the mambí bugler Pepito are as cunning, eager, and patriotic as any adult mambí.

Yet what has truly rendered the series so enjoyable and memorable is its humor. In nearly every episode Elpidio and his comrades make off safe and sound through clever and humorous ruses that leave their adversaries irate or sullied. They use disguises, spies, and decoys; slyly infiltrate forts and garrisoned towns; cut telegraph wires and derail trains; sabotage artillery; lead Spanish troops into mosquito-infested woodlands; or comically harass soldiers at night so that they cannot sleep. In doing so, the cleverness and ingenuity of the Cuban people stands out as against the idiocy or arrogance of their enemies. Cuba Libre's enemies are wealthier as well as more numerically and technologically endowed. A mambí ethic of resourcefulness must, thereby, accommodate for these asymmetries. And this, too, can be rendered humorous. Nowhere is this more emphatically the case than with the mambí inventor Oliverio. All of his devices (e.g., bullet-loaded cigar, boomerang machete, manually pneumatic cannon with nitroglycerin balls) are fashioned from whatever is readily at hand and, however preposterous, somehow work. Often, in fact, they are decisive in a dramatic escape or a seemingly ill-fated battle. And Oliverio's aesthetic only accentuates their comical efficacy: his scientific jargon, shrill voice, diminutive stature, and thick spectacles all invite levity and laughter in the midst of war and momentous stakes. Nor is Elpidio any less touched by the comical. His physique is marked by softer, corpulent lines that render him more huggable than fearsome, and his jovial temperament and folk sayings befit a trickster more so than a chivalric knight or classic epic warrior. Nor do his horse Palmiche's goofy faces and Don Juanesque antics resemble the "noble stallion" or "trusty steed" of a Cid or an Abdala.

Duping and cunning are of course no strangers to the epic. One need only think of the Trojan Horse, recalled by Aeneas in Virigl's *Aeneid,* or of Odysseus in Homer's *Odyssey.* What makes *Elpidio Valdés* so comically gratifying, by contrast, is that the foiled enemies are always sinister or dishonorable. The viewer wants to see the imperialist Spaniards and Americans of *Elpidio Valdés* foiled, for their deeds are neither gallant nor their intentions virtuous. Were it otherwise, the viewer would mourn for or sympathize with their losses: it would be tragic, not comical. One does not laugh at Hector's last stand for his family and the city of Troy, for instance, precisely because he and his deeds are praiseworthy. Nor would one laugh at the Spaniards or Americans were the mambises to mercilessly avenge themselves. The series relies, instead, on ridiculing laughter. As Russian folklorist Vladimir Propp explained, laughter as such renders the one laughed at intellectually and morally inferior to she or he who laughs. Insofar as the viewer identifies with the trickster or comedic hero (the mambí) and, especially, insofar as the enemy is villainous, the viewer enjoys her quota of pleasure in seeing vice succumb to ridicule, if not virtue. The comical as such offers the viewer not only amusement but also a vicarious hope that justice shall prevail.[36]

The Spanish officers Resóplez, Cetáceo, and Andaluz are series regulars, always ridiculed and foiled. *Elpidio Valdés contra Dólar y Cañón,* 1983.

The series' enemies are, thereby, not only idiotic and cowardly but also greedy and malicious. These inwardly moral flaws are outwardly matched by caricatured ugliness. Spanish soldiers are almost always drunkards who talk like imbeciles or a faceless mass of blue khaki uniforms. But the brunt of the jokes always falls heaviest on the Spanish officers General Resóplez and his aides, colonels Andaluz and Cetáceo. They are mocked as pompous bourgeois officers with their fine military regalia and an exaggerated Castilian accent that makes them sound as if they have a lisp. They are mocked, too, as cowardly and doctrinaire. In every battle they shield themselves behind their superior numbers and technology (i.e., their infantry, machine guns, artillery, gunboats, and forts), and whenever their by-the-book field strategy falters, they grovel on their knees for mercy or flee hysterically.

Nor are Americans flattered. In the second film, *Elpidio Valdés contra dólar y cañón,* Americans are represented by a corrupt sheriff who conspires to rob the mambises of their revolutionary funds and rifles. The sheriff is a portly, pig-faced man whose two deputies are all but faceless, their eyes covered under their oversized cowboy hats. His voice is a groggily deep bellow that sounds like a monster and theirs like that of minions. The most notorious of Americans is, however, the wealthy sugar and tobacco baron tellingly named Mr. Chanes—pronounced "chains." He has a vampire-like physiognomy—slender face, buzzard nose, angular eyes and eyebrows, sharp teeth that glimmer when he grins—and sports a cloak-like coat and Monopoly-style top hat. If that were not unsightly enough, he speaks an absurdly "gringo" Spanish that would make any native speaker's skin crawl—or laugh out loud. And his morality matches the aesthetic: he cares only about his exploitive wealth.

A greedy Mr. Chanes and his tycoon brother cheer their sinister plot. But the joke is on them. *Elpidio Valdés contra Dólar y Cañón,* 1983.

Elpidio and his fellow mambises could not differ more starkly. As against the Spaniards' pomposity and cowardliness, Cubans are jocular and improvisational tacticians, and all are known for their defiance and poise, whether when held in captivity or at the lead of a machete charge. As against the Americans' bigotry and greed, Cubans are an economically humble alliance that commissions Afro-Cubans and women as officers and never falls prey to material incentives. This is not to say that *all* Cubans are virtuous. Arguably the most hideous of foes are the *contraguerrillas,* the Cuban mercenaries that the Spanish army enlisted in their worst war crimes. Elpidio's most fierce nemesis in the first film is Mediacara (literally, "Half-face"). Leader of the contraguerrillas, he is a gorilla-like mestizo with an unkempt beard and hair that cover most of his face and render him scarcely recognizable as human. He is slovenly, vice ridden, and every bit the wicked criminal he is visually made out to be. And although he and his motley crew speak in Cuban vernacular and hail from the campo, they are rogue anti-Cubans. They have no scruples whatsoever about placing unarmed women and children in harm's way or betraying the Patria for some proverbial silver—as the ugly Cortico does in the first film.

Granted, the series could be read as nationalistic propaganda. And no doubt it is meant to speak to contemporary audiences and their lived reality. For all its historical fidelity, the series cues its viewers in to the structurally analogous exigencies of the socialist present. Contemporary Cubans can identify with the material austerity and imperial hostilities heroically endured by Elpidio and his comrades, who "emulate" for youth viewers the resourcefulness, loyalty, solidarity, and rebel spirit that is their mambí patrimony. As Guevara would have it, Elpidio and his mambí comrades are the vanguard, except that with Juan Padrón's touch the vanguard and the masses are indistinguishable: the Cuban people are the revolutionary vanguard. And however "nationalist" the series may seem to the disenchanted critic, it must not be lost on us that "nation" in this case is synonymous with egalitarianism and anti-imperialism. The *Elpidio Valdés* series revels as such in the biblical-cum-revolutionary trope of David versus Goliath—repeatedly invoked in Fidel Castro's oratory. It emulates for Cubans that the virtuous shall prevail over the villainous. And in this regard the series exploits the compensatory logic that is ridiculing laughter by rendering Cuba Libre's financially and technologically superior foes nonetheless intellectually and morally inferior.

For all that, the series likewise solicits Cubans to laugh at themselves. Its heroes are quotidian and fallible Cubans. They are not GI Joe special forces or Marvel Comics superheroes—much less demigods or divinely ordained kings and knights. Nor are they exactly handsome and endowed with stellar physiques. Their bodies, vernacular, and ethos are all comically inflected and communicate that to be a revolutionary one need not be unbearably serious. There can—if not *must*—be joy, laughter, and festivity. So while *Elpidio Valdés* is not exemplary of "grotesque realism," it does exploit folk humor (choteo) and the comical's capacity to "lower" and "travesty," as Mikhail Bakhtin famously theorized. The choteo of *Elpidio Vadlés* is particularly seductive because it lowers not just the enemies of Cuba Libre but also the revolutionary epic itself. With its populist profile and laughter, it abjures the impossibly heroic and somber Martí and Maceo—as well as Che and Fidel—for an epic more participatory and festive. It is as if the series says that the true enemy of Cuba Libre—which is to say, the Revolution—is the dogmatically serious. *Elpidio Valdés* can be read as such as a series in which, in Bakhtin's words, a "new, free, and sober seriousness" comes alive.[37]

That said, *Elpidio Valdés* never disavows the epic altogether. Whatever the series' levity and comical ruses, nearly every episode ends with a climactic battle in which the iconic machete charge is heavily featured. The series is, after all, about historic wars. But as a series for youth, violence and death are comically leavened. When Spanish soldiers are shot or cut down by machetes, they merely freeze stiff, make a silly face and fall to the wayside—a death more laughably "theatrical" than anything else. No blood, wounds, severed limbs, corpses, agony, or mourning damper the overall excitement and humor that is a machete charge and the sight of Spanish officers fleeing hysterically or throwing childlike tantrums. There is loss and the occasional somber note. Elpidio's father dies in the first film and his mother in the second. Yet both die heroically and, tellingly, off screen. Never, in short, does tragedy meaningfully displace the comical, at least not in the first two films and the first two cartoon series. Elpidio's jovial temper, María Silvia's lovely smile, Eutelia's mischievous pranks, Palmiche's silly snicker, Marcial's hearty laughter, the bulger Pepito's anxious eagerness, and the battle scenes that end to euphoric cheers all cumulatively bespeak an army and a war that were as enjoyable as they were just.

Elpidio (and the Epic) in "Parasocialist" Times

The first two *Elpidio Valdés* films were created when the Revolution and ICAIC could count on Soviet subsidies and at a time when the Third World and the Tricontinental were lively historic projects.[38] By the early 1990s, this was no longer the case. Cubans now lived in a period characterized by hunger, scarcity, and disenchantment. The dramatic losses in revenues and strategic allies affected the Revolution's literary and cultural institutions, too. Many publishing houses and periodicals were discontinued or consolidated, and ICAIC produced fewer films than ever. Like the state and everyday Cubans, ICAIC now had to finesse foreign investors and international audiences to underwrite its solvency. And with this came a loss of autonomy.

One sees the effects of these processes most plainly in the third *Elpidio Valdés* film. Coproduced with Telemadrid, it aired on Spanish television in 1995 under the uncharacteristic title *Más se perdió en Cuba* (More was lost in Cuba), and the next year in Cuba under the title *Elpidio Valdés contra el águila y el león* (Elpidio Valdés against the eagle and the lion). Whatever the title, it was not like its predecessors. Most notably, whereas the first two films relied almost exclusively on caricatured Spaniards and Americans, this film offers nuanced and favorable portrayals. Conspicuously absent are the lampooned Spanish officers Resóplez, Andaluz, and Cetáceo and the hideous contraguerrillas Mediacara and Cortico—all stock characters in the 1974–92 cartoons and films. Nearly all Spanish officers and soldiers are now relatively complex humans and adept soldiers. Rather than drunkards or doctrinaire, they fight honorably and are depicted as reluctant and homesick.

There are villains, of course, but the heroes now include a Spaniard and Americans. Other than Elpidio, there are the Spaniard Manolo and the African American Sergeant Washington. The young Manolo is a lieutenant in the Spanish army who is demoted and sent to a penal battalion for having refused orders to kill a convalescent and unarmed mambí. His sympathies with the mambises are redoubled by his love for Rosita, a Cuban mulata, whom by film's end he has married and had children with. Manolo is tantamount, thus, to an honorary Cuban. Married to a mulata—quintessential symbol of the nation—he stays after the war to live in Cuba and fights alongside Elpidio in 1933. His archenemy is the corrupt Colonel Porrones, a Spanish officer who colludes with the United States—so much so that upon this return to Cuba in 1933 he goes by the name Mr. Johnson. Sergeant Washington and his Black Buffalo Soldiers are the virtuous Americans. As soldiers, they fight bravely, and Washington in particular comes to Manolo and Elpidio's aid at crucial moments. The key adversary herein is Mr. Chanes Jr., heir to his father's sugar and tobacco wealth and now a media tycoon. Like his father, Jr. has a vampire-like physiognomy, speaks an exaggerated gringo Spanish, and is obsessed with trying to kill Elpidio. In his quest to amass wealth, he counts not only on Porrones but also on Miranda, a Cuban. Lanky and with a whiny voice, the cowardly Miranda spies for Chanes Jr., an act for which he is handsomely rewarded.

The film's plot is driven by a quest on all sides to seize an American watch with encryptions of the order to sink the *USS Maine* in Havana's harbor. As Cuban historians have argued for years, this was precisely the pretext Americans used to intervene in the war.[39] Jr. and his cronies kill dear friends to Elpidio and Manolo in order to destroy the incriminating evidence. But their deaths are avenged in 1933. As such, the film accentuates Cuba's capacity to resist all odds and rearticulates the lesson that virtue shall triumph over vice. When the American flag is ceremoniously raised at El Moro in Havana 1899, a Cuban flag likewise appears in the sky. Affixed to a kite and cushioned by the sun's light, the Cuban flag flies higher and brighter than that of the occupier's and rouses cheers from Cubans in the streets. So although the dream of Cuba Libre is tragically deferred in the "pseudo-republican" years, Elpidio and his comrades see to it that Jr. and his cronies pay their debts in 1933.

But not all is settled. The film's closing scene is a freeze frame of Elpidio hanging outside the window of his getaway car, sleeves rolled up and teeth clenched, with semiautomatic rifle blasting at the police in pursuit. He hollers out to Manolo, "One of these days we're going to win!" One way to read Elpidio's comment, if not the film in its entirety, is that it anticipates what the viewer already knows (or is expected to know), namely that the victorious day arrived January 1, 1959 with the Revolution. But that would be to neglect the ways in which the film rearticulates 1898 and the mambí ethos as an intergenerational and *contemporary* address. That the film ends with a middle-aged Elpidio, with salt-and-pepper hair and wrinkles around his eyes (and a silver-haired María Silivia), is no idle detail. For Elpidio was not the only graying revolutionary. Whichever barbudos were still alive were shadows of their youthful bravado selves, not least El Commandate Fidel (age seventy when the film was aired). Hence, the presence of a son, Elpidio III, in this episode. The telltale (patrilineal) epic must go on.

Never, after all, had the Revolution endured more dire and distraught years than these. And never had its youth been exposed to greater provocations. The newly organized tourist economy yielded much-needed foreign currency revenues, but so, too, did it tempt Cubans to embrace capitalist and cosmopolitan vices. The state and Party knew they had to renew their commitments to the youth. This they did via a series of reforms in youth organizations as well as ceding power to a younger cadre of technocrats, civil service officers, and academics.[40] The Elián González affair was only the most sensationalized symptom of this larger "battle" for the Revolution's wayward or endangered youth. And herein the symbolic power of Elpidio was explicitly enlisted. The Cuban journal *Cine Cubano* (no. 147) and the nation's daily, *Granma,* published a letter allegedly written by Elpidio himself to seven-year-old Elián, who was in the custody of relatives in Miami. Elián's mother had drowned in her attempt to bring him to Florida, but this she did against his father's wishes to remain in Cuba. In the letter, Elpidio—that is to say, ICAIC personnel—beseech Elián to resist American culture (e.g., Mickey Mouse) and to fear not: should they not release him, Elpidio and his mambí comrades would head to Miami, machetes in hand, and rescue him themselves![41]

Either way, *Elpidio Valdés contra el águila y el león* left much to be desired and was poorly received. Not only are its portrayals of Spain and Spaniards overly generous, but so, too, is it characterized by a decidedly muted humor. Elpidio is more stoic and classically heroic than ever, as are the handsome and stoutly built Manolo and Sergeant Washington. Granted, ridiculing laughter is not altogether absent. Teddy Roosevelt and his Rough Riders are hilariously mocked. Roosevelt is a dandy and inept military leader, whereas his Rough Riders are a skinny, ugly lot of racists with hooked noses and gnarly teeth. In southern drawl, they badger and taunt the Buffalo Soldiers with slurs (e.g., "smoked Yankee") and cower when Spanish rifles are turned on them. But overall the film's deaths are more tragic, the betrayals more sinister, and the drama more serious than either of its predecessors. It has scarcely any of the jocular humor and vanguard aesthetic that had come to so decisively mark the beloved *Elpidio Valdés* series, its animated "imperfections" and all.[42]

This of course could (and should) be read as symptomatic of its time. The more classically dramatic and stoic epic that the film depicted was, presumably, better suited to Cuba's besieged present, but it either fell on fatigued revolutionary ears or underestimated the allure of the comical. For humor had not withered. Cubans continued to look to laughter to make light of—and, obliquely at least, decry—their daily tribulations. The Special Period was, in fact, renowned for its jokes: "All of Cuba's problems are, in reality, only three: breakfast, lunch, and dinner." Such a joke rendered talk of sacrifice and revolution utterly superfluous, if not obscene, and "lowered" the transcendent to the realm of the immanent, namely the carnal and hungry body. Even Elpidio was enlisted in such humor. Another popular joke had Elpidio trying to enter the Habana Libre Hotel but kept out because he looked too Cuban (i.e., not a paying tourist). Elpidio is irate and insists on speaking with the manager, who turns out to be none other than General Resoplez, the Spanish commander from the cartoon series whose sole mission is to kill Elpidio! It is an ironic commentary on the period's tourist economy and its ambivalent effects, drawing in much-needed revenue but also a flock of Spanish investors and bachelors who "reconquer" the island. One is reminded of Freud's treatise on jokes: they "bribe" us, he argued, with a "yield of pleasure" in order to voice that which cannot openly or consciously be voiced.[43]

So, too, is one reminded of Bakhtin's claim that laughter has the remarkable power to "uncrown" and "dismember" the epic as heroic narrative and pious past. It is that which lays bare the revered object and opens space to "fearlessly" scrutinize it.[44] But, as Mañach warned, such comical powers can be "salutary," or they can be "toxic." The earlier *Elpidio Valdés* series could be read as more salutary and carnivalesque than vulgar or toxic. The yield of pleasure that it offers opens space for the heroic and for the critically humorous to coexist. Elpidio and his fellow tricksters are populist "antiheroes," but heroic nevertheless. They embody a politics of sacrifice and solidarity yet never take themselves too seriously. The series constitutes, accordingly, a critical alternative to the sober asceticism and dogmatic self-righteousness that could stifle the Revolution. We might say that *Elpidio Valdés* is "ruled unruliness," to borrow Gustavo Pérez Firmat's apt phrase.[45] For such differences matter. As Hayden White argued, comedy promises only *provisional* victories and *partial* liberation.[46] On that count, *Elpidio Valdés*'s humor and festivity inflect the epic hope for liberation with a more amiable and meager hope for *occasional* reconciliations. As a consequence, the animated *Elpidio Valdés* is not only a more pleasurable but also, ironically, a more "realistic" text.

4 *¡Al machete!*

On Epic Violence

When the slaughter ended, we could see mounds of little Spanish heads along the pineapple grove. I've seen few things more striking than that.
—Esteban Montejo, *Biography of a Runaway Slave* (1966)

IF EVERY epic has its hero, every hero has his weapon—and rarely is it an ordinary one. Like the classic hero himself, the epic weapon is almost always of divine or royal stock and its significance to the drama neither trivial nor accidental. Rama felled the wicked Ravana with the Brahmastra; Achilles's and Aesneas's shields possessed genealogical and prophetic wisdom; Beowulf's and el Cid's swords were royal heirlooms. Such weaponry says something about the hero's violence. As divine or royal gifts, they symbolize the noble and the good. Theirs is a violence employed in the service of the vulnerable and the wronged. Rama rid Lanka of the demon king Ravana; Beowulf rid Scandinavia of the monstrous Grendel and his mother; Sundiata liberated Sosso from the evil sorcerer Soumaoro. But the violence of the epic and its heroes is not necessarily "civilized." Indeed, it can be ferocious. Achilles disgraced Hector's dead body; Aeneas was merciless with Turnus; Beowulf tore Grendel's arm out and decapitated his mother. Such violence communicates potency and solicits awe, all the while coded as just, redemptive, and emancipatory.

The mambí epic has its prized weapon, too: namely, the machete. But like the mambí, it is neither divine nor royal. And this has made all the difference insofar as Cuba's is a *subaltern* epic. For while the machete was once a tool synonymous with exploitation and toil, in the midst of the nation's wars for independence it came to signify prowess and liberation. In the hands of the formerly enslaved, it was symbolically endowed with redemptive powers—as that humble yet deadly weapon by which the "slave" became "soldier" and the "colony" a "republic." A catachrestical revolt, so to speak. But its violence could be fetishized, even if merciless.

The Republic in Arms may have touted the discipline and "decorum" of its soldiers, but Cubans were (and remain) enamored with their mambises as machete-wielding furies. No other epic "scene" was as sensational(ized) as that of the mambí charging into the Spanish lines with his machete held high, crying out "¡Viva Cuba Libre!" The propagandistic value of this scene could not be overstated. The mambí as fierce *machetero* emboldened the emasculated colonial subject and endowed him with a sense of bodily prowess and consequence—the corollary of which is that it terrified Cuba Libre's foes. Not surprisingly, thus, did the mambí epic become the tale of a dispossessed people who reclaimed their dignity and the Patria's sovereignty one machete charge after the next.

That narrative, however, belies how the wars were actually waged. For all its mythic grandeur, the machete charge was a tactic used sparingly. The mambises were most successful as an army that waged war not on conventional or "heroic" fronts but on the colony's infrastructure, especially its lucrative sugar plantations. To this end, not the machete but the torch was the mambí's most decisive "weapon," as was the mosquito his deadliest. The mambises were their most formidable not as machete-wielding furies, that is, but as guerrillas that sabotaged the colony's sugar estates and protracted the war so that Iberian soldiers could fall prey to tropical diseases. As a case in point: nine out of every ten Spanish casualties fell not to the blade of the machete but to the pathogenesis of microbes—yellow fever, above all else.

But such guerrilla tactics did not as alluringly evoke the classic epic hero. They all but equated the mambí with an arsonist or saboteur, one that *avoided* epic battles. To memorialize the mambí as such was to repudiate the "grandeur" of the epic and its venerable hero. Little wonder, then, that Cubans opted to memorialize the mambí (not the mosquito) as a mounted warrior with machete (not torch) in hand. The republic conceived of itself as free thanks to Homeric valor and sacrifice, not devious sabotage and a "friendly fever." In doing so, many orators, poets, and sculptors also subtly euphemized or ennobled the mambí's ferocity, disavowing any of its populist connotations. The mambí was to be remembered as a respectable soldier, not a dissident Afro-Cuban or dispossessed guajiro (peasant).

The reverence bestowed on the mambí kept alive, moreover, the mystique of armed violence as the truest means by which to liberate the Patria. To wit, the so-called republican era was riddled with armed revolts, each rhetorically cast as a fulfillment of the mambí epic: the Liberal Party revolt of 1906, the Independent Party of Color's revolt of 1912, the Veterans and

Patriots' Movement revolt of 1924, the Revolution of 1933, the Moncada attacks of 1953 and the revolutionary war of 1956–58. With the Revolution, the barbudo came to signify the glamour and efficacy of guerrilla warfare. The story of Cuba Libre became a tale of citizen-soldiers as savvy as they were valorous. Mambí chronicles and memoirs were reissued to stress *guerrilla* tactics and a people's army. But never were such tactics as dramatic or seductive as the mambí's machete heroics. No account of arson or sabotage could rival the "enthusiasm" and prowess of the mambí in the throes of battle. And so for all its populist and anti-imperialist storylines, the national epic remained narratively and aesthetically tethered to armed violence, even when such a "necro-aesthetic" seemed least likely to be salient, namely in the Special Period.

Discipline and Decoro

The Ejército Libertador Cubano (Cuban Liberation Army, or ELC) was not a *professional* army. It did not boast an officer corps trained at military academies or well-provisioned battalions. Nor was it conjoined with a state that could tax its citizens, issue bonds, legally contract arms, and conscript soldiers. Granted, the ELC had commissioned officers and combat divisions, and it deferred to a civilian government that, albeit in exile, raised funds and smuggled weapons to the island. But all told, the ELC more closely resembled a *people's* army. And this mattered ideologically. The mambí was an impromptu volunteer, and his war a war for independence. It was neither state coercion nor financial incentives that explained his sacrifices: it was the desire for a Cuba Libre.

That, at least, was how the Republic in Arms projected its armed forces and narrated its wars. And not without a quota of plausibility. No one could doubt the sincerity with which some mambises forsook their careers, worldly possessions, and lives for a greater good—be it racial equality, women's dignity, national sovereignty, or a family's honor.[1] And no one can deny that the army did at least *resemble* a professional army, with its cavalry, artillery, infantry and chains of command. But the truth is the ELC was a motley ensemble of small farmers, artisans, anarchists, merchants, ranchers, licensed professionals, maroons, recently manumitted slaves, and even notorious bandits. It is inconceivable that their motives were as coherent and as consciously accessible—let alone as noble—as the wars' hymns, manifestoes, and testimonials avowed. The circumstances of the war in fact render it practicably undecidable to what extent avowals like "love of Patria" were ad hoc, opportunistic, or sincere. Whichever the case, such diverse and "nonprofessional" constituencies meant the Republic in Arms faced noteworthy obstacles in fielding an effective army. To meet this objective, it had to recruit a stock of healthy and sober citizens and train them not just how to fire a rifle or mend a wound but also how to obey orders and adhere to codes of conduct. These were no trivial matters, lest lives be needlessly lost or the ELC be vilified as barbaric. Generals such as Máximo Gómez, Antonio Maceo, and José Maceo did not tolerate improper conduct. In their camps, vices such as alcohol consumption, cock fighting, gambling, and prostitution were discouraged or altogether prohibited. Disciplinary measures could range from extra work details and demotions in rank to corporal punishment or outright execution. Martí's *War Diary* (1895) recounts the court-martial and execution of the notorious bandit, Masabó, for the crime of rape. The diary quotes Commander Gómez's unequivocal disgust at trial: "This man is not our comrade, he is a vile worm."[2]

Military efficacy was, after all, at stake in such executions, as was the Cuba Libre cause. Colonial officials and the Spanish press scorned the mambises as "negro hordes" and "anarchist terrorists." Any vile deeds that could corroborate these slanders were a threat to the army's credibility. This the Republic in Arms knew it had to counter, on the island and abroad. Without the sympathies of island residents and of the North Atlantic powers, the war was not as winnable and the Republic's legitimacy not as secure. The Republic in Arms had every incentive, in other words, to project *and* enforce an ethically circumscribed violence. Addressed to the island residents of Cuba, the "Manifesto of Montecristi" (1895) pledged a "civilized" and "humanitarian" war. The "revolution" sought to institute a "moral" and "industrious" republic, it said, and to do so with an "abhorrence of sterile vengeance and futile devastation." In fact, the Manifesto lamented that war should be necessary at all: "More than saluting him [the Spanish soldier] in death, the revolution would like to welcome him in life[. . . .] This is the heart of Cuba, and in this way will the war be carried out."[3] The army's circular known as the "War Policy" (1895) stipulated in greater detail the "heart" of mambí violence. The Cuban soldier was to welcome "with affection" the Spanish defector and treat with "benignity" any neutral Spaniard. Cubans who refused to serve the "revolution" were not to be harmed: one must "always keep open [to the noncommitted] the path towards Revolution." And prisoners of war were to be released unharmed.

The Cuban soldier was, thereby, to embody a "strict discipline and decorum [*decoro*]."[4] The importance of this policy was as strategic as it was humane. It was no doubt admirable in its own right, and leaders such as Martí and Maceo morally ascribed to it. But it was also the strategically superior choice. Civilians on the island were key assets to the ELC as spies, saboteurs, propagandists, cooks, couriers, and nurses. Were they to be treated too "rigorously," sympathies would subside, and such valuable services would be harder to procure—let alone make it easier for Spain to vilify and discredit the Republic in Arms.[5]

The rhetoric of "decorum" did not, of course, always coincide with its tactical reality.[6] The War Policy stated that the Revolution would "respect all those who respect us." The unsaid corollary was that of reciprocal hostility. Those who did *not* respect the Republic in Arms were met with "rigor." This left much to the discretion of local commanders and the exigencies of war. One could levy a "revolutionary tax" or "commandeer" the property and services of civilians to feed, cloth, and quarter the ELC's troops. Whether such civilians had a choice in the matter, let alone be justly compensated, was not likely the case. Moreover, the ELC was pitiless with defectors, spies, and enemy collaborators. In fact, it was an anomaly to be executed as mercifully as was Masabó, that is to say, by firing squad. The scarcity of bullets compelled the ELC to employ more "affordable" options, which included death by machete strikes or by "trees of justice."[7] As the War Policy stated: when it comes to enemies, "one must wage inexorable war."[8]

The Machete Mystique

Despite Martí's avowal that this would be a "civilized" and "humanitarian" war, the Liberation Army was not legendary for its civility or placidness. Quite to the contrary! The literary, oratorical, and testimonial odes to the mambí exalted him as a fierce machetero. Luis García Pérez's play *El grito de Yara* (1874) has Céspedes declare: "The machete will be the arm/fierce, terrible, rife with fury/that extermination and death/everywhere spreads."[9] No other symbol was as fecund and no other scene as enthusiastically memorialized as were the machete and the machete charge.

The machete is, after all, a *phallic* symbol. In the hands of stoutly built men, it symbolized physical prowess. The fact that it was wielded against a numerically and technologically superior foe rendered it all the more so. Spanish forces outnumbered the mambises roughly ten to one and were armed with Mausers, a rifle with unrivaled range, velocity, and accuracy. By contrast, Cuban rebels had either a single-shot Remington or Winchester or, all the likelier, a machete. But the fact that the mambí would wield a mere machete against such treacherous odds was choice material for epic emplotment: what better evidence was there that Cuba Libre's soldiers were driven by a transcendent creed to die rather than live enslaved? The machete was a *populist* and *redemptive* symbol, too. As the everyday tool of the Cuban guajiro, it was synonymous with the humble campesino. This buoyed the ELC's profile as a *people's* army and their claim to the (is)land. Arguably all the more fecund was the fact that the master's oppressive tool became the slave's emancipatory weapon. For the machete went hand in hand with a mambí epic in which slavery was abolished and an ethos of racial equality instituted.

Not all such tributes were purely rhetorical. On December 15, 1895, the Liberation Army fought and decisively won its most famous battle, the Battle of Mal Tiempo. Maceo's and Gómez's troops entered Santa Clara province and received notice of a Spanish detachment in nearby Mal Tiempo. The generals had their cavalry flank the enemy troops and ambush them with machetes drawn. It is said that the terrified Spaniards lost their nerve and either ran for their lives or knelt for mercy. José Miró Argenter referred to it as a "frightening mutilation."[10] Bernabé Boza wrote: "We men became beasts starved for blood and slaughter!"[11] And Esteban Montejo recalled: "We started to chop off their heads. But really chopping them off. The Spaniards were scared shitless of the machetes."[12] With sixty-four enemies dead and forty more wounded, Cubans walked away only four men lighter and with a bounty of Mauser rifles, bullets, pack mules, and, most importantly, a heightened morale.[13] It was an auspicious start to Maceo's and Gómez's historic "invasion" of the Cuban West, and no other battle would more vividly attest to the mambises as macheteros who struck terror into the hearts of Spanish soldiers.

There was, thereby, historical facticity to the storied machete charge. Mal Tiempo was neither the first nor the last. But as Lawrence Tone has pointed out, the machete charge was not as tactically valuable or as widely practiced as Cubans have been led to believe. Mambí commanders quickly noticed how ineffective or disastrous it could be, if not used selectively. Insofar as their troops rode directly into Spanish lines, they and their valuable horses became easy prey to the Spanish infantry and its Mausers. It was smarter for Cubans to *dismount* their valuable horses, leave them on standby for retreats, and lure Spaniards into tactically advantageous sites such as open fields or bottleneck trails, where they could fire at them from concealed positions. Not exactly an "epic" scene, but Cubans were all the wiser (and less dead) for it. The machete charge was in reality a tactic of last resort. As a case in point: the number of Spanish casualties treated for machete wounds was a small fraction of the number treated for rifle wounds.[14] But its efficacy in the realm of psychological warfare cannot be overstated. The tales, theatrical verses, and army cadences of the mambises as fearsome macheteros emboldened Cuban soldiers. This was no small dividend. With imperial odds stacked against them, the outnumbered and poorly armed Cuban mambí needed to believe such odds could be surmounted—hence the portrayals of the mambises as "ferocious panthers" and "titans." Such portrayals, moreover, terrified and demoralized Cuba Libre's foes. As it was, Spaniards thought of the mambises in bestial racist terms such that publicized accounts (and rumors) of battles like Mal Tiempo "corroborated" their prejudicial fears.

Needless to say, there was a risk herein: the "barbarity" of a macheteo did not exactly evoke "decorum." But the mambí did enjoy an aura of heroic nobility thanks to the horse. Horses were in fact more valuable to the war than machetes. Cuba's cattle ranchers were known for breeding fine horses, which they tended to let roam freely to forage and round up when necessary. This made them easy for the ELC to "commandeer." That Cuba's cattle ranchers were concentrated in Camagüey, just on the border of rebel-teeming Oriente and east of the Júcaro-Morón *trocha* (fortified trench), made it even easier. Spain by then was better known for its pack mules than its horses and could not so readily acquire and restock quality horses from the Peninsula or from any of its former viceroyalties in the Americas, most importantly Mexico. As a result, the ELC had a monopoly on horses, whereas the Spanish fielded a large army with relatively few cavalry units. Militarily, their value at the time was as such quite handsome. Without horses, the Spanish could not flank marching troops or lead an advance, could not properly scout ahead for intelligence, and could not pursue retreating forces to effect a larger number of casualties. The ELC, by comparison, was able to move swiftly and elusively about the island as it wrought a saboteur's havoc on railways, bridges, telegraph lines, outposts, and sugar estates.[15] In the end, the mambí's tactics and violence were more guerrilla than they were classically "epic."

The horse, nevertheless, bolstered an iconography that evoked the epic. Gonzalo de Quesada's *The War in Cuba* (1896), the official account by the Republic in Arms' chargé d'affaires, is embellished with illustrations such as *Spirited Charge of the Cuban Cavalry,* a wood engraving every bit as faithful to the machete charge mystique as its successors.[16] That the horse's symbolic value is more classical than guerrillero should be

The epic machete charge illustrated. Gonzalo de Quesada, *The War in Cuba,* 1897.

little wonder. Within the Occidental collective consciousness, the soldier on horseback conjures up the sense of a medieval knight or a modern cavalry officer, icons of nobility and gallantry. As a mounted warrior, the mambí thereby enjoyed greater respectability than if he were to be rendered a mere infantryman—let alone the ELC soldier's truer identities as saboteur and arsonist. Rather than bespeak a "dastardly" or "irregular" war waged in the shadows—elusiveness made possible by the horse!—the imagery of a mambí with flaunted machete bespoke a romanticized scene of war and a more classically heroic protagonist.

The "Blessed Torch" and the "Black Vomit"

Whatever its charms, the machete and the machete charge were not the winning protagonists of the war. It was, after all, only because of chronic shortages that the typical mambí was armed with little other than a machete or a hopelessly antiquated Remington or Springfield. Given such arsenals and such numeric odds, Gómez and Maceo knew well that they could not defeat the Spanish army in a traditional war of "open fronts"—no matter how heroically they wielded their machetes.[17] An altogether different repertoire of military insight and strategy would have to be called on in order to counter, if not surmount, the war's disparities.

And the disparities were bleak. At war's outset in February 1895, Spanish forces numbered nearly 80,000. By December of that same year, another 70,000 Spanish regulars had been sent to the island, and by war's end Spain had deployed a massive force of 190,000 regulars and 60,000 irregulars.[18] By stark contrast, the ELC was never greater than 30,000 combat-effective soldiers at any given time in the war. Worse yet, they were chronically short on rifles, ammunition, and field supplies. Even when resupply expeditions did make it ashore, the medley of rifles and ammunition that was sent often did not match, rendering them worthless.[19]

Gómez and Maceo thus had to exploit the *conditions* of war. With the reluctant blessings of the Republic in Arms, Commander Gómez had his ELC enact a "total war" and systematically assault the colony's infrastructure. This meant first and foremost the colony's prized commercial asset, namely its sugar. ELC circulars were issued July 1 and November 6, 1895, stating the following:

> Article 1. That all plantations shall be totally destroyed, their cane *and* outbuildings burned and railroad connections destroyed.
>
> Article 2. All laborers who shall aid the sugar factories . . . shall be considered as traitors to the country.
>
> Article 3. All who are caught in the act, or whose violation of Article 2 shall be proven, shall be shot. [20]

In a letter to Delegate Estrada Palma, Gómez explained that he sought out "the total paralyzation of all labor in Cuba."[21] The Maceo brothers, as had Martí, thought it wiser to be selective in their desolation so that the Republic in Arms would not be "needlessly" deprived of financial resources and productive capabilities *post*bellum. But Gómez, quite justifiably, was weary that it would lead to class favoritism and fail to bring the economy to enough of a halt. At any rate, wherever the ELC had a monopoly on the use of violence, they could charge planters a "revolutionary tax" in lieu of absolute desolation. They also made it a practice of "confiscating" any absentee planter's property and redistributing it to the small farmers of the region. This enabled them to grow crops and care for livestock that would feed the revolutionary army. Nor should one overlook the fact that these policies were consistent with Gómez's and Maceo's outspoken antipathy toward social inequalities and class privileges. Gómez had once confessed to a colleague in arms:

> When I arrived in this island and saw the plight of the poor workers, I felt wounded with sadness. There was this poor wretchedness working beside magnificent grandeur; beside all that beautiful richness was so much misery and so much low morality. When I saw the wife and children of the poor worker covered with rags and living in a battered hut, I was touched with the enormity of the contrast. When I asked for the school and was told that there had never been one, and when I entered innumerable towns and saw no culture, no morality, no clean people, no acceptable living accommodations [. . .] then I felt indignant and profoundly disgusted against the elevated classes of the country. And in an instant I exclaimed to myself, 'Blessed be the torch!' [*¡Bendita sea la tea!*].[22]

It would be no exaggeration to say that *la tea,* the torch, was the most efficient weapon in the ELC's arsenal. To torch a plantation did not require costly-to-feed and difficult-to-maneuver brigades of armed soldiers. Rather, small dispersed cells of guerrillas could wreak havoc at little expense and with minimal operational "friction." It compelled, moreover, the Spanish army to undertake a soldier-intensive and militarily disadvantaged effort to guard plantations and outlying towns from their incendiary demise. In so doing, the strategy of the torch generated a *social* as much as a financial crisis. Sugar was the colony's largest revenue source and its largest employer. Every newly unemployed worker was now either a potential recruit for the ELC or yet another disgruntled colonial subject in need of food, shelter, and security. Usually he and his family were the latter. The ELC would no doubt welcome and put to work a "compatriot," but it could only afford to "employ" so much of Cuba's rural peasantry and agro-industrial proletariats. Not many in the loyalist West wanted to join its ranks anyway, if only because the Spanish had depicted the ELC as savages and terrorists. Rural noncombatants tended to hedge their bets and flee for Spanish-garrisoned towns and cities, involuntarily yielding the equivalent to a general strike.[23] The colony thereby became a colossal financial liability to Spain—all of which Gómez had strategically foreseen and tactically precipitated.

Insofar as this is how the war progressed, the mambises retained the initiative and the odds were not as disparate. Especially in the central and eastern provinces, the ELC was able to convert tens of thousands of otherwise "neutral" bystanders into vital auxiliaries who repaired weapons, raised crops, tended to livestock, cared for the infirmed, and gathered intelligence. The ELC seemed to know the whereabouts and capacity of every advancing Spanish force and their relief columns, enabling them to set up roadblocks and ambushes or to altogether avoid a much too risky encounter. Confidant José Miró Argenter credited these near-mystical sounding words to Gómez on the subject: "I know where the sucking insect lays its egg in Cuba. I know where the fat bull is and where the best water is. I know the hour the Spaniard is wakeful and the hour when he sleeps most deeply. I divine his moments of fear, and then I am courageous and daring. And I quickly recognize when he is fearless, and then I prudently let him pass, so that he expends his bravery in a vacuum."[24] Of course, Spanish officers soon realized that every Cuban in their midst was a potential spy. Within due course, they began to deliberately "leak" misinformation and to plan their stratagems through the confidence of whispers.[25] But such measures could not counter the most lethal of ELC "recruits," namely, in Gómez's words, the "sucking insect."

Indeed, the ELC's most effective killer was not the mambí: it was the mosquito. As a vector for yellow fever and malaria, the mosquito devastated the Spanish army, whose combat-ready forces were cut by anywhere from a third to as much as half at different junctures in the war.[26] The aggregate figures tell part of the story: for every Spanish serviceman killed in combat proper, nine died to disease alone. Yellow fever, malaria, typhus, pneumonia, dysentery, smallpox, and other diseases killed off 22 percent of the Spanish forces and accounted for 90 percent (41,288) of all Spanish fatalities.[27] Yellow fever in particular took the largest toll and was a dreaded end. Its signature symptoms were, initially, jaundice and fever and, in later stages, bleeding from the gums, ears, rectum, and genitals and vomiting up a mixture of internal organ tissue and blood that looked like wet coffee grounds—hence its colloquial names among the Spanish and Cuban troops: the "black vomit" and the "friendly fever," respectively.[28]

Again, this was not serendipity as much as foresight and strategy. It had not yet been "scientifically" validated that particular species of mosquitoes were vectors for yellow fever and malaria, but two things were popularly known: that *peninsulares,* those from Spain, had a heightened susceptibility to tropical diseases and that there was a correlation between epidemics and the rainy season.[29] It had been no mystery to Toussaint, Dessalines, and Christophe in their revolutionary war against the continental French forces sent to Haiti (1793–1804), and it was certainly no mystery to Gómez: "My three best generals? June, July, and August," he told an inquisitive reporter.[30] If Gómez's and the ELC's estimates are to be trusted, throughout the rainy season Spanish servicemen were falling at a rate of a thousand per day. And such diseases did not have to be lethal to be effective. For every fatality to the "friendly" fevers, roughly another four servicemen were temporarily out of commission to illness and recovery in the rear.[31] Little wonder that Gómez would reassure his officers with a routine farewell: "Another day, gentlemen, and another battle won."[32]

It was largely thanks to the torch and the mosquito, thus, that the Republic in Arms was a force to be reckoned with. The machete killed very few Spanish soldiers and was no threat whatsoever to the imperial economy. But the mounted mambí with machete in hand would continue to enjoy a cachet that no arsonist or saboteur—let alone insect—could rival. The epic would live on in the popular imaginary as a series of wars cumulatively won one machete charge after the next. To get a sense for its importance, one has only to imagine the reaction to the historically fastidious Cuban who recommends that the torch (in lieu of the machete) or, worse yet, the mosquito (in lieu of the mambí) become the heroic icons of the national epic.[33] Sacrilege of most peculiar sort!

Republican Odes and Bearded Reenactments

The ostensibly independent Cuba of the early to mid-1900s had no time for fastidious details about torches and mosquitoes. Nor did it wish to memorialize Black and guajiro dissidents—which is to say, their populist agendas. The new Republic reiterated a narrative of decorum and euphemized the mambí's violence. Generals Antonio Maceo and Máximo Gómez were memorialized with large equestrian statues in Havana. In 1916, Maceo was *literally* rendered a bronzed titan, with his signature stout shoulders and a machete at hand. The viewer looks up at Maceo, mounted on a stallion that rears, and the stallion's enormous testicles. The monument bespoke thereby an ambivalent potency, that which can make life (a virile male body, robust testicles, etc.) and that which can take life (the machete). His violence was not, however, flaunted inasmuch as ennobled: there is no bloodshed; his machete is at his side; and he sits atop an elegant marble pedestal. Years later (1931), Gómez was mounted on a stallion, one that stands disciplined and regal as if on parade. There are no testicles flaunted, nor does Gómez bear a machete. The elder Gómez, known affectionately as El Viejo (the Old Man), holds his hat to his side in what amounts to a gentleman's salute. Out of the marble pedestal emerge a spell of horses that render Gómez a kind of charioteer: he who steered the Republic to its independence. Not surprisingly do Greco-Roman and Hellenic references abound. On the pedestal is a smaller replica of *La República,* the Cuban republic as the Greek goddess Athena.

Such monuments, epic in scale and neoclassical in aesthetic, bestowed on the Republic and its heroes an aura of grandeur and honorableness. And they did so, it should be noted, in ways that disavowed the mambí's Afro-Cuban and guajiro profiles—which is to say, the utopian impulses repressed within that mythical account. This was not unique to monuments. Bonifacio Byrne's *Lira y espada* (1901) was typical of a poetics indebted to Hellenic referents and their more "respectable" connotations.[34] The lyre (*lira*), for instance, connotes classical Greece as much as the euphony and pleasures of poetic expressivity: it was the musical instrument that Greek poets strummed as they sang none other than the Homeric epics! That Byrne opted to frame his poetics under the trope of the "sword" (*espada*), moreover, spoke volumes. As opposed to the more worldly (and populist) machete, the sword conjures affiliations with the epic hero and noble knight.

In Bryne's poetics, the mambí (a word, quite remarkably, never used) is more akin to a Spartan than to an African or Taino warrior—let alone a saboteur or an arsonist. In other words, no bestial or cunning violence and, similarly, no emancipatory desires. Only trite nationalistic odes and Occidental aesthetics. "Beautiful is he who wields the sword," opens "The Young Ones," and "More beautiful and noble, when he dies/in the front lines of combat!"[35] The poem "On a Shield" invokes the well-known Spartan creed, attributed to mothers who told their sons before battle: "Come back with your shield, or on it."[36] Its narrator, which one presumes to be an older man, looks on and recounts, enviously as much as reverently, the citizen-soldiers' return from battle: "Here they come, those who confident and pleased/fled to battle/to feel in their noble thoughts/the sharp and patriotic spur,/turning their back to the dear city/and with their heads held high;/looking for another horizon,/like the condor the daring summit/they went to the bitter, impenetrable mount,/to bring death or to give their lives!" It is a poem dedicated to the "young patriot" who has "returned on his shield," now held in the "interminable embrace" of his coffin.[37]

For all that, many Cubans felt that the *epic* of Cuba Libre had ceded to the *tragedy* or *farce* of the so-called "republic." Grievances abounded: electoral fraud, embezzlement schemes, clientelist politics, racist immigration policies, economic dependency, the Platt Amendment, and so forth. Such scandals did foster a melancholic malaise that Jorge Mañach analyzed, but so, too, did it arouse what poet Cintio Vitier called a "redemptive impatience."[38] No greater evidence of this were the periodic armed revolts in the name, invariably, of Cuba Libre: the Liberal Revolt of 1906, the Independent Party of Color's armed protest of 1912, and the Veterans and Patriots Movement uprising of 1924. That each of these was repressed did not conceal the fact that the mambí sentiment was still alive.

By the 1930s, revolutionary newsletters took on titles such as *Cuba Libre* and *El Machete,* as did revolutionary poetics evoke "mambí epicness" and the aura of *emancipatory* violence.[39] Rubén Martínez Villena's "Mensaje lírico civil" (1933) declared: "What is lacking is a [machete] charge to kill scoundrels/to fulfill the work of the revolutions."[40] Only such an act could excise the "tenacious scab of colonialism" and realize the "marbled dreams of Martí." It is to they who fell and died for such "dreams" that Villena pledged his poetic oath: "And I swear by the blood that flowed from so many wounds,/to yearn for the salvation of this beloved land."[41]

If that revolutionary moment (1933) was curtailed, its emancipatory promises and the mambí's rebelliousness had to be kept alive, if only poetically. Manuel Navarro Luna's *Poemas mambises* (1943) was precisely such a project.[42] In it, visceral imagery and a vitalist prose pay tributes to and evoke mambí epicness. "Campana" referred to the Demajagua bell rung in October 1868 when Céspedes declared his slaves free and Cuba independent. Luna addressed the bell's "bowel" and "mouth" as if a conscious and carnal subject and implored it to recall the "fire" it once possessed, the "delirious cry" (*grito delirante*) that made the earth tremble and alight in "flames." And this he did not so that it would oratorically pander to the living, for as he said: "Your bronze was not forged/for useless words!"[43] "Racies bravas," whose title could be translated as "Valiant Roots," likewise invokes fire, flames, and the vocation of a heroic death: "We have to die, before anyone else;/we should die, before anyone else . . . !" But the nation's roots are not found under the soil. They are, poetically at least, at El Torquino in the Sierra Maestra: "For what are we [if not] the sons/of the Sierra Maestra . . . ?" it asked rhetorically.[44] As Cuba's highest peak and a vast mountain range, El Torquino and Sierra Maestra bespoke the heights of the (biblical) sublime as well as the actual place where the nation's heroes found refuge in the wars for independence. In short, Luna poetically summoned the sacred and the prophetic, the mythical and the heroic.

And such associations were capitalized on by Fidel Castro and the barbudos in the 1950s, as they waged (and broadcast) their war from the Sierra Maestra. No other revolutionary organization inscribed itself as convincingly in the national epic as did the MR 26-7 movement. As armed rebels affiliated with historic Oriente and headquartered in the Sierra Maestra, the barbudos fashioned themselves as the mambises reincarnate.

The barbudos as reincarnated mambises. *La Caballería, Cuba,* Raúl Corrales Forno, 1960. (Museum of Fine Arts, Houston, gift of the estate of Esther Parada, 2006.471)

With a newsletter titled *El Cubano Libre,* battalions and platoons named after heroes such as Antonio Maceo and Mariana Grajales, and historic reenactments such as the torching of sugar cane and the "invasion" of the West, the resemblances were historically salient and at times outright uncanny. Camilo Cienfuegos's column went so far as to ride on horseback (not on a tank or jeep) and wear straw hats (not berets) in their victory procession toward Havana, in what amounted to an irresistible homage to the mambises.

Whatever the seductiveness of such reenactments and resemblances, however, it was just as crucial that the barbudos resembled and reenacted the mambises' "decorum." Not unlike the ELC's "War Policy," the Rebel Army was "benevolent" toward civilians and lenient with prisoners of war, who were not tortured and would be released (or exchanged). As in the 1870s and 1890s, such practices were as strategically wise as they were ethically just. The Rebel Army depended on civilians as spies, cooks, couriers, nurses, and recruits, and its small guerrilla army could not afford to house, quarter, or be tactically encumbered by prisoners of war. Wiser (and more humane) it was to treat civilians with dignity and release captives unharmed. Without the lethal capabilities (or capital) to subdue populations and annihilate foes, the objectives were to enlist services and sympathies. The barbudos projected themselves to national and international audiences as freedom fighters trying to take down a "tyrant." The Rebel Army was keen to demoralize Batista's army and solicit as many defections as possible, a tactic that saved many lives and eased postwar transitions. The "enemies" in this war were, after all, fellow Cubans, not Spaniards. There were, of course, lives *not* spared. Like the ELC before it, the Rebel Army was pitiless with spies and deserters. A utilitarian calculus deemed it a strategic necessity: spies jeopardized the lives of fellow soldiers, and desertion could put an end to the rebel forces. Were commanders too lenient, recruits would flock back to civilian life once the odds and hardships of the war proved too dismal. "Luckily" for the convicted, rifles and bullets were more abundant in this war, so an execution by machete was far less likely.[45]

It is crucial that the barbudos compellingly projected themselves as morally endowed heroes and, at least provisionally, embodied a "decorum" that would have pleased Maceo and Martí. This was their most important victory, a victory consolidated all the more decisively through the postwar people's trials. As much by de fault as by popular consensus, the barbudos oversaw the prosecution of the dictatorial state's worst war criminals—save for, needless to say, those who fled. The evidentiary force of witnesses and photographs that testified to torture and mutilations made clear to everyone a violence that did not abide by the dictates of "civilized" warfare. The violence associated with Batista was gratuitous and cruel. It exceeded what was militarily necessary and targeted civilians. It was also repressive, for it kept at bay the emancipatory promises of the MR 26-7 movement. The corollary of these trials, thus, was that they cast the barbudos' violence as justified and civilized. The barbudos were they who targeted only armed and uniformed adversaries; they who conceded amnesties and renounced torture; they who fought and died for the People. That the trials were public (and televised) no doubt lent itself to politicized spectacle. But the spectacle was not that of barbaric executions inasmuch as a measure of due process and justice served: a martial tribunal and a formal execution. The cry of *paredón* (the wall) and the firing squads were neither a novelty nor mob vengeance. They and the tribunals were a violence rendered ethically tempered, juridically sanctioned, and politically emancipatory.[46]

Vanguard Aesthetics

In 1961, Luna's *Poemas mambises* (1943) was reprinted under the title *Odas mambisas,* except that this time the collection included poems dedicated to Cuba's "new mambises." "Fidel," one poem declared, "could give lessons to the Homeric heroes."[47] The barbudos were characterized as the heirs to the mambises and the socialist future as a consummation of Cuba Libre. Much was at stake. As fellow poet Roberto Fernández Retamar put it, "true revolutions conquer not only the future, but also the past."[48] And the mambí past was no frivolous past. It was abundant in virtues such as discipline, austerity, sacrifice, and martial prowess—virtues, all told, deemed necessary to build that socialist future. For the path to a socialist paradise was not likely to be paved on leisure and promiscuity.

Not surprisingly, thus, did the Revolution cultivate a militant ethos. From its militias, volunteer "brigades," and compulsory military service, an ethos of sacrifice and military preparedness now governed Cuban life. It was, admittedly, not without its glamor and credibility. Cubans could identify with their young charismatic leaders and as an internationalist vanguard with a historic mission, a mission worthy of their mambí ancestors. To that end, the year 1968 was an opportune one. As centennial to the Grito de Yara and onset to the nineteenth-century wars for independence, 1968 was subsumed under the trope "One Hundred Years of Struggle for Liberation," a trope that stimulated a bloc of films on the mambí epic's relevance to the historical present: *Lucía* (1968), *La odisea del general José* (1968), *1868–1968* (1968), *Hombres de Mal Tiempo* (1968), *La primera carga al machete* (1969), and *Páginas del diario de José Martí* (1971). It was not the first time the mambí epic had been conjured to cinematic life. Cuban filmmaker Enrique Díaz Quesada had done so in the early republic: *Manuel García o el rey de los campos de Cuba* (1913), *El capitán mambí o libertadores y guerrilleros* (1914), *La manigua o la mujer cubana* (1915), and *El rescate del Brigadier Sanguily* (1916)—albeit all lost. Critic Michael Chanan tells us, however, that we should be suspicious of their critical credentials. They were endorsed by President Mario García Menocal. A major general in the mambí army, Menocal was educated at US universities, served as the administrative head to the Cuban American Sugar Company, and, later, became a staunchly pro-American president. Chanan suspects Quesada's films were works that legitimized a fraudulent republic.[49]

In any case, the context of the late 1960s was remarkably different. This was the era of Third World liberation and of "Third Cinema," a cinema abundant in militant rhetoric and violent motifs. But violence of a particular sort. As Brazilian filmmaker Glauber Rocha put it, "the [new cinema's] aesthetics of violence are revolutionary rather than primitive." For insofar as the subject is immiserated and starved, violence is a "noble act." It restores to the "colonized" precisely what the "colonizer" has taken away, namely her or his power and dignity. "The first policemen had to die," Rocha pointed out, "before the French became aware of the Algerians."[50] Argentine filmmakers Fernando Solanas and Octavio Getino echoed this sentiment when they said that Third Cinema was "guerrilla cinema" and the film a "detonator." As they put it most memorably: "The camera is the inexhaustible expropriator of image-weapons; the projector, a gun that can shoot 24 frames per second."[51] These were the years of decolonial wars and revolutions throughout the Third World, with Cuba at the vanguard. Solanas and Getino's three-part documentary, *The Hour of the Furnaces* (1968), ends with a section titled "Violence and Liberation." It highlights armed liberation fronts and guerrilla soldiers throughout the Third World, punctuated by images of Fidel Castro at the head of mass rallies and, at film's end, a close-up still of the martyred Che Guevara. But these sequences are juxtaposed with montages of civilian deaths and bombardments in Vietnam. In other words, it cinematically *qualifies* violence—the one heroic and revolutionary, the other abhorrent and repressive.[52]

Violence and military preparedness were, after all, matters that the Revolution could not take lightly: the Bay of Pigs invasion of 1961; the October missile crisis of 1962; the war against the "bandits" in the Escambray mountains (1959–65); and the Revolution's internationalist missions throughout a tumultuous Third World—from Algiers and Vietnam to the Congo and Bolivia—all bespoke its relevance. That said, like the mambí's violence, the Revolution's violence was touted as anti-imperialist and anti-racist. Cuba's historical cinema made such continuities unmistakable. Alejandro Saderman and Miguel Barnet's 1968 documentary *Hombres de Mal Tiempo* (The Men of Mal Tiempo), for instance, did not didactically recount a famed battle inasmuch as host a "fiesta of memory," as the narrator puts it. The liveliness of the work is found in the exchanges between mambí veterans and the actors tasked to play them on screen. Esteban Montejo, the subject of *Biografía de un cimarrón,* and four other elder veterans to the Battle of Mal Tiempo (1895) are consulted for historical fidelity. Once the actors proceed with the reenactment, though, the unassuming elders become animated and interject. They in effect assume the role of directors and mentors, both to the actors and to the viewer. This enables the anonymous heroes of the mambí epic to emulate for and enthuse the anonymous heroes of the socialist epic. The younger men on screen who are dressed (and expected to act) like the mambises are, as such, intergenerational metonyms, and the film's subtext that of a willingness to die and kill for the Patria, no matter how raw or visceral the violence.[53]

This was a familiar predicament, both ethically and aesthetically. As in the wars for independence, *revolutionary* violence had to be dramatized to an extent that it could be rendered both thrilling and ethically justified. Such matters were finessed in the critically acclaimed film *La primera carga al machete* (1969), directed by Manual Octavio Gómez. The film is fictional but stylistically crafted as a documentary—or, better yet, what Latin American critics call *cine encuesta,* a film that, like *Hombres de Mal Tiempo,* "investigates" or "inquires" about (rather than just reenacts) the historical past. Here the event in question takes place October 25, 1868—literally, the first known and resoundingly victorious machete charge. The film actually opens at the scene of the battle's aftermath, exposing the viewer to visually high-contrasted images of corpses sprawled about a roadside creek. The viewer is also introduced to the film's deliberately anachronistic "aesthetic" of newsreel reportage, with hand-held cameras and portable "on the spot" sound relaying an interviewee on screen speaking to an (anonymous) interviewer off screen—a technique that puts past and present in touch with one another. In this first of many interviews to come, weary-looking and heavily bandaged Spanish soldiers tell the interviewee: "They [the mambises] don't fight like soldiers; what we were [militarily] trained for does us no good here." Other constituencies will be called on throughout the film to answer for the war: patriotic citizens of Bayamo, headquarters to Cuba Libre and the national anthem's namesake; Spanish authorities, such as the governor and latifundista gentry, who refer to Cubans as "lazy, insolent, and ill-suited for combat"; civilians in Havana, who are beaten by the police for openly debating the desirability of independence; and mambises themselves, from officers to rank-and-file soldiers. These scenes are punctuated by a wandering troubadour (a young Pablo Milanés), who sings a ballad, tellingly enough, to the machete.

All of this leads us, retrospectively, to the film's final scene, the battle itself. Taking up no less than ten minutes of screen time, the "machete charge" is portrayed as an almost feverish slaughter. All that is heard are agonizing cries and a metallic tish-tish as an unsteady camera delivers a visually delirious spectacle. Throughout the ten minutes no image holds the screen for much longer than two seconds, making it difficult to watch not just for its violent content but also due to its visual form. Of all the imagery, a "counterpoint" stands out, that of alternating high-angle to low-angle close-ups—the one of a mambí striking downward and the other, a Spanish soldier crawling away, eyeing the mambí over his shoulder with a look of terror on his face. As such, Cubans are portrayed as fierce, even merciless. But their ferocity has been contextualized as an

An "imperfect" cinema's rendition of the machete charge. *La primera carga al machete,* 1968.

act of liberatory violence, as if to visually depict the "purging" effect that Frantz Fanon attributes to decolonizing violence and that Jean-Paul Sartre prefaced as follows: "For [Fanon] shows clearly that this irrepressible violence is neither sound and fury, nor the resurrection of the savage instincts, nor even the effect of resentment: it is man recreating himself . . . to shoot down [or slay] a European is to kill two birds with one stone, to destroy an oppressor and the man he oppresses at the same time: there remain a dead man, and a free man."[54]

For we ought not overlook the fact that however mercilessly they kill, the mambises' victims here are Spanish cavalry and infantrymen—uniformed and armed with bayonets and rifles. What else could the mambises be, if not fearless and virile, to dare take on such a superiorly armed foe? And what else could they be, if not clever, to have lured their foes into an ambush? By stark contrast, the Spaniards enact the most loathsome and cowardly of violence, namely rape. In an earlier scene depicting a town's pillage, a woman's testimonial voices over the imagery of Spanish soldiers cornering Cuban women and wrestling them to the ground. It is obvious what transpires next, although it is neither shown nor narrated (the woman's voice, or language, fails her). The viewer walks away with a sense that the mambises have avenged and redeemed her (allegorically, the Patria) and villains gotten what they deserved.[55]

That such a film came in 1969 was no doubt significant. The world's revolutionaries had lost Che Guevara (October 1967), and Cuba's economic woes grew worse by the day. As head of the central bank and minister of industry and production, Guevara had pushed for Cuba to diversify and technologically advance its economy so as not to be dependent on sugar exports. Sugar was, after all, on the wrong side of history. Unlike the "proud cigar band," as Fernando Ortiz put it, the "lowly sack" of sugar denoted colonialism, slavery, racism, seasonal (under)employment, drudgery, and economic dependency.[56] Of all things, however, the machete was its iconic tool. With the wars for independence, it had come to signify liberation, but thereafter it was used to cut sugar cane—just as before, albeit now in an industry largely American owned. Even the Revolution's nationalized economy could not rid itself of sugar. The Revolution came to terms with this painful reality in the late 1960s, when it decided to invest its militant fervor and hard labor in a record harvest. Fidel Castro prophesied ten million tons of sugar for the 1970 harvest, a "heroic" feat. Not incidentally does this become a time of triumphant speeches, mass mobilizations of volunteer labor, and a film about the machete. In many regards, *La primera carga al machete* was a cinematic ploy to confer on to the machete "redemptive" qualities and a vanguard glamor that in reality and the historical present it did not possess. It belied the fact that the economy was still dependent on sugar and that the machete remained an implement of drudgery more so than "liberation."[57]

Textual and Tactical Memory

Whatever its economic frailty or faults, the epic romance of the machete had value in the realms of morale and military preparedness. The Revolution had credible threats and, accordingly, the need for well-trained armed forces and a vigilant citizenry, one that was savvy in the ways of guerrilla warfare. The fact that US Marines were stationed on Cuban soil (Guantánamo Naval Base) made this threat all the livelier.[58]

Other than amass armaments, it was advisable to foster militias and teach guerrilla warfare. For should the island be invaded and occupied, it would be a familiar war of David-versus-Goliath odds and the need to tactically recalibrate those odds, just as the mambises had done. This fact was not lost on the Revolution's cadre or its Book Institute, which reissued and distributed literatura de campaña texts for Cuban readers. Manuel Piedra Martel's *Memoria del mambí* (1966) was one of its earliest releases and quite apropos, for it reads like Che Guevara's *Guerrilla*

Warfare (1960), except that it possesses a drama and mythical aura that the latter does not. Unlike Guevara's manual, Piedra Martel's memoir-chronicle has the literary and psychological qualities one might expect (and crave) in accounts of war: a participant narrator; vividly described locales, settings, and battles; and the affective lures of danger, suspense, mood, and heroic deeds. These attributes make for a dramatic narrative that embellishes the historic and tactical "lessons." One such lesson was the "system of war" that the mambises had to adopt: constant movements, partial actions, fast retreats, evasions, ambushes, harassment, and sabotage.[59]

The reader was not to be led to believe, however, that the mambises avoided battles altogether. Piedra Martel was a soldier in none other than Antonio Maceo's regiment, and the Bronze Titan was not to be dissociated from the machete and combat. Albeit a heavily edited text, the editors were sure to include Piedra Martel's account of the Battle of Mal Tiempo: "The sound of machetes against bayonets resounded, but more frequently still was the sound of our machetes against the skulls of the enemy soldiers. [. . .] Very few escaped, and the field of battle, from one end to the other, was left littered with hundreds of [Spanish] corpses."[60] What the Battle of Mal Tiempo taught was that the mambises had more than guerrilla savvy at their disposal. It taught that greater than cunning was the "imponderable" factor of "enthusiasm." This most precious asset was what distinguished the mambí from his imperial foes. It was that which elevated the mambí's potential to an "indominable caliber," that which could compel him to answer the clarion call: *¡Al machete!*[61]

If literatura de campaña was "testimonial," thus, revolutionary enthusiasm was that to which it testified—or, more exactly, that which it hoped to rouse. From versed drama and epic vignettes to battle hymns and cadences, literatura de campaña lionized a folk hero and bore witness to the repercussions of his "enthusiasm" on the field of battle. It was "mythical," too, affiliated with the nation's birth and, presumably, its most virtuous ancestors. Hence came other collections. An anthology of plays written and performed between 1868 and 1898, *Teatro mambí* (1978) is well-stocked with patriotic speeches, valiant soldiers, and machetes. This was theater, editor Rine Leal said, as a "weapon," theater that roused a willingness to pay one's "quota in blood and sacrifice."[62] Later came *Los poetas de la guerra* and *Heroes humildes,* both reissued in 1981. The former was a collection of Ten Years' War battle hymns and cadences first published in 1893, compiled and edited by none other than José Martí. It is mostly décimas, a ten-line rhymed verse set to folk music, and its value is in its authenticity of voice and epic commitment. "Their literature is not in what they wrote, but in what they did," said Martí. These "poets" may have "rhymed poorly, but only pedants and scoundrels would scold them for it, for they knew how to die well."[63] Serafín Sánchez's 1894 *Humble Heroes* was, similarly, an elegy to the popular classes and to the mambí epic as a participatory epic. Composed of six vignettes, the book tells of the heroic deeds and sacrifices of "humble" Cubans from the Ten Years' War. But all the same it articulates a stark and familiar choice: better to die heroically and be remembered than to suffer humiliations and die in oblivion.[64]

The stakes in 1890s Cuba were not, after all, frivolous. Cubans on and off the island conspired for war, and there was a need to organize, collect funds, and, especially, recruit soldiers. This latter requisite could not be fulfilled through conscription nor with generous material incentives. What the Republic in Arms had to offer was the *immaterial:* dignity for having stood up to one's oppressor and the utopian promise of a "moral" and "industrious" republic to come. But the "republic" had already been to war, extensively and intensively (1868–78, 1879–80), and there were those who were worn and weary. The war that Martí so fondly referred to as "sublime" was in reality a war rife with desertions, surrenders, strife, corruption, and untold sacrifices that did not amount to independence—let alone collective welfare. Naturally, some veterans were cautious of a renewed war effort. That weariness was voiced in Lieutenant Colonel Ramón Roa's *A pie y descalzo* (1890). A memoir-chronicle of the Ten Years' War, the title itself spoke volumes—literally, it reads "Walking and barefoot."[65] As its title recommends, the book offers a bleak account of war: harsh living, tragic deaths, faulty strategies, intrigues, and discord. If not tragically emplotted, it is at least *anti-romantic.* For while it does applaud mambí sacrifices, war is rendered all duty and no glory. In fact, one is left with the impression that the war was futile, if not worse.[66] And so while some celebrated the book for its sober realism, others did not take kindly to it. In November 1891, while campaigning in Ybor City, Florida, for war funds, Martí issued his thinly veiled rebuke: "Will the fear of war's tribulations make us turn back, scared by sullied people on the Spanish government's payroll, by the fear of walking barefoot, which is already quite common in Cuba, because only thieves and their accomplices now have shoes? Well, [. . .] I say to those who wish to frighten us with the very sacrifice that we crave: They lie!"[67] Enrique Collazo and three other mambí veterans fired back with an open letter in the Havana newspaper *La Lucha:* "It does not surprise us that you [Señor Martí] have misunderstood the nature of *A pie y descalzo:* the book must have terrified you." The authors ridiculed Martí as an effete civilian who fled to Madrid and thereafter lived in exile. The letter's farewell was particularly harsh: "If the hour of sacrifice should arrive anew, we might not be able to shake hands in Cuba's *manigua;* surely because you will then still be giving lessons on patriotism to the emigres, under the shade of the American flag."[68]

The emasculating sarcasm of Collazo was not lost on Martí, whose most conclusive retort was his death at Dos Ríos in March 1895. But that "retort" did little more than illuminate the commensurate criteria held by Collazo and Martí. Martí would have never earned the honorary title "martyr," much less "Apostle," were it not certified by the "unassailable title" of his death on Cuban soil. Neither Collazo nor Martí would dispute that. Instead, what was in dispute was *how* to properly narrate the war: What *tone* and *plot* should such narratives possess? What *sentiments* should they evoke? What *meaning* should they attribute to armed violence? To *whom* are they addressed? And for what *sake?* These were normative questions that one could not settle via strictly epistemological criteria. As we have discussed, the facticity of the wars could tolerate epics, tragedies, jeremiads, romances, parodies, satires, and so on—each empirically verifiable, yet each with its own "lessons" to bequeath. On that count, Roa's *A pie y descalzo* (1890) and Collazo's *Desde Yara hasta Zanjón* (1893) were anti-romantic narratives that made it clear what hardships new recruits could expect and what "tragic flaws" the Republic in Arms would have to surmount. This made them valuable texts. One could look to Roa's and Collazo's works for insights on how to better orchestrate the coming war.[69] But with their sober tone, dry prose, and a proclivity for logistical details, such texts were hopeless bores (or worse) when it came to recruitment. What the renewed war needed were not *pedagogical* inasmuch as *pathological* narratives, which is to say, ones that could rouse the pathos of "enthusiasm."

To this end, what was necessary were stories that could dignify and sensationalize armed rebellion, stories that stressed glory and adventure. Manuel de la Cruz understood this well when he wrote *Episodios de la revolución cubana* (1890), almost certainly the most popular of the literatura de campaña in its time.[70] De la Cruz confessed to fellow writer and mambí officer Manuel Sanguily that he set out to write an "epic legend," one that would "stir and touch the Cuban heart."[71] And, indeed, its riveting style and epic sentiment pleased even the most erudite of readers. "How could I begin to tell you," wrote Martí to de la Cruz, "the affection, agitation, reverence, and joy with which I read [. . .] your *Episodios de la revolución.*"[72]

These were still timely affairs in the early 1980s, when the Revolution reprinted not only *Los poetas de la guerra* and *Héroes humildes* but also de la Cruz's *Episodios.* With the socialist revolutions in Nicaragua and Grenada, active guerrilla movements in El Salvador and Guatemala, and the "African epic" in Angola, Cubans were called on to aid and abet comrades at arms. Under such circumstances, tragedy would not suffice. One *had* to believe that such revolutions were plausible, maybe even pleasurable, and one's sacrifices meaningful, maybe even heroic. In doing so the grandeur of the revolutionary epic was conferred on "small" nations and their "humble" peoples. And this, rhetorically, was on a par with the guerrilla tactic to recalibrate strategic odds and exploit the "imponderable." For what was more enthusing than the tale of the dispossessed who set the scales of justice aright? Of those whom history would not only absolve but venerate?

As history marched on, however, such tales lost their viability. By the 1990s, nearly all revolutions had fallen (Grenada in 1983 and Nicaragua in 1990), and Cuba's no longer shrouded in an epic luster. For some, this meant it was precisely the hour for "revolutionary intransigence"—the hour, as it were, for the machete. What else could hold the Revolution together? And were these not centennial years? Was it not their duty to live up to their mambí patrimony?

The irony was that the War for Independence did bear some uncanny resemblances to the Special Period, but not as epic emplotment would have it. For in both cases, Cubans were largely reduced to a famished nation at the mercy of an imperial power. In the historic war, the worst off were the *reconcentrados,* those interned in what Spain called "camps of reconcentration." It was they who died at rates far in excess of any "heroic" mambí. This discrepancy is worth a closer look. For the *scale* and *peculiarity* of the camp's violence was such that it defied what epic emplotment could readily accommodate. How, for instance, could one speak of "sacrifice" or the "heroic" when it came to the reconcentrado—or, for that matter, to the everyday Cuban of the Special Period? Did she or he not render such notions laughable or perverse? How Cubans have reconciled the two—the mambí and reconcentrado, machete and camp, the sublime and the catastrophic—is the subject of the next chapter.

5 The Epic (De)Sacralized

Sacrifice and the Specter of the Camp

La doctrina del sacrificio es la madre de lo poco que somos
—José de la Luz y Caballero

ARGUABLY THE most seductive and venerable quality of the epic is the heroic death. It is a species of death both dramatic and almost always sacralized, a death with elective affinities to a martyred prophet. For the epic hero knowingly wagers his life and does so for the sake of some greater good. But unlike the prophet, the hero dies in the throes of battle. This is essential. The Occidental world's heroic archetype is, after all, none other than Achilles: the consummate warrior who forsook a peaceable life for a violent death that would forever crown the Greek's name in glory.

More exactly, it is not violence or killing inasmuch as *being killed* that shrouds the epic in an aura of sublimity. For the heroic death is best understood as a *sacrificial* death. One dies willingly and in doing so purifies and redeems a wronged or wayward nation. Indeed, it is as if death itself is vanquished: "fear not a glorious death/for to die for the patria/is to live," resounds "La Bayamesa," Cuba's national anthem. That anthem was written in the hour of the nation's birth (1868), and its author, Perucho Figueredo, sang it aloud as he faced down his executioners. As sensational as it sounds, Figueredo's story was not so exceptional. For the story of Cuba Libre reads like a litany of epic *deaths*. The nation's most revered names are those of men who died in combat (e.g., Ignacio Agramonte, Carlos Manuel de Céspedes, José Martí, Antonio Maceo). Nor is it any less telling that era's most routinely invoked phrase was "sublime abnegation." Patria was that secularized deity to which one sacrificed. "Patria is altar, not pedestal," proclaimed Martí. And that sacredness was derived not from philosophical ideals or the poetically beckoned beauty of the island inasmuch as these epic deaths, these sacrificial offerings. Patria called for bloodshed, and the more bloodshed the holier.

The nation's "sublime" and "necessary" wars produced, nevertheless, an entirely different species of deaths, namely the *reconcentrados,* the name for those interned in Spain's "camps of reconcentration" (1896–97).[1] As a military strategy, Spain forcibly relocated Cuba's rural populations to garrisoned "camps" near or inside towns and cities. With inadequate food, shelter, medicines, and waste disposal, these densely populated camps became nuclei for starvation and epidemics. No fewer than 400,000 were interned and as many as 200,000 died—or, rather, were strategically *let to die.* This was a number that far exceeded (i.e. by a factor of as much as 20) deaths on the battlefield. But its significance was not just quantitative. What mattered at least as much were its qualitative attributes: the camps were conspicuous for their *absence* of war, conventionally conceived. Those that died therein were unarmed civilians, mostly women and children. In other words, no "sublime blood" was shed.

The epic as genre and sentiment could not, thereby, so easily account for reconcentrados. But account it did, however inadequately. Reconcentrados came to symbolize ineradicable proof of Spanish barbarism, of a tyranny that brutalized an innocent Cuba. And the mambí was her valorous and redemptive savoir. He coincided with the classic hero (male, armed, virile) and his death in battle was the archetype of sacrifice and the sublime. Little wonder that in the postbellum years it was to the mambí's honor that monuments were erected, streets renamed, holidays declared, and poems recited. For all its scale and "unspeakable" horror, that is, reconcentration and the reconcentrado were mere footnotes to an otherwise glorious epic. It was the mambí titans and apostles that Cubans learned to admire, if not emulate. Fidel Castro and his fellow barbudos professed to do precisely that. But it was no trivial irony that the Revolution itself made use of forced labor camps from 1965 to 1968. Those deemed not fit for or insufficiently committed to the Revolution were liable to be sent to such camps, in which prison-like conditions and abuses of power prevailed—not least for gay men and Jehovah Witnesses, those who did not abide by the martial and hyper-masculine credo or who refused to defer to the secular deity known as Patria. That said, this scandal was a relatively quiet (and small-scale) one. The Cuban popular imaginary remained invested in the historic mambí and the bearded guerrilla as archetypes of "revolutionary intransigence."

With the scarcities and uncertainties of the 1990s Special Period, however, Cubans writ large came to resemble not the mambí inasmuch as the famished reconcentrado. This was not lost on the state. The oratory and historiography of the era likened the refortified US embargo (*el bloqueo*) of the 1990s to the US naval blockade of 1898, responsible for as many as half of the reconcentrado dead. If the analogy was fair, its corollary was less so: the reconcentrado was resignified as patriotic "resister" and her or his death a sacrifice. In other words, the Revolution continued to be narrated in the epic terms of a willingness to die (and kill) for the Patria. That reconcentration and the reconcentrado could constitute the basis for a different story—a story about the precariousness of life and an ethical summons to care for it—was, evidently, unthinkable.

Sacri-Ficium, "Making Sacred"

Shortly after the Ten Years' War (1868–78) commenced, José Martí wrote his drama in poetic verse titled *Abdala* (1869). Against the agonized pleas of his mother, the play's protagonist takes up his spear and leads his fellow Nubians to war against would-be conquerors, only to return from the battlefield mortally wounded. In the presence of fellow warriors and his inconsolable mother, he declares: "Nubia [i.e., Cuba] is victorious! I die happy: death/Little does it matter, for I was able to save her [. . .]/Oh, how sweet it is to die when one dies/Struggling audaciously to defend the patria!"[2]

A fifteen-year-old white Havana student—son, moreover, to a Valencian father and Canary Islander mother—Martí had conjured up a sense of identity with the Afro-Cuban men of Oriente's swamplands and mountainous jungles, where the war for Cuba Libre was most alive and treacherous. He had also, literarily at least, rendered their deaths a "happy" and "sublime" affair. The young romantic was not alone in glorifying a certain manner of dying. Fifty-year-old "Perucho" Figueredo, Oriente lawyer and landowner, wrote the words and melody to what became (and remains) the Cuban national anthem: "La Bayamesa" (1868). A battle hymn that liberation soldiers chanted in the field, "La Bayamesa" called on Cubans to bear arms and reassured them to fear not a "glorious" death: "for to die for one's country is to live."[3] That the authors of *Abdala* and "La Bayamesa" died in these wars only made such prose all the more majestic, as dying for the Patria took on a moral grandeur in Cuban rhetoric and consciousness that little else could rival.

Why death holds such sway within nationalist literature and consciousness is not, however, entirely self-evident. Benedict Anderson has pointed out that modern nations write their "biographies" through a peculiar inversion of genealogy, that is, they are marked not by a series of births inasmuch as deaths. Not ordinary deaths of course: "exemplary suicides, poignant martyrdoms, assassinations, executions, wars, and holocausts."[4] Deaths of a "special kind." That death is such a lively issue within nationalist "imaginings," Anderson argued, bespeaks a close affinity with religious modes of thought. For nations, too, transmute the facts of fatality and finitude into matters of transcendence and continuity, beyond the earthly body and biological time of any given citizen or generation—the "mystery of re-generation," Anderson called it. Nations, in other words, have the capacity to evoke love and kinship between the dead, the living, and the yet unborn—despite their lack of "natural" (i.e., blood) ties. And so dear is that attachment that it makes it possible for millions not so much to kill as to willingly die and tender all manner of "colossal sacrifices."[5]

Mid- to late nineteenth-century Cubans were no strangers to violent deaths and the idiom and ethos of sacrifice. "Everything, absolutely everything, has to be offered to the Patria," exhorted Fermín Valdés-Domínguez, mambí colonel.[6] And whether voluntarily or otherwise, Cubans did precisely that: their careers, savings, harvests, livestock, worldly belongings, and lives were offered up to that phantasmal Patria. "We prefer to see our Cuba converted into a mound of ashes, and the cadavers of its sons reduced to charred remains, before consenting to the continued rule over this unhappy land by Spanish domination," said Salvador Cisneros Betancourt, provisional president to the Republic of Cuba.[7] His colleague, Manuel Sanguily, Ten Years' War veteran and mambí colonel, pledged that Cubans were ready to see "[their] land transformed into an immense tomb, covered in ashes, bespattered with stains of blood."[8] And so it was. By war's end, in the summer of 1898, hundreds of thousands had either perished or scarcely survived what proved to be the longest and most catastrophic of liberation wars in the Americas.

As morbid or hyperbolic as their prose may sound to disenchanted ears, it was not so unusual. Ashes, charred remains, tombs, blood—are these not the artifacts of ritual sacrifice and the sacred? While Cuba's official proclamations read like secular republicanism, the wars' and revolution's larger discourse abounded with mythico-religious referents and connotations. To this end, burnt offerings and spilt blood were *the* metonyms in the *sacri-ficium,* the "making sacred," of the Patria. Be they Catholic, Lucumí, or Palo Monte, each is tied to the sacred for Cubans. Whether in a biblical sense or otherwise, that is, offerings made by fire (e.g., burnt incense, oils, herbs) and by bloodletting (e.g., the ritual slaughter of "clean" animals) are understood to fulfill salutary or sanctifying functions: to expiate sin, cleanse the defiled, heal the sick, give thanks, or to bless.[9] And by way of both, sacrifice by fire and by bloodletting, Cubans came to figure and understand their revolution, their Patria, and themselves as sacralized.

As discussed in chapter 4, the torch (la tea) was pivotal to the Liberation Army's strategy. In the war of 1895–98, Generals Máximo Gómez and Antonio Maceo had their mambí armies set ablaze the island's sugar estates. With minimal risks and resources, they could reduce the colony's most lucrative industry to ash. And while worthless to wealthy Spaniards, a torched island was an act and thing rich with symbolic connotations to Cuban nationalists. Salvador Cisneros Betancourt reiterated in 1897 that Cubans would "*purify* the atmosphere with fire and leave nothing standing from San Antonio to Maisí [i.e., from one end of the island to the other]."[10] Commander Gómez would go as far as to refer to the torch as a "blessed" object, possessed of a power to cleanse the island of an accursed industry, the industry with the closest ties to slavery, dependency, and exploitation.

Bloodshed, too, was a salient constituent in the war's *symbolic* economy. The independentista newspaper, *La República,* stipulated that those entitled to the name "Cuban" were "those who have shed their blood in combat after having been despoiled of what they owned, those who have sacrificed on the altar of the patria their family, their positions, and their possessions."[11] It was not the killing of another, thus, that constituted a sacred act inasmuch as offering one's *own* blood. For just as religious sacrifice calls for "clean" and "worthy" offerings (e.g., first-born males), so, too, did the Patria call for the blood of her "true and good sons." On this count, arguably no other act could as forcefully endow the wars and Patria with an aura of the sacred and the sublime than could the sacrifice of one's own beloved. This took on mythical and biblical proportions in the cases of Carlos Manuel de Céspedes and Mariana Grajales, known respectively as the "Father" and "Mother" of the nation.

In 1870, Céspedes, first president of the Republic in Arms, received word that his son, Óscar, had been captured and sentenced to death. Spanish commander Antonio Caballero informed Céspedes that his son's life would be spared should the president surrender. Céspedes's reply is legendary: "Óscar is not my only son: I am father to all Cubans who have died for the Revolution."[12] Óscar was then executed. The parallels with the biblical story of Abraham and Isaac (Genesis 22) would not have been lost on Cubans. Céspedes was, accordingly, framed as a prophet who proved his faith and devotion to the secular deity known as Patria.

He was to sacrifice what he presumably cherished most, except that here Patria does not intercede and spare Óscar/Isaac's life, a sacrificial fact that accentuates all the more emphatically Céspedes's faith and the cause's sanctity. Playwright Francisco Javier Balmaseda, in his play *Carlos Manuel de Céspedes* (1900), retold the tale with these words: "Tell your coronel that all of my family will perish, and I [Céspedes] with them, before I betray my patria."[13] In the play, Céspedes is then tested again, when faced with the decision whether to execute ninety-four Spanish prisoners of war as retribution for his son's death. Instead, he grants them clemency. The soldiers cheer and join the mambí army. Had Céspedes done otherwise, he would have sullied the sacredness associated with the sacrificial, reducing his son's death to a logic of mere vengeance. The patriarch Céspedes is framed as just and merciful and his son's death a sacrifice, if not a *gift*.

No one, in this regard, was as sacrificially "generous" to the nation as was Mariana Grajales, whose husband and nine of eleven sons died in the wars for independence. As discussed in chapter 2, her truest renowned was not merely the quantity of her loss, but the *quality* with which she bore that loss. In the celebrated scene where she tended to her wounded titan (Antonio Maceo), she turned to her youngest son (Marcos) and said: "And you, stand tall, because it's time for you to fight for your patria."[14] Like Céspedes, Mariana's sacrificial ethos vis-à-vis her sons echoed the biblical narrative of Abraham and Isaac, except that herein mother and Patria are surrogates for father and Yahweh. This aura of the sacred resounded in the account (also publicized by Martí) of how Mariana reacted to war's outbreak in 1868. Mariana is said to have run to her room, come out with a crucifix, and say, "Everyone on their knees, father and sons, before Christ [. . .] and let us swear to liberate the Patria or die for it."[15] The theological credentials that were the biblical parable, the crucifix, and Mariana's namesake (as mother to Jesus) were not lost on Cubans. Nor, especially, was the moral cachet of a sacrificial death.

That said, of all the wars' deaths none was as retrospectively revered as was José Martí's fall at Dos Ríos. The author of *Abdala* rode to his "happy" death on March 19, 1895. After twenty-four years in exile, Martí returned clandestinely to Cuba as chief delegate to the Cuban Revolutionary Party (PRC) and, once on Cuban soil, was named major general in the Liberation Army. Commander Máximo Gómez had no illusions about Martí's lack of military experience and his truer value to the Republic in Arms as orator and chief delegate. Going against Gómez's order that he stay in the rear guard, a forty-two-year-old Martí "audaciously" (others said carelessly) charged into the Spanish line of fire at the Battle of Dos

Ríos. He was shot dead. He had fallen far enough into the field of fire that his body could not be recovered. At first buried in a mass grave, his corpse was exhumed the next day and placed in a coffin with a small window over Martí's face—a morbid display meant to demoralize the rebels.[16] Martí's death did not, however, demoralize inasmuch as "certify" and embolden his and others' capacity for "sublime abnegation." His patriotic prose and oratory were now beyond reproach. Cuba Libre's official history, Gonzalo de Quesda's *Cuba's Great Struggle for Freedom* (1898), no longer referred to him as the "Delegate" but as "our new redeemer" and, most lastingly, as the "Apostle."[17]

Hence, of all the epic motifs, sacrifice, especially in the mode of a heroic death, was the wars' most renowned. And not surprisingly so. As anthropologists Henri Hubert and Marcel Mauss stated, "There is no sacrifice into which some idea of redemption does not enter."[18] The words *Cuba Libre, mambí,* and *Patria* were as if a liturgy of redemption and the acts of "sublime abnegation" the rituals that endowed such words with a capacity to enthrall and enchant. For if sacrifice was redemptive and the nation sublime, it was because it was attributed a power to transcend death itself. The nation *as* sublime, to quote Terry Eagleton, "allows us vicariously to indulge in fantasies of immortality, flaunting our own finitude."[19] In Martí's words: "To die is to live, is to sow."[20] It was a transcendence within the reach of even the humblest of Cubans. Even the lowest ranked mambises would enjoy honorary tributes, however generic or anonymous, as "heroes" within the nation's annals. Martí's "Manifesto of Montecristi" (1895) referred to those who had fallen (and would soon fall) as "warriors of independence" whose "memory shall forever be blessed."[21] Generalísimo Máximo Gómez echoed with an elegy that ranked his soldiers as the "apotheosis of humanity," never to be forgotten before the "sacrosanct altar" of history and Patria.[22] Whether dead or alive, impoverished or mutilated by the war, the mambí and his loved ones at least enjoyed the solace that he fought for the Patria's liberation and would live on in exalted oral and official histories. He would forever signify valor, cunning, sacrifice, and redemption, and his memory would forever be affiliated with hallowed names and events such as Céspedes, Martí, and Maceo and the Gritos of Yara and Baire.

Catastrophe

The rhetoric of Cuba Libre would have one believe that only the mambises risked or lost their lives in the wars. But the truth is that Cuban women and children were calculatingly engulfed by the war and that between 1896 and 1898 their tribulations far outweighed those of any mambí: for every mambí who died in the war, as many as twenty so-called reconcentrados were strategically let to die. Of these civilian casualties, approximately 80 percent were women and children and every other a child under six years of age.[23] Starved, stricken, and unarmed, at the sovereign's mercy in what were called "camps of reconcentration," they were beyond the pale of "battle laurels" and the "crown of martyr." They would not—indeed, *could not*—enjoy such solace. Their memory would forever be tied, rather, to the diabolical name Weyler and to a decidedly anti-heroic death.

Valeriano Weyler y Nicolau was governor general of Cuba during 1896–97. At the time, he enjoyed many aristocratic titles: Marquis of Tenerife, 1st Duke of Rubí, Grandee of Spain. Yet the sobriquet that would haunt his otherwise decorated career and pedigree was "the Butcher." In Cuba his infamy as a man "without scruples" (*sin contemplaciones*) was already well known. During his tour in Cuba's Ten Years' War, he distinguished himself as leader of a unit nicknamed *Los Cazadores de Valmaseda,* "the Hunters of Valmaseda," in honor of his old commander and fellow aristocrat (General Blas Villate, Count of Valmaseda). The "Hunters" were mostly Cuban volunteers (not Spanish conscripts), handpicked from among the most fanatical of Spanish loyalists and disguised as Cuban rebels. Governed by little other than orders to hunt down mambises, Weyler's cazadores gave no quarter to the wounded, tortured prisoners, mutilated corpses, and terrorized villagers throughout Oriente.[24] They were the Spanish army's most feared and effective "counterguerrilla" force.

Accordingly, as Gómez and Maceo made their way across the island with near impunity in late 1895, all hopes for Spain were in the hands of Weyler. With the blessings of Prime Minister Antonio Canovás, Weyler set out to redeploy the Spanish army in Cuba as a counterinsurgency, rather than constabulary, force and, as he famously said, to wage "war with war." Many measures were taken to this effect, but it was Weyler's orders for all "rural inhabitants" to be relocated into garrisoned "camps of reconcentration" that would irrevocably taint his name. The first of Weyler's decrees (*bandos*), dated February 16, 1896, ordered all "rural inhabitants" of eastern Cuba to "reconcentrate themselves" (*reconcentrarse*) in the nearest fortified town or city. They were told to vacate their homes and were given eight days to comply, lest they be subject to the "responsibilities" attendant with disobedience to the law. A generic preamble to the bando reassured them that the measure was meant to "prevent resolute dangers to the honorable inhabitants of this Island."[25] That same day another bando was issued. This decree detailed all of the crimes now punishable by death or life imprisonment: sabotaging train tracks, cutting telegraph or telephone wires, destroying bridges, burning commercial properties or army barracks, smuggling arms or munitions, spreading rumors favorable to the "rebellion," providing rebels with horses, or acting as a spy, guide, or courier to the rebels.[26] The bando evidenced as such the guerrilla style of war that the Cuban Republic in Arms had victoriously waged since February 1895. It also evidenced, if elliptically, that the guerrilla strategy could work only insofar as Cuban civilians were free to act as an auxiliary force to the Liberation Army (ELC). Hence, Weyler outlawed and severely punished pro-rebel activities, cutting the ELC off from its nurses, cooks, spies, smugglers, recruiters, and any number of other vital functionaries that the *pacíficos*—literally the "peaceful ones," the name for Cuba's peasantry—were or could become for the Revolution.

Weyler likewise reoutfitted the trocha (militarized trench) system. Two major trochas were cleared and armed—one from Júraco to Morón and the other from Mariel to Majana. A militarized line that ran north to south across the center of the island, the Júraco-Morón trocha cut off rebel-friendly Camagüey and Oriente from sugar- and tobacco-rich western Cuba. Its efficacy in the first year of the war was the butt of many mambí jokes, but once at capacity (late 1896), the trocha kept Máximo Gómez's columns at bay in the east while Weyler tore apart Antonio Maceo's forces in far-off Pinar del Río of the west. This was no ordinary "trench." It consisted of a two-hundred-yard-wide clearing in otherwise dense jungle or forest, and the trees felled were mounted on each side to constitute a barrier at least five feet tall. Down its center ran communication wires and a single-track railway equipped with armor-clad cars to transport men and supplies from one post to the next. Every half-mile or so stood a fort encircled by trenches and barbed wire, and between these stood smaller blockhouses at variable intervals. 20,000 soldiers manned its fifty miles. The Mariel-Majana trocha had searchlights, artillery, and 14,000 soldiers across twenty miles that insulated imperial Havana from Maceo's columns to the west in Pinar del Río. Weyler as such parceled out three "departments" (west, center, east) that he would "pacify" one after the next.[27]

If Weyler never had his opportunity to pacify the east, his "reconcentration" strategy nevertheless jeopardized the revolutionary war like no other foe had. By early 1897, all provinces were under reconcentration orders, the Maceo brothers had been killed, imperial Havana was no longer under siege, and mambises were left to fend for themselves. The mambises no longer enjoyed or could coerce services out of Cuba's peasantry, nor could they forage or commandeer as once before. Weyler had his forces despoil the island of its bounty: they torched or confiscated all crops and grains; slaughtered any cows, pigs, chickens, or goats they could not consume or easily transport; contaminated fresh water sources; torched or pillaged outlying trading posts, homes, cottages, and ranches; cut down fruit trees; and shot any hogs they found in the wild.[28] With Weyler's orders to redouble naval patrols and fortify ports, moreover, the mambises received fewer supplies from abroad. In short, the mambises and their Revolution had entered their most dire hours.

If the mambises were at risk, reconcentrados were in peril. Estimates have it that no fewer than four hundred thousand Cuban pacíficos flooded major cities such as Matanzas, Havana, Cienfuegos, and Santa Clara—"voluntarily" or at gunpoint. Thereafter, they were known as reconcentrados, literally the "reconcentrated ones." Old, structurally unsound warehouses or crudely improvised corral-like structures were used to house them at first. But they filled to capacity so quickly that the reconcentrados crowded the cities' courtyards and plazas. Within weeks the cities were riddled with human feces and reconcentrados begging for morsels of stale bread or boiled rice. Shortly thereafter corpses began to litter the streets. Cemetery lands were expanded, but the toll was so hefty and so swift that mass graves (and bonfires) became the Spanish regime's method of choice for disposal.[29]

Not all, but the majority of reconcentrados were women and children. Adolescent boys and adult men had, by and large, already been recruited, imprisoned, or killed by either of the armies. Reconcentrados hailed, moreover, from communities and families of meager financial means. Their wealth and subsistence were intimately tied to their rural lives: homes, tools, livestock, and farmlands that were left behind or overwhelmed by either of the armies. Nor were they warmly welcomed to the cities. Many urban dwellers blamed their woes on the pacíficos, believing that the war would have already ended were it not for their "auxiliary" services to the mambises. Consequently, reconcentrados had only their bodies to sell and mercy to pray for. With rations and charity not sufficient, many were exploited for their labor, sexual and otherwise. It is true that small details of reconcentrados were allowed to forage nearby lands and (abandoned) estates under the watch of a soldier's escort. But within months, the well ran dry, as it were. Weyler then issued (belated) orders to set aside "cultivation zones" near Spanish forts so that reconcentrados could grow their own food. How this policy was enforced was left to local juntas and subject to graft. What yields they could muster, for instance, were almost always used to feed the Spanish soldiers first.[30]

Plagued by starvation and epidemics of beriberi, malaria, yellow fever, tuberculosis, and typhoid, reconcentrados began to die by the dozens on a daily basis. Records were not methodically kept and were subject to the vagaries of local juntas. In certain cases a dedicated mayor or citizen's charity council pooled resources and saw to it that as many reconcentrados as possible could receive as many rations as could be hoped for under the circumstances. But mortality rates never fell below 26 percent in the least-worst cases (Matanzas) and soared to as high as 50 percent in the worst of the worst (Pinar del Río and Havana).[31] All told, the most reliable estimates say that no fewer than 157,000 and as many as 200,000 died in the camps—of these the majority where children under five years of age.[32] With the dramatic fall in natality rates per annum, one could impute an additional 59,000 *unborn* victims to reconcentration.[33] Even after the bando was officially rescinded (November 1897), at least another 200,000 ex-reconcentrados were left to wander listlessly as homeless, jobless, landless, and half-starved on a despoiled island: commerce had been brought to a halt; the once lucrative sugar estates were now rubble and ash, as were many villages and towns; agricultural fields and orchards were barren; grain stockades were emptied; many freshwater sources were spoiled; livestock had been systematically slaughtered—no ox to plow fields, no chickens to lay eggs, no pigs for meat; and families had been irrevocably torn apart: no other country in the Americas had a higher percentage of orphans and widows than did postwar Cuba.[34] All told: catastrophe.

The Unsacrificeable

It was hoped that the morbid spectacle that was reconcentration would compel the clandestine Cuban rebels to surrender. But no such surrender came, only more misery and hundreds of thousands living under the sentence of death—a death that could only perversely be described as "sublime" or "happy." For the epic emplotment of Cuba Libre could not convincingly confer any dignities onto the reconcentrado nor account for such catastrophic loss and so peculiar a violence. None of its transcendental connotations were applicable: not the martial prowess of a Titan, the eloquence of an Apostle, the romance of the machete, the purifying powers of the torch, the cunning of the guerrilla, the "decorum" of the mambises, the grandeur of a Revolution, nor the sacredness of sacrifice. The reconcentrados were a world apart.

As a *modality* or *technique* of violence that was neither conventional combat nor senseless slaughter, so-called reconcentration did not coincide with normative senses of "civilized" and "savage" violence—and, for that matter, what constituted the "heroic" and the sacred. It killed en masse without modern weaponry and, technically, without shedding blood. Those who were strategically let to die teetered, thereby, at the thresholds of the sacrificial motif and nationalist honorariums. They bore no arms and were interned in a space conspicuous for its *absence* of war, conventionally conceived. Nor were they subject to trials or formal executions. They were not criminals. Spanish war decrees (bandos) professed the measure was in fact to "prevent resolute dangers to the *honorable inhabitants* of this Island."[35] For those dying of hunger and disease and under the pretext of a humanitarian measure, how could their deaths count as either murder or as capital punishment? No rifle or artillery fire, no bayonets, no garrotes, no iconic torture devices—only undernourishment and pathogens to blame.

And how could one speak of martyrs and martyrdom? Derived from the Greek word for "witness" (*martis*), "martyr" and "martyrdom" were terms coined by the early Christian Church to refer to those who, facing tortuous deaths at the hands of Roman authorities, refused to renounce their faith. Yet it would seem quite misled to refer to the reconcentrado dead as having "bore witness" to something sacred. They were not known to have defiantly professed their faith in Cuba Libre, nor were they known to have faced their drawn-out (bloodless) deaths with "sublime resignation." Did their deaths constitute, thus, the "scandal of a meaningless death"—to borrow Giorgio Agamben's phrase?[36] Agamben, in *Remnants of Auschwitz* (2002), took care to critique the will to make sense of the senseless. He quoted Bruno Bettelheim, a Dachau survivor, on the matter: "By calling the victims of the Nazis 'martyrs,' we falsify their fate."[37] Let us be clear, however, that reconcentrado deaths and "living-deaths" were not senseless per se. It may have been "senseless" that one particular family or child suffered as they did and that others were spared, but their interment as a whole was a calculated war measure with punitive and preemptive objectives. The fact that Cuba's "rural inhabitants" were targeted was no coincidence; no other class of Cubans was better situated to serve as auxiliaries to the Liberation Army and rebel cause—and serve many did, whether voluntarily or by the force of circumstances. Hence, whether or not they had ever aided and abetted a Cuban mambí, their "living-deaths" as reconcentrados were far from senseless or inconsequential to Spanish as much as Cuban war officiates.

But their fates as the "living-dead" of the camps situated them a far cry from constituting martyrs or "sacrificial offerings" to the Patria. Reconcentrados were unarmed civilians who died anonymously and silently, with no heroic deeds or dictums to their credit. Their deaths may have been "tragic," colloquially put, but not exemplary or sacral. After all, if they could not be likened to fierce Spartans (as were the mambises), nor could they be likened to a Socrates or a Jesus. Both Socrates and Jesus freely faced their deaths and permitted miscarriages of justice to be carried out: Socrates forgoes the opportunity to flee in exile and voluntarily drinks his hemlock; Jesus prophesies his betrayal and solemnly bears his cross. Their deaths "bore witness" and were endowed with sacrificial power. Yet it would be an utter absurdity to speak of reconcentrados as having freely, let alone graciously, sacrificed themselves "before the altar" of the Patria. Had sacrifice thereby "lost all rights and dignity," as Jean-Luc Nancy said of the victims of the Shoah?[38]

Jean-Luc Nancy is not alone in trying to make sense of the ethical and epistemological peculiarities of concentration and death camps. Agamben, in *Homo Sacer* (1995), argued that within the "the camp" life is but "naked" (*nuda*), a mere existence one kills but does not as such murder or desecrate.[39] Hannah Arendt, in *The Origins of Totalitarianism* (1951), provocatively figured colonial Africa as that "phantom world" in which "natives" are to Europeans "just another form of animal life" that one killed but did not murder.[40] Her final chapter concludes, as near parallel, that "the abstract nakedness of being nothing but human" was the ghettoized and encamped European Jews' "greatest danger."[41]

Whether Spanish reconcentration was structurally analogous to Nazi labor and death camps is not what is at stake herein. It suffices to note that Americans and Cubans alike chose to refer to the event as "inconceivable," "unimaginable," "unspeakable," and "indescribable." Not only its scale but also its mortality rates, the agonized and belabored deaths it meted out, and the *profile* of its victims (i.e., women, children, noncombatants) all rendered it a representational as much as moral scandal. The reconcentrado's pitiable existence went hand in hand with the ways in which witnesses portrayed them and the progenitor of their misery. Weyler soon became the name and face of evil in the North Atlantic press and political oratory, spoken in the same breath as Herod and Nero. These were no idle associations to any Christian reader or addressee. Herod, the Roman client ruler of Judea, was he who ordered

John the Baptist's death (by decapitation) and the "Massacre of Innocents," the slaying of all boys two years of age and younger in Bethlehem in hopes of killing the newborn "King of the Jews" (Jesus). Roman Emperor Nero was also renown as one of the first Christian slayers, so much so that early apocryphal writings identified him as the Anti-Christ. Obviously, if Weyler was placed on a par with the Anti-Christ, Cubans were eo ipso Christian martyrs.

Christian tropes no doubt outnumbered any others when it came to rhetorically fleshing out what Americans called the "Cuban Question." Cubans were repeatedly figured as "our neighbors," with all of the biblical connotations of duty and covenant this entailed. Americans, accordingly, were called on to be the "Good Samaritans" to their distraught neighbors.[42] And when it came to visual tropes, illustrators turned to the Christian *pietà* as their aesthetic of choice. In this respect the victim was not likened to a *man* robbed, beaten, naked, and half-dead on the Jericho road inasmuch as an aggrieved and saintly *mother.* The cover-image to Stephan Bonsal's *The Real Conditions of Cuba To-day* (1897) was exemplary in this regard. The reader beheld a (Cuban) mother on her knees, in tattered dress and with her sickly, if not dead, child's head on her lap. To her rear is a Spanish soldier who looks on indifferently to the vast sea before him. For this, too, is noteworthy: they are at the seashore, not in a "camp." This situated her plea such that the proximity of Cuba to the United States was recalled to the reader—such that the reader did not mistake to whom her plea was addressed.

And mistake they did not. Frank Bruce's poem "Free Cuba" evidenced as much:

> Fair Cuba, we have heard thy cries,
> Have seen thy pain and anguish,
> And now we come to bid thee rise,
> Thou needn't no longer languish,
> Beneath the cruel tyrant's power,
> Deliverance comes to thee this hour.[43]

One is reminded of Gayatri Spivak's thesis that the *portrayal* of an (subaltern) Other bears within it the choice of and need for a *proxy*—and not unusually a heroic or paternalistic one.[44] For what else could a portrait of Cuba as a pietà-style dolorous mother or as a damsel in distress call forth if not the need for a heroic proxy? It was no secret to Americans *who* that heroic proxy was or would be. If Cuba was to be free, it would be thanks to "Uncle Sam" and the "sons of Columbia." Bruce, of course, was but one poetic voice in a larger public discourse that framed American military intervention as a "war of humanity." Poetic titles alone spoke volumes: "Set Cuba Free," "Cuba Shall be Free," "To the Rescue," "Cuba's Cry is Heard."[45]

The cruelest of ironies is that *nearly* all was as the Cuban rebels would have it. The Republic in Arms had headquarters not only in Florida but also in New York and D.C. They had strategically situated themselves not only for "filibuster" expeditions but also for press releases and lobbying campaigns. It was hard to know, in fact, to whom one should credit the "news." The Republic in Arms gave daily press releases of "Spanish atrocities" in Cuba and, in turn, cited senior US diplomats and journalists who reported on the horrors of reconcentration. Just like Americans, Cubans portrayed Weyler as a diabolical villain and employed all the sobriquets and adjectives Americans had or in due time would: "Murderer," "Butcher," "Inquisitor," "monster," "bloodthirsty," "perverse," and "inhuman." They mocked him in animalistic terms: as a crow, symbol of death; as a serpent, symbol of evil in all its biblical connotations; or as jackal, a scavenger and symbol of piracy. And not unlike Americans they taunted and mocked Weyler's stature: at five feet tall, he was known not only as the Butcher but also as the "sinister dwarf."[46] Weyler was, in other words, the moral and physical inferior to the mambí, Cuba's manlier savoir.

If there was any disagreement, thus, it was not on *how* to discursively represent the victims and perpetrator. It was merely on the count of *who* would redeem the damsel in distress that was Cuba. If for Americans it was a gallant Uncle Sam or the sons of Columbia, for Cubans it was the mambí with "redemptive torch" and "fearsome machete." "Hail, the redemptive torch/whose red splendor/is that shimmering radiance/that announces the new dawn!," announced one poem. "Send if you like/your Weylers and your Pandos/with their butcher's decrees [. . .] For Cuba shall greet your fury/with the machete's blade."[47] Americans had, after all, written the mambises out of the melodrama: Cubans were (feminized) victims to a villainous Spain, not belligerents in a revolutionary war. But if Cubans disagreed, it was only insofar as they touted their own prowess and decorum as "warriors of independence." For they, too, spoke of "atrocities," "shocking indignities," and "unspeakable cruelty," and they, too, spoke of reconcentrados in generic terms such as the "defenseless woman" and the "innocent child."[48] Never, consequently, did the reconcentrado problematize inasmuch as *supplement* and *endorse* the epic of liberation. It was she and her children's victimhood and suffering—an allegorically captive and imperiled Cuba—that rendered Cuba Libre's foes cruel and repressive and, by corollary, the mambises virtuous and emancipatory. The reconcentrado was narratively valuable insofar as she served to define *revolutionary* against *imperial* violence, to distinguish the valorous and the "endowed" from the cowardly and the effete.

The scandal herein was that these tropes and mythoi elaborated on an innocence that never was. Americans never contextualized their outcry at Spanish atrocities in relation to their *own* nation's history of violence—not least Native American dispossession and the enslavement of Africans and their descendants. General Weyler would do precisely that, years later (1910) when he chronicled his career. He stipulated that General Sherman's "March to Atlanta" in the American Civil War and the US Army's strategy against the Plains Indians were precedents to his "system of war" in Cuba. Nor did he miss the opportunity to point out, quite glibly, that those who most censured his use of concentration camps—the British and the Americans—subsequently "copied" him in South Africa and in the Philippines.[49] But the cruelest of ironies was that as Americans marveled at their "war for humanity," they did not censure their navy's blockade of Cuba in that war—a blockade that has been credited with as many as half the reconcentrado dead.[50]

Cubans were not as innocent either. As they reveled poetically at their "sacred" torches and "redeeming" machetes, they never meaningfully reckoned with the effects of their incendiary war, a strategy that left Cuba's peasantry and agricultural laborers unemployed, endangered, and fleeing to towns and cities that could neither employ nor feed them. Nor, as they decried the reconcentrado's misery, did they critically reflect on the coercive measures undertaken by the Liberation Army in order to "enlist" the peasantry, measures that rendered them targets of choice for reconcentration. In fact "reconcentration" was first employed, albeit on a smaller and less lethal scale, in the Ten Years' War, and veterans at the highest command (including Máximo Gómez) rightly anticipated its reuse in the 1890s.[51] Granted, the Republic in Arms many have calculated that the Spanish would not reenact reconcentration so thoroughly and tenaciously. But the fact is that pacífico lives were wagered as collateral in a war deemed "calamitously necessary," and it was precisely calamity that befell them. Needless to say, the Republic in Arms was not on a par with Weyler and Madrid in terms of responsibility for the reconcentrado dead. Yet nor was it as innocent—let alone as "decorous" and "redemptive"—as the epic's mythoi would have one believe.

From *Pietà* to *Piedad*

Reconcentration, thus, was a wholly *anti-heroic* affair that postbellum Cubans would rather forget. And forget they did—institutionally at least. The national calendar filled with commemorative dates devoted to the wars' "sublime" events and "heroic" dead: from the Grito de Yara (October 10) and the Grito de Baire (February 24) to the deaths of Céspedes (February 27), Agramonte (May 11), Martí (May 19), and Maceo (December 6)—each the occasion, as Louis Pérez Jr. has said, to "remind the living of the debt owed to the dead."[52] Not just any dead: the mambí dead. February 16, the date of Weyler's first reconcentration bando, was never declared a day of solemn observance, for instance. Nor would any of the reconcentrado dead count among the nation's esteemed martyrs and *próceres* (founding fathers). Such an act would be just shy of "unthinkable" insofar as the nation's past was epically emplotted. Instead, the era's memorials, eulogies, hymns, speeches, and lectures were dedicated to the machete charges and heroic deaths that were the story of Cuba Libre.

This was no idle project, of course, not least in the midst of two US occupations (1898–1902, 1906–9) and the Platt Amendment (1901–33). Cubans were to learn of their epic past so as to emulate, not just venerate, it. As mambí veteran and historian Luis Rodolfo Miranda put it, "It is our desire to make known the achievements of the men who, with a smile on their face, were happy to die for Cuba Libre. We wish our youth of today to learn of the sacrifices and glory of the past, knowledge that serves as a source of pride to our people so that they will continue to struggle to complete the noble work begun by those men [*sic*]."[53] The anticlimactic end to the wars and the farce that was the early republic were not an outcome worthy of so much sacrifice. Under such circumstances, the mambí epic was not irrelevant inasmuch as all the more valuable. For it was the mambí who constituted the archetype of the prowess, valor, and sacrifice it would take to redeem the Patria.

The reconcentrado could not compete with so dramatic and so "classical" a hero. Streets were not renamed after reconcentrados, nor monuments erected in their honor. No one recited reconcentrado poetry or read reconcentrado memoirs, for there were none to speak of! The bleak truth is that there exists scant documentary evidence that can attest to reconcentrado lives (not only deaths) in anyway other than generically and sorrowfully. We know so few names and have even fewer stories. As is the case with written archives, the voices of a largely illiterate and dispossessed multitude are barely audible in the published sources that do exist.

But the bleakest of truths is that their lives—and, especially, their deaths—simply did not coincide with what counted as a *venerable* death. For only perversely could they be said to have sacrificed themselves. Nor did their bodies or deeds coincide with the classical epic hero, so intimately affiliated with the youthful male body and armed combat. Despite the vital services that they (as pacíficos) performed for the Republic in Arms as reconcentrados, that is, they were condemned to an abject vulnerability and obscene death that was likeliest to arouse pity, not awe or reverence.

Francisco Machado's 1917 *¡Piedad!: Recuerdos de la reconcentración* (Pity!: Memories of reconcentration) was one such text. It is the most extensive memoir-cum-testimonial devoted to the "horrid spectacle" that was reconcentration. As its former mayor, Machado wrote the saga of Sagua la Grande's travails to feed and shelter—and later, apprentice and employ—the "sickly ambulant skeletons" in their midst, especially all the orphaned girls. At times, Machado's prose is wrought with the most insufferable of scenes: the mother, pleased to see her child die at her milkless breast; the child, "suckling at the flaccid and cold chest of her dead mother."[54] But grief and cruelty are neither the text's plot nor its protagonist. Rather, *¡Piedad!* tells the story of how the "noble sentiments" of Sagua's bourgeois citizenry overcame cruelty and saved innocent lives. In truth, reconcentrados never speak or act in the text inasmuch as constitute an adversity that "Charity, Compassion, and Pity" must overcome. What one encounters are a series of vignettes on Sagua's charitable juntas and their distinguished members: names are listed, virtues and sacrifices are respectively detailed, periodicals to their credit are cited, and faces are honored with full-page illustrations. For *¡Piedad!* is a richly illustrated text, but its illustrations are not symmetrical. On the one hand, Sagua's charitable ladies and gentry: each a singular bust with captioned name and title, dressed in Victorian attire, and willingly posed as a respectable man or woman. On the other, Sagua's reconcentrados: a dejected nameless collectivity, emaciated and nearly naked, with empty gazes that do not welcome the camera's eye (and that this author will not reproduce). The images thereby work in tandem to signify bourgeois "civility" (*civismo*) against the reconcentrado's mute precarity. The reader walks away from the text without any sense for reconcentrado lives, talents, or virtues—only that they suffered en masse or died horribly were it not for Sagua's clinics and asylums.

A rare, if not singular, work written by a former reconcentrado is Ramiro Guerra y Sanchez's 1957 memoir, *Por las veredas del pasado* (Through the paths of the past). But what is noteworthy is that even here the reader must parse through telling equivocations. Guerra's family did not suffer as others did. They came to Batabanó with a milking cow, two oxen, cooking supplies, clothing, and all of their harvested vegetables in tote. And within short order, they were gainfully employed. Guerra's mother found work as a cook for the port city's military commander; his father made and sold sugar cane syrup (*melado*); and the young Guerra, who was literate, would write letters on behalf of Spanish soldiers to their loved ones back in Spain—services that earned him the privilege to freely forage for fruits and vegetables. All in all, it was "tolerable," as Guerra put it. His family's services for the Spanish military ensured that when the young Guerra contracted typhoid and, later, yellow fever, he had sufficient nutrients and quinine to survive it. Their relative fortune did wear thin: their milking cow was killed in a shoot-out with rebels; the region's sugar cane for his father's melado was torched by rebels and Spaniards alike; and foraging was doomed to diminishing returns. Guerra's family also dealt with their share of loss. He spoke of cousins and uncles that were imprisoned or had been killed by Spanish forces for having aided the rebels. And this is key to the text's narrative: Guerra never truly identifies as a reconcentrado.

Guerra knew "reconcentrado" to be an identity one affixed to the living dead of the camps. And understandably, he resisted it. At a telling moment in his text, he described a most "pathetic scene." In the outskirts of Colón, Guerra, in the company of Spanish soldiers, came across a reconcentrada who, barefoot and half-naked, held out a tin plate to beg for food. Her green eyes, her youth, and her "silent supplication" moved him to make a "defensive gesture" on her behalf. At the sight of this "gesture," a Spanish soldier called out, "*¡mambí!*" The accusation was aimed at Guerra, who reminisced: "His supposed insult I took as a great honor."[55] Guerra thereby identified with, if not *as,* a mambí, not reconcentrado. He knew the latter to signify the meek and starved, whereas the former was the hallmark of patriotic valor and, as this scene attested, a defiant benevolence. It was a familiar script: the reconcentrados as an allegorically innocent Cuba, brutalized by imperial villains, and her only hope, the virile and honorable mambí.

The Specter of the Camp

Such was the historiographic and symbolic milieu in which Fidel Castro and 1950s rebels were educated. Castro's apologia for the armed assault on the Moncada Barracks evidenced as much: "We were taught from early on to venerate the glorious example of our heroes and our martyrs. Céspedes, Agramonte, Maceo, Gómez, and Martí were the first names engraved in our minds."[56] The assault on Moncada was, of course, a *tactical* disaster. Some would say it was suicidal. Indeed, it resembled a machete charge, except with semi-automatic rifles. But such resemblances were precisely what were at stake, so much so that the assault was translated into a *symbolic* victory. For akin to the *romance* of the machete and the *epic* of Cuba Libre, Castro framed the act not as suicidal inasmuch as sacramental and the dead as not dead: "My comrades, anyway, are neither forgotten nor dead; they live today more than ever and their assassins must be terrified at how from their heroic cadavers arise the victorious specter of their ideas. May the Apostle speak for me: 'There is a limit to mourning the graves of the dead, and that limit is the infinite love for patria and the glory that is sworn over their bodies [. . .] because the bodies of martyrs are the most beautiful of altars to honor.'"[57] History would soon absolve Castro, but it would not absolve Batista—as with Weyler. Castro in fact likened Batista's commanders to Weyler, who was merciless with prisoners of war. Almost all of the armed rebels who assaulted the Moncada (and Bayamo) barracks were tortured and killed as captives. But no one, least of all Castro, mistook the dead for reconcentrados. The dead of Moncada and, later, the barbudos of the Sierra were categorically narrated as heirs to the mambises, as patriots and revolutionaries comprehensible under the mythopoetics of the sublime and the sacrificial.

With the Revolution, such heroics were to be emulated, whether as a member of the Revolutionary Armed Forces, the militia, or the Communist Party. An ethos of sacrifice and military preparedness could not be taken lightly, after all—not with all the sanctions, sabotage, and propaganda meted out against the Revolution. But not all such sacrifices and preparedness were voluntary, let alone welcomed. Other than *morally* sway citizens to participate in mass rallies and organizations, the Revolution passed laws that *compelled* service and penalized noncooperation. One such mechanism was compulsory military service for all males, enacted in 1961. Cuban men (ages seventeen to twenty-eight) would be trained to abide by discipline and the chain of command and learn how to use firearms. That said, the largest share of their "service" was in public works projects, whether to build housing, schools, or clinics, or to do agricultural labor. Like their counterparts around the world, conscripts were paid a meager wage, housed in austere barracks, and fed rather bland food. It was neither glamorous nor "glorious."

There were, however, those who were deemed "unfit" for military service or insufficiently devoted to Patria and the Revolution. For such constituents, coercive and punitive measures were employed, none as notorious as the UMAP camps. Euphemistically termed Military Units to Aid Production, these UMAP "units" were in fact forced-labor camps. Internees, or *confinados,* were subjected to prison-like quarters and feed, grueling agricultural labor of as many as ten to twelve hours a day, and regular sessions of indoctrination. Hemmed in by ten-foot barbed-wire fences and with only 120 men per camp, the camps were relatively small and dispersed throughout Cuba's east-central and largely rural Camagüey province. In a larger context, they were meant to address national security and economic imperatives. The early 1960s were plagued with CIA-sponsored bombings, sabotage, armed rebellion, and assassinations such that community vigilance organizations (CDRs) were formed and entrusted to report on the "counterrevolutionary" activities of their neighbors. It is generally agreed that the majority of UMAP internees were victims of CDR prejudices and abuses of power. Equally important was Cuba's dire need for greater productivity in order to adjust to the US embargo and rising military and social expenditures. UMAP yielded the cheap regimented labor of as many as thirty-five thousand men precisely where ranch lands were being converted into sugar cane fields. Like other military conscripts, UMAP internees received a meager seven pesos a month for their services—one-tenth the state's monthly minimum wage for agricultural labor at the time.[58] But unlike official conscripts, the confinados were stigmatized and despised.

Victims of the UMAPs included Catholic priests, farmers who rebelled against state appropriations of their lands, religious minorities associated with criminality (e.g., Abakuá) or "yankee" intrigues (e.g., Pentecostals, Gideons, and Jehovah's Witnesses), nonconformist university students, government officials accused of corruption, persons who were illegally self-employed, drug addicts, prostitutes, "hippies," and "homosexuals." Of all these, the two most frequently interned were religious minorities and gay men.[59] In this regard, one cannot explain UMAP solely in terms of national security and economy, for Jehovah's Witnesses and gay men were not just overrepresented but also treated the worst. According to Hector Santiago, who was interned in a gay camp, "With us, they were terrible, but let me tell you the truth, they treat you like a lady compared to the Jehovah Witnesses. Oh my god, they really, really were terrible with them, terrible. The things that they did to them . . . horrible, horrible."[60] It is said that Jehovah's Witnesses were subject to all manner of cruel treatment: beaten; deprived of food, water, family visits, and leaves; forced to stand at attention in the hot sun until they fainted; tied up naked outside and left for the mosquitoes and sun; or forced to stand in latrines filled with excrement. Closer scrutiny recommends that Jehovah's Witnesses were not treated so inhumanely because of their religiosity per se. Other religious minorities were not systematically tormented inasmuch as intimidated and exploited for their labor. The truly revealing matter is that Jehovah's Witnesses *doctrinally* refuse to work in military industries or serve in the armed forces. So, too, do they refuse to salute or pledge allegiance to flags or sing national anthems.[61] At a time when revolutionary identity and ethos were so spectacularly tethered to the figure of the patriotic guerrillero, such refusals were tantamount to sacrilege. They communicated that there was a calling and entity more sacred than Revolution and Patria. That Jehovah's Witnesses refused, moreover, to wear the UMAP camp uniforms of olive-green pants, blue denim shirt, and military boots only made (corporeal) matters worse for them.

But revolutionary identity and ethos in the 1960s were understood to entail more than militarized patriotism. Just as with the mambises of the 1890s, revolutionary identity and ethos of the 1960s was a deeply *moral* affair with, as Antoni Kapcia has put it, a "*martiano* pedigree."[62] Martí routinely invoked the "decorum" of the mambises as exemplary of the "moral republicanism" the liberation army fought to install. Mambises were those who not only sacrificed their lives and worldly possessions but also those who embodied the virtues that should come to characterize the everyday citizens of a Cuba Libre. Commanders Gómez and Maceo did not tolerate gambling, cock fighting, alcohol use, or prostitution within their ranks or army affiliates. Cuba Libre was, in short, to be free not only of imperialism but also of moral "vices." Drawing on this "pedigree," the revolutionary regime of the 1960s sought to eradicate the vices of a brothel- and casino-ridden Havana through "offensives" such as Operation P (1961). A secret police identifying itself as the "Scum Squadron" raided Havana streets and establishments for "pederasts, prostitutes, and pimps" in order to push out the mafioso sex and drug lords of Batista-era Cuba. Nearly all of the economically marginalized (and socially stigmatized) women they rounded up were then trained and reemployed as seamstresses and other occupations in the formal economy.[63]

Operation P was, however, only one such offensive in a larger moralistic campaign to "sanitize" Cuba and its people of their neocolonial and capitalist vices. For it was one matter to structurally adjust an economy with hopes to undermine dependency and boost technological development, and another matter to alter the consciousness of the "masses." To this end, Che Guevara insisted that moral (in lieu of material) incentives would pave the way toward non-alienated labor and noncommodified human relations. Rather than overtime pay, bonuses, or raises, for instance, excellent workers would be offered symbolic tributes such as national awards, certificates, and honorariums that paid off in other respects such as a gratifying sense of duty or peer admiration.[64] Yet while men *and* women were expected to foster this "new scale of values," it was clear that for the revolutionary vanguard moral virility was as if a derivative of masculine virility. Fidel and Che were models of this revolutionary *hombría* (manliness). With their signature bravado and gallantry, they conveyed a sense that to be physically weak was tantamount to being morally weak. It was easy, as such, to draw out the corollary that the effeminate man was less, if at all, revolutionary.

Within this heteronormative bigotry, the least tolerable of all were the so-called *maricónes* (faggots) and *locas* (queens). Cuban writer and painter Samuel Feijóo, in an *El Mundo* editorial of 1965 titled "Revolution and Vices," declared: "No homosexual represents the Revolution, that is a matter for men [*varones*], of fists and not of feathers, of fury and not of trembling, of sincerity and not of intrigues, of creative valor and not of candy-coated surprises [*sorpresas merengosas*]. . . . We are not talking about persecuting homosexuals but of destroying their positions in society, their methods, their influence. Revolutionary social hygiene is what this is called."[65] But persecute they did. Gay men in particular were systematically purged from the universities and press, officially prohibited from joining the military or the PCC, and forcibly sent off to UMAP camps under the pretext of "antisocial" behavior. In the camps, they were subjected not only to exploitive labor but also to "rehabilitative" experiments that included electroshock therapy. There were public trials and assemblies for "outing" politically unreliable peers, but gay men were thought to be easily identifiable for their tight pants, sandals, and flamboyance. These were no idle metonyms. The true revolutionary, identifiable by his olive-green fatigues, military boots, and disciplined body, was he who stood for moral integrity and productive labor against the alleged promiscuity and vagrancy of queer (or ascriptively queered) Cubans.[66] The mambí was, after all, a desexualized, if not asexual, archetype. His only "sexualized" identity was conveyed via camaraderie in phallic arms. It was clear, in other words, that if a man *received*—rather than *made use of*—the phallus (be it a penis, a machete, or a rifle), his moral as much as sexual integrity was suspect and grounds for internment or other "hygienic" measures.

The UMAP camps lasted from November 1965 to July 1968. They were condemned internationally and domestically, with Cuba's National Union of Writers and Artists (UNEAC) and its Council of Churches among their most vociferous critics.[67] It is said that some commanders were subject to court-martial and convicted for their brutality.[68] But this did not spell the end for gay (or religious) persecution in Cuba. In 1971 the Congress on Education and Culture concluded that "homosexuality" was "sociopathological" and that gays and lesbians should be denied employment in any institution in which the corruptibility of Cuban youth was at stake. It is generally agreed that such openly hostile purges and provocations ended in 1975, with the next five years seeing many of the persecuted financially, if meagerly, compensated and many others finding a more hospitable milieu in the arts.[69] But no apology for the camps and purges came, and gay and lesbian Cubans were not openly recognized for their contributions to the Revolution.

It would not be until the 1990s that Cuba's historic and the Revolution's institutionalized homophobia would be more earnestly reckoned with. This was most sensationally the case with the 1993 film *Fresa y chocolate* (Strawberries and chocolate). The film won the prestigious Silver Bear prize in Berlin and was the most sought-after screening at film festivals in Brazil, Argentina, Mexico, Italy, and Spain. It even enjoyed the honor of being the first Cuban film nominated for an Oscar. But what was truly remarkable was that it caused a stir in Cuba itself, winning the Critics' and the People's Choice Awards at the Havana Film Festival and playing to packed Havana cinemas for the unusually long tenure of eight months.[70] This was so not least because it licensed discussions on culturally and politically taboo issues.

Nominally set in 1979, though with an uncanny feel of the contemporary, the film is about the unlikely yet heartfelt friendship that buds between David and Diego. David and Diego are stark, if clichéd, contrasts: David the atheist, heterosexual university student and member of the Union of Communist Youth; Diego the gay photographer and eclectic intellectual who prays to the Virgen de Caridad. Diego spots the younger David at the Coppelia, Havana's famed ice cream parlor, and lures him back to his apartment. The reluctant David, a would-be writer, is drawn to Diego's knowledge and possession of literary and artistic works rarely found in Cuba. Diego becomes David's mentor, not only in matters of art but also in sex and politics. For David is a virgin in every sense—culturally, sexually, and politically—and it is Diego who initiates his metamorphosis into a revolutionary with a liberal and artistic sensibility.

It is not *with* Diego, however, that David sexually "consummates" his maturity. This he does with Nancy, Diego's neighbor and close friend.[71] Nancy, too, is older and, like Diego, symbolizes a Cuban outcast. A former prostitute who prays to the Virgen and trades illegally in dollars, Nancy is a kindred rebellious spirit to Diego. It is to the film's credit that David is drawn to them instead of Vivian and Miguel. Vivian, David's ex-girlfriend, and Miguel, his roommate and fellow militant, are portrayed as cold, dull, and doctrinaire Cubans who wish only to fulfill their socially prescribed roles—Vivian as married with children, Miguel as Communist Party bureaucrat. Against this, David (and the viewer) encounters Nancy and Diego, who, despite their socially stigmatized lives, are loving and gregarious.[72] And while it may be the case that Diego's character is stereotypically "gay"—that is, flamboyant and has a passion for (bourgeois) culture and the arts—it is by virtue of Diego that David matures culturally and politically. Diego's apartment is, after all, the place of erotic and dialogical fecundity in the film. An ensemble of art gallery, library, and shrine, Diego's apartment symbolizes the forbidden and the repressed, and its on-screen portrayal is akin, as Emilio Bejel has argued, to a "coming out" of sorts.[73] It is where, for instance, José Martí and Lezama Lima can be equally revered and where David and Diego can openly debate the "errors" of the Revolution while they nurse their glass of contraband whiskey, the "enemy's drink."

This is not to say that David and Diego's interactions are frictionless. David's liberality does not come easily. It takes time for David to work through his ambivalence toward Diego and whether he should, as Miguel recommends, spy on and denounce him or, as his heart and intellect evidently tell him, trust and befriend him. Diego, too, must work through an ambivalence all his own: whether to seduce David or to be his mentor and, ultimately, friend. As this narrative arc from *eros* to *philia* unfolds, there are fiery disagreements. One such disagreement was, notably, over the topic of the UMAP camps:

> David: "What I'm trying to say is that it's lamentable but understandable if mistakes are made like sending [the famous troubadour] Pablo Milanés to the UMAP."
>
> Diego: Not only him! What of all the *locas* who don't sing."
>
> David: The mistakes are not the Revolution. They're part of the Revolution, but not the whole of it, understand?
>
> Diego: And the bill? Who should that go to? Who's going to answer for them?

That a taboo subject like the UMAP camps would be aired out in such a highly visible forum—an ICAIC film directed, no less, by Cuba's premiere filmmaker, Tomás Gutiérrez Alea—was remarkable in its time. That the openly gay Diego gets the last word makes it all the more poignant.[74] In many respects it is prophetic because for Diego there is no happy ending. Diego's protest letter to the Ministry of Culture, which has censored his loca friend Germán's art exhibit, gets him fired, leaving him no other viable option but exile. This leaves, as Emilio Bejel has noted, Diego "in disgrace and solitude," whereas David and Nancy enjoy their heterosexual happy ending in their homeland.[75] And while Diego does not leave with the Mariel boatlift, as so many other gay Cubans did, the fact that the film is set in 1979, a year prior to the 1980 exodus, situates Diego's exile in dialogue with the historic *marielitos*.[76]

Fresa y chocolate could be read, thus, as a critique of what we have named the mambí epic. One need only consider the fact that the film's most rebellious spirit is, unquestionably, Diego. And Diego, rather than occupy the position of the patriotic soldier who enacts redemptive violence, articulates a *critique* of violence and a bid for reparative justice. Granted, it is not Diego, the queer libertarian, with whom the Cuban viewer is meant to identify. That honor goes to David, the heterosexual communist. But David has no real allure until *after* Diego has recrafted him into a revolutionary with sensitivity for artistic beauty and political difference. It was a film that questioned the *revolutionary* identity and ethos itself. And the fact that it stirred such enthusiastic debates was probably the greatest evidence that the mambí sublime had become a hackneyed, if not defunct, paradigm.

El Bloqueo as "Reconcentration"

Indeed, the 1990s were not years hospitable to talk of epic glory. Adrift in a world where history had come to an end, so to speak, Cuban socialism had to fend for itself without the aid, quotas, solidarity prices, and foreign exchange reserves it once enjoyed as strategic ally to the Soviet Union. To make matters worse, the United States did not lessen its embargo, colloquially known in Cuba as *el bloqueo* (the blockade). Rather, it enforced harsher punitive measures that, as they were designed to do, made life in Cuba all the more miserable.[77] In fact, the embargo was never more akin to a blockade than in these so-called times of peace. The Torricelli (1992) and Helms-Burton (1996) Acts, among other things, penalized US-subsidiaries, extended US prosecutorial powers over foreign countries and corporations that invested in Cuba, deterred credit and international lending agencies, and financed dissidents on and off the island.[78] The cumulative effects of these losses and renewed hostilities left Cubans suffering deprivations and hardships that bore uncanny resemblances to war, none more pressing or ubiquitous than food scarcity and hunger. Rations for staples such as coffee, rice, bread, and beans had never been more limited; meat and spices were scarce or nonexistent; and recipes for typically discarded, yet edible foods were concocted (e.g., fried grapefruit or plantain peels, salads made from sweet potato leaves, rice with egg shells, etc.). Caloric consumption fell dramatically, and an illicit market for food (re)emerged as its prices soared.

All told, the Revolution was in peril and could not subsist as it once had. At the material level, it dollarized the economy; handed state farms to cooperatives and families who could sell their surplus in farmer's markets (*agropecuarios*); permitted Cubans to rent out their rooms to tourists and to open small restaurants (*paladares*); and contracted with foreign investors to revitalize the island's tourist industry.[79] This strategy afforded the state much-needed revenues and foreign currencies and was done in hopes that Cuba could carve out a niche market as one of the world's last socialist republics with unique attractions. It was hoped that the Revolution could promote an ensemble of politically conscious tourism alloyed with health and eco-tourism. But, sadly, what proved most financially viable was the same formula for all other Third World countries—namely, the exotic and the erotic. Most tourists came for the salsa dancing, son music, mojito drinks, cigars, guayaberas, antique automobiles, and, needless to say, the sensual bodies, especially the coveted mulata.

That Cuba, or especially Havana, soon came to resemble its 1950s prerevolutionary days of tourist hedonism and social inequality was a cruel irony. The even crueler irony, however, was that it also resembled 1890s Cuba, with all its famished citizens and so many impoverished women with little else to sell but their bodies. As Cuban historian Francisco Guzmán noted, it was common for reconcentradas to receive food from Spanish soldiers in exchange for sexual favors.[80] It was no coincidence that in these years Guzmán wrote and published a book on reconcentration, a book tellingly titled *Herida profunda (*Deep wound*)*. Scholars and officials did not squander the opportunity to flesh out the denunciatory and disciplinary value that the national epic had to offer. The same year the Torricelli Act was passed (1992) and as Cubans began to feel their post-Soviet precarity in earnest, Fidel Castro avowed: "We cannot forget that this is the people of 1868 and of 1895, that we are the descendants of those who struggled for ten years, those who endured the reconcentration program of Weyler, which tried to do what the US seeks to achieve today: to force us into submission through hunger."[81] Military historian Raúl Izquierdo Canosa, in *La reconcentración, 1896–1897* (1997), made a bolder case for placing the 1990s blockade on a par with the naval blockade of 1898. Used, ostensibly, to prevent enemy soldiers or arms from entering the island, the US naval blockade of major Cuban ports not only isolated the Spanish army and navy but also blocked Cubans' access to foods and medicines. The effects of this were disastrous. While reconcentration had been annulled de jure in October 1897, its structure lingered well into 1898 such that the naval blockade aggravated what was an already miserable situation. Even Clara Barton's Red Cross committees were denied access to their humanitarian cargo. Consequently, no less than half of the total two hundred thousand reconcentrado dead can be attributed to the Americans' "pitiless and criminal" tactic, as Canosa put it.[82]

What was most striking about Carnosa's rhetoric, however, was not its polemic against Yankee imperialism; it was the newly deployed identity attributed to the reconcentrado: a patriotic resister! In an echo of Fidel and Raúl Castro, Canosa said he wrote his study as a "tribute to those hundreds of thousands of anonymous victims who enriched [literally 'fertilized,' *abonaron*] with their blood and mortal remains the land where they were born." "Through its resistance and stoicism," he clarified, "the suffering Cuban people demonstrated its will, its capacity to struggle and disposition to face the greatest sacrifices, including that of surrendering [*entregar*] the life of nearly 20 percent of its population."[83] We have already problematized whether one could say such lives (and deaths) were "surrendered" or constituted "sacrifices." But the real issue here was neither the dead nor the historical. For it was the living (and calorically deprived) that these belated "tributes" were meant to dignify—if not discipline. For what else *could* it mean to identify with the reconcentrado, except as one who shall suffer any such hardships "stoically," that is to say, mutely and obediently?

It should come as no surprise, all the same, that the reconcentrado was never taken up with any seriousness as an icon of resistance. One did not encounter billboards with images of emaciated reconcentrados aside a slogan that read, *¡Patria o muerte!* Nor were any grand or solemn monuments erected for the reconcentrado dead. The Special Period's billboards and monuments carried the usual faces and connoted the usual epic motifs: Martí, Maceo, Camilo, Che, loyalty, valor, prowess, and so forth. The frail, sickly female and child bodies of the reconcentrados could not possibly cohere with an iconography of resistance and emancipatory power that called for stout, youthful men's bodies—bodies almost always adorned with symbols of phallic and martial power: horses, beards, machetes, rifles. For whatever "dignity" and "resistance" one wished to attribute to the reconcentrado, Cubans were not likely to identify with a mute, anonymous mass of the ignobly dead. Far likelier were they to be enchanted by the Spartan-esque warrior and the myth-cum-fantasy of a heroic death. The only real rhetorical value of the reconcentrado in these years was to distinguish the stoic and patriotic from the fickle and disloyal. She could be invoked to denounce the violence of imperial *others* and ennoble the sovereign self, but never as a figure that embodied a decidedly anti-epic sentiment and critique of *revolutionary* violence.

For the reconcentrado could be narrated as other than mere abject victim, other than as she or he who died a horrific death and, thereby, corroborates the mambí's decorum and the Patria's sanctimony. To wit, not a few mambises laid down their arms and left the Liberation Army's ranks for the sake of their reconcentrado kin. They helped them escape to the wilderness or smuggled in what meager foods and medicines they could offer or surrendered and pled for mercy toward their wives and children who were otherwise "marked."[84] That mambí commanders had to grant more and more temporary leave and harshly punish deserters are symptoms of its toll on the rebel army.[85] Nor, crucially, were the reconcentrados as powerless as they have been historically portrayed. Many mothers and older siblings did not—or more exactly, *could* not—wait around for charitable relief or for a mambí savoir to feed and care for their endangered loved ones. While many were forced to beg for alms, many others (also) sold the only thing they had to sell, namely their labor, their bodies. This could range from the more dignified work of a cook, nursemaid, or laundress to the least desirable of all, cane cutter or prostitute.[86] Surely this was exploited labor, and surely these were acts of survival. But were they not also "sacrifices" in their own right? They did not entail bloodshed, arms, love of Patria, or the stout, youthful bodies of soldiers inasmuch as sweat, tears, love of family, and the frail, sickly bodies of children and the elderly. They did not symbolize the liberatory power of the people or the sanctity of Patria inasmuch as the precariousness of life and the ethical summons to care for it. That is to say, they may not have embodied the epic, classically conceived, but there was a dignity and sacrifice to what they either defied or had to endure. It was the reconcentrado, *not* the mambí, who had the most asked of her, namely to tend to her children and loved ones as they died merciless deaths, deaths for which patriotic consolations could only ring hollow. And while his virility and rebelliousness have accordingly enjoyed all reverences due, her labors and torment have never truly registered in Cuban historiography and the popular imaginary except as tragedy—which is to say, except as an *alibi* for revolutionary violence and "stoic" allegiance.

Epilogue

On Moral Equivalence in the Twenty-First Century

Could it be that foolishness bore me
the foolishness of what is today foolish:
the foolishness of confronting the enemy
the foolishness of living without a price.
—Silvio Rodríguez, "El Necio" (1992)

As WE have come to understand, the words *mambí* and *Cuba Libre* convey possibilities that far exceed a mere historical referent. Not just the name for a flesh-and-blood soldier or for wars that occurred in the nineteenth century, *mambí* and *Cuba Libre* bespeak virtues and sentiments as lively and as quintessential as rebelliousness, camaraderie, dignity, stoicism, hope, and the radical generosity we call sacrifice. Indeed, they bespeak that most seductive of desires, namely liberation.

So, too, do they tell a story, a story of mythical proportions and utopian horizons: of ancestors who wagered their lives for a republic "with all and for the good of all." It is the story of from whence Cubans came and of what virtues they possess and most cherish. It insists that Cubans are worthy of the dignity and grandeur of words such as "heroic," "sublime," and "revolution." And all the more daringly, it teaches that justice had (or will have) its day, that its pursuit is the worthiest of "callings" and not to be jettisoned as futile. A story, in short, not to be trifled with.

Whatever its pleasures and dignities, it is also a story not always consonant with the historical present or its foreseeable futures. The early republican years were far from "epic" times. The catastrophic tolls of the War for Independence (1895–98) and its anticlimactic end did not bespeak emancipatory promises. It was US soldiers who paraded through Cuba's streets and the American flag that was hoisted at Havana's El

Morro. Thereafter came the Platt Amendment and a republic far less "moral" than the one prophesied in the wars' manifestoes. Not all was lost, of course. In the 1920s, veterans revitalized an epic sensibility that coalesced in a younger generation's "revolution" (1933) and a decidedly populist Constitution (1940). The Platt Amendment had been annulled and Cubans' rights as citizens and workers were legally recognized. But a host of familiar foes saw to it that the 1933 Revolution would be curtailed and the new Constitution feebly, if at all, enforced. Cubans would have to wait until the Revolution of 1959 to enjoy a sense that a Free Cuba was at last at hand. Never in the nation's history had so many radical reforms been pursued, and not since the nineteenth-century wars had words such as "epic" and "liberation" been so copiously invoked—and befittingly so: in due course that "small place" became the vanguard of world revolution.

But the story, needless to say, does not end there. In the 1990s socialist Cuba was left to fend for itself in a world inhospitable to "liberation," except as synonymous with the so-called free market.[1] Rather than invest in the island's infrastructure and economy, the United States all the more eagerly sanctioned and subverted it—with few regrets, evidently, that Cubans all the while starved. It was not a period amenable to heroic rhetoric. As poet Reina María Rodríguez asked, incredulously, "and still you demand of me my quota of faith[?]"[2] For it was not easy to reconcile the period's "special" circumstances with the epic's most crucial affect, namely hope—the hope that virtue shall prevail, that one's sacrifices and death are not in vain. Instead, disenchantment or, at best, bewilderment prevailed. Filmmaker Fernando Pérez's dystopian *Madagascar* (1994) and Leonardo Padura's series of detective novels were symptomatic of the era's sentiment, an aesthetic in which gray skies, urban squalor, and existential doubt stood out—starkly in contrast, that is, to the island's tropical lushness and its revolutionary aura. Fidel and his cohort of iconic revolutionaries, moreover, were no longer their youthful virile selves, a fact that many critics (in ableist terms) cast as a metaphor for an ailing Revolution and its "anachronistic" ideology. What was once grand and sacred was now reduced to the inglorious and the profane, especially hunger. Irony now thrived where hope once dwelled. To wit, by the end of the century the so-called Revolutionary Armed Forces were likelier to be managing tourist companies than slaying imperial dragons.

Opportunities for "glory," in other words, were scant. But the mambí came out of this period no less an obligatory and revered referent. In 2017, the late Roberto Fernández Retamar, president of Casa de las

Américas, avowed: "It pleases me to confirm that I believe the most venerated word in Cuba continues to be *mambí.*"[3] This is not to say that the mambí and Cuba Libre are aesthetically rendered as they once were. One work that illustrates a new sensibility is Fernando Pérez's *José Martí: El ojo del canario* (2010). Unlike the usual hagiography, *El ojo del canario* (Eye of the canary) renders Martí utterly human—a Martí "neither sanctified nor statue-fied," as Joel del Río has nicely put it.[4] In fact, for the first half of the film Martí is a meek and bullied schoolboy warmly known as "Pepe." Only in the last quarter of the film does he, as a seventeen-year-old pupil, bear any resemblance to the fiery orator Cubans have come to identify as their "Apostle." This alone distinguishes it from earlier cinematic accounts, whether the melodramatic *The White Rose* (1954) or the vanguardist *Pages from Martí's Diary* (1971), both of which end with Martí's epic death at Dos Ríos.[5] In lieu of the all but compulsory need to reenact and mourn Martí's death, *El ojo del canario* invites the viewer to reckon with a young "dissident" still very much alive. He is neither illustrious warrior nor dead martyr. The (Cuban) viewer sees no Liberation Army or, for that matter, a machete. For violence in *El ojo del canario* is not a guerrilla violence that liberates: it is only ever a state violence that executes and imprisons. The viewer does not walk away visually roused by erect phallic objects (machetes, rifles, etc.) in the hands of virile men that shout *¡Viva Cuba Libre!* Rather, she or he bears witness to an incarcerated youth who abides by civil disobedience and a cry for free speech and the rights to assembly.[6]

El ojo del canario was not alone in such disavowals of the (classic) epic. The film *Cuba Libre* (2015), directed by Jorge Sánchez, also has no victorious battles or dramatized machete charges.[7] Nor is Cuba a lush or vividly colored tropical island. It is an arid and drab (urban) milieu where grays and light browns stand out. This aesthetic is reinforced by a soundtrack that is symphonic, where mostly cellos and violins (not brass) conjure ominous, unhappy times. Overall what stands out thematically are despair, deception, and opportunism. The story is set in the year 1898. A truce has been called, but there is a frail rapport between the mambises and the American armed forces that now occupy the island. Intrigues and betrayals ensue, all of which we see through the eyes of two Afro-Cuban boys named Simón and Samuel. And this, too, is what stands out about the film: virtue and vice do not meaningfully correlate with nationality inasmuch as race. Nearly all Black and mulatto characters are sympathetically portrayed and constitute the majority of the lead cast: the innocent Simón; his patriotic father, José María; his wise grandmother, Julia; and the American rank-and-file soldiers, who are none other than an all-Black regiment, known popularly as the "Buffalo Soldiers." This latter choice is exceptional. For rarely, if ever, have Americans been sympathetically portrayed in Cuba's revolutionary era historiography and cinema. In *Cuba Libre* they are handsome and noble Black soldiers—whether Freddy, who acts as an adoptive father to Simón, or the lieutenant who is dismissed by his white superior for having treated the mambises as equals. The film's most treacherous and least likeable characters are, by contrast, almost all phenotypically white: the hypocritical Father Gabriel, the heartless Doña Alfonsa, the opportunistic Mayor Lamberto, and the icy and deceitful American colonel. In a sense, the film resembles the work of Sánchez's predecessor and fellow Afro-Cuban filmmaker, Sergio Giral, whose "slave trilogy" was discussed in chapter 1. But the Afro-Cubans of *Cuba Libre* are not rebellious maroons who exact a righteous vengeance, let alone prefigure a national epic. Nor does their mambí leader, not too subtly cast as a variant of the Bronze Titan, die a heroic death in battle. Rather, he commits suicide. This, too, is exceptional. A character encoded as Antonio Maceo would fight to the bitter end. But herein Colonel Armenteros dies an inglorious death, and the Liberation Army is, by film's end, disarmed. The film reads, accordingly, more like a tragic requiem for the (socialist) epic, an epic laid to rest not just in 1898 but also in the early twenty-first century. For what we see postulated in its stead is an ethics of hospitality, a cue to contemporary Cubans who anticipate Americans "invading" the island anew, except this time as tourists.

If the film's Colonel Armenteros is its Antonio Maceo, then the (grand) mother Julia is its Mariana Grajales. The blind and elderly Julia is an impeccable patriot. But while she is portrayed as noble and wise, her role is the familiar one of the matriarch who stoically bears her son's death. Besides her, the only other women in the film are the cruel and racist Doña Alfonsa and Fela, a prostitute. In other words, *Cuba Libre* reiterates the familiar trope of women in subordinate, if not unflattering, roles. Nor, sadly, was this unique to Sánchez's film. The mothers and wives of the five counterespionage agents (all men) caught and imprisoned in the United States, known as los Cinco (the Cuban Five), were all awarded the Mariana Grajales Award. At the award ceremony of March 8, 2002, in the Marx Theater, Fidel Castro praised "the spirit of sacrifice" of these men and "their mothers and wives" as consistent with the "legendary heroes" of Cuba's history.[8] Consistent indeed. It was a familiar (patriarchal) logic that valued women *by virtue of* their filial and faithful relations to "heroic" men. It is the *men* who are endangered and, thereby, heroic. It is they who embody the sublimity of sacrifice, and it is they who decide on and confer recognitions. The Mariana Award and the flowers and condolences sent to these women each Mother's Day reaffirmed as much. So, too, does Julia, the allegorical Mariana of Sánchez's *Cuba Libre*. She is the wise elder to whom others caringly defer, but that deference is restricted to the space of the home (domesticity) and to her identity as (grand)mother to a mambí son and grandson. The absence in the film of any daughters or, for that matter, mambisas is striking to this end.

That said, the project to revitalize Black consciousness and women's equality has not been tossed to the wayside, least of all by Black women scholars and artists on the island. Gloria Rolando's *1912: Voces para un silencio* (*1912: Breaking the Silence*) was one such intervention. A three-chapter documentary, *Breaking the Silence* tells the story of the Independent Party of Color (PIC) and the racist massacre of 1912, a history not regularly taught in Cuban schools. Drawing extensively on archival imagery and the voices of Black scholars, it tells the story of that historic tragedy and, obliquely, of the "frustrated" project that is Cuba Libre. More than a tribute to the unjust dead, it is an address to the *living*. Each of the three chapters opens and closes with images of contemporary Afro-Cubans who stare proudly and soberly back at the camera. That these images are set to Cuban hip-hop is just as relevant. The film is rich with classic son and trova music, not least the spectral "Clave a Maceo," but its theme song is the revealingly titled "Afrolucha contínua" by Anónimo Consejo. "Afrolucha contínua" is an elegy to Afro-Cuban freedom fighters, with a roll call that includes Antonio Maceo and the mambí veterans and PIC leaders Pedro Ivonnet and Evaristo Estenoz—each name met with a Yoruban-derived honorary salute, *aché*. Visually and lyrically, the film points to a struggle that continues. "Do not fear asking about the past or the present" are its narrator's last words.

Albeit independently produced, *Breaking the Silence* was screened at prestigious events and venues such as the Santiago Alvarez Film Festival and Casa de las Americas and awarded the Walterio Carbonell Prize from the Cofradía de la Negritud in 2012 and the Caracol Prize from UNEAC in 2013. And it is just one of many works, committees, forums, and initiatives dedicated to more earnest dialogue and inquiry on existent racism, no longer the "taboo" subject it once was.[9] Nor is it the only recent work produced by or about women of color in Cuban history.[10] The tellingly titled *María Cabrales: Una mujer con historia propoia* (Maria Cabrales: A woman with her own history) is a long overdue biography of the mambisa María Cabrales, usually remembered as little more than "Maceo's wife." Author Damaris Torres Elers introduces us to a woman with ethical conviction, political savvy, and the valor to take on extraordinary risks. A similar commitment is voiced in the 2015 edited collection *Mariana Grajales: Doscientos años en la historia y la memoria* (Mariana Grajales: Two hundred years in history and memory) (2015), which includes retrospectives on Mariana's significance to her family and to the nation beyond mere motherhood.

If Black and women's dignity are issues as timely as ever, so, too, is the issue of revolutionary youth. On this count, Cubans continue to enjoy their *Elpidio Valdés* comics and cartoons and to bestow their gratitude on the late Juan Padrón, lovingly known as "Padroncito," recipient of the 2008 National Cinema Award. But not all is so straightforward. In 2010, Cuba's premiere children's theater group, La Colmenita, debuted the musical *Elpidio Valdés y los Van Van* in the Marx Theater, with Juan Padrón and musician Juan Formell as guests of honor. The performance featured children dressed as famous *Elpidio Valdés* characters with dance sequences set to the music of one of Cuba's most popular son and timba groups. The irony, however, was that while the comedic spirit of the animated series was incorporated, the musical rendered the mambises more akin to entertainers than to soldiers—perhaps a fitting metamorphosis in a Cuba dependent on tourist dollars! Another dubious honor are the parodies of *Elpidio Valdés* in exile communities. Among others, the Miami-based Los Pichy Boys created the video *Elpidio se fue* (Elpidio left), posted to YouTube. In it, the clownish duo dub clips from authentic cartoon episodes and make a Hollywood-like trailer to an action thriller: "This is a story of a man who everyone thought was a patriot . . . Don't miss it this summer . . . Elpidio left [Cuba]!" In the trailer Elpidio flees the island on a small boat in hopes to be employed at none other than Disney, with Mickey Mouse. It is funny, no doubt. And it unwittingly reminds us that humor is universally accessible and is not intrinsically revolutionary or reactionary.

It also unwittingly reminds us that Cubans continue to live in the shadow of imperialist hostilities and that the epic is not, accordingly, so easy (or advisable?) to surrender. At stake, after all, is *what kind* of epic the next generations will (or should) write with their lives and deaths. Fidel Castro understood this nuance. In 1962, in what is known as the "Second Declaration of Havana," he proclaimed:

> Great as was the epic of Latin American Independence, heroic as was that struggle, today's generation of Latin Americans is called upon to engage in an epic which is even greater and more decisive for humanity. [. . .] This epic before us is going to be written by the hungry Indian masses, the peasants without land, the exploited workers. It is going to be written by the progressive masses, the honest and brilliant intellectuals, who so greatly abound in our suffering Latin American countries. Struggles of masses and ideas. An epic which will be carried forward by our people, despised and maltreated by imperialism, our people, unreckoned with till today, who are now beginning to shake off their slumber. Imperialism considered us a weak and submissive flock; and now it begins to be terrified of that flock; a gigantic flock of 200 million Latin Americans in whom Yankee monopoly capitalism now sees its gravediggers.[11]

Whatever became of that epic, today's generations are, as they must, "writing" new stories for new times. At the outset of the twenty-first century and in the context of the Americas, the most lively of these stories were those that initiated new emancipatory plots and utopian horizons: the "good governance" caracoles of the Zapatistas, the "communal state" in Bolivarian Venezuela, *buen vivir* (*sumak kawsay*) in Ecuador, *vivir bien* (*suma qamaña*) in Bolivia.[12] Granted, these and affiliate projects have faltered—or, more exactly, have been battered and sieged. They have had to weather not just human fallibility but financial blockades, artificially induced scarcities, paramilitary violence, parliamentary coups, and prejudicial media—none of which is unfamiliar to revolutionary Cuba and Cubans. That said, like Cuba's revolutionary processes, one cannot reasonably say that these historical projects were a futile exercise in liberation praxis. They brought housing, land, schools, and health care to low-income families and communities of color; audited and dramatically reduced public debt; advanced unionized labor and worker-owned cooperatives; and diversified their economies, even if still largely "extractive." So, too, did they elect or appoint unprecedented numbers of women and peoples of color as ministers, governors, generals, judges, mayors, spokespeople, executives, and presidents. And this is to say nothing of the new ministries, feminist agendas, decolonial curricula, community-operated media, and participatory networks fostered by and within these processes.[13]

That Cuba had a hand in this "Bolivarian alternative" for the Americas was no coincidence. But it was not armed guerrillas that they had to offer; it was their medical "brigades" of internationalist doctors. Those doctors have served the underserved and have trained new doctors, whether abroad in Venezuela's barrios or on the island at the Latin American School of Medicine (ELAM), which has trained over forty thousand doctors from underserved communities and countries since its inauguration in 1998.[14] The tragically emplotted story of Cuba's turn to tourism is not, thus, the only story to be told about the Special Period and what has come in its wake. Amid those distraught years and with so few resources at its disposal (let alone the temptations to sell out), revolutionary Cuba stayed committed to its "social medicine" and its internationalist ethos. It invested not only in hotels, that is, but also in hospitals, doctors, and research for novel vaccines, biotechnology, and medical procedures. It even scientifically validated and invested in medicinal herbs, colloquially known as "green medicine." That such medicines can be affordably grown and not patented is no idle detail, and that they vindicate ancestral wisdom no less so. Nor was this the only green initiative to come out of the Special Period. Without access to the synthetic fertilizers and chemical pesticides it used to receive from the Soviet Union, the Revolution had to innovate its agriculture. And innovate it did: land and technical aid was redistributed to cooperative and small farmers as those farmers (re) learned how to cultivate foods using more ecologically sound methods, the results of which include more resilient and fertile land, healthier ecosystems, nutritious fruits and vegetables, socially useful employment, and greater food sovereignty.[15] A word could be said, moreover, about innovative biofertilizers and biopesticides; the strides made in energy conservation and efficiency; and an agenda for tackling the climate emergency, named Tarea Vida (Life Works).[16]

But, again, the story does not end there. The cumulative tolls of US sanctions against Venezuela as much as Cuba and the global pandemic have been decisive in recent years. They have led to dramatic falls in Venezuelan oil imports and in remittances and tourist revenue, which in turn have created scarcities, blackouts, and malcontent at a scale and intensity not seen since the Malecón protests and *balsero* (rafter) crisis of 1994.[17] The difference, however, is that Cuban dissidents now have smartphones, social media, and even a "hip-hop anthem," namely "Patria y Vida" (Homeland and life). Featuring Yotuel Romero of Orishas fame, Descemer Bueno, Alex Delgado and Randy Malcolm of Gente de Zona, and a cameo by Havana-based Maykel Osorbo and El Funky, the song and its video went viral after the July 11, 2021, protests and has been credited with "fueling a New Cuban Revolution."[18] It is indeed no trivial artifact. From its catchy slogan to Yotuel's sexiness and Gente de Zona's gritty swagger, it is a potent (counter)revolutionary hymn. Its brilliance, to be exact, is that what once was attributed to Cuban revolutionaries—the bravado, youth, and virility of a bearded Fidel or bereted Che—is now attributed to Yotuel and his comrades. It is now they who are marketed as the defiant David versus the communist Goliath; it is now they who embody liberation and the new.

But aesthetic form (like racial identity) does not in and of itself stipulate political content or consciousness. Consider the video. It opens with an image of the Cuban peso, which features Martí, the nation's most beloved martyr. That peso begins to burn, exposing underneath the US dollar, which features George Washington. Within seconds, the two currencies share the screen, and we witness a hybrid subject, half Martí–half Washington. What this could mean is anyone's guess. Arguably, it is a call for a harmonious pact between the two countries and their economies, with a nod to each founding father. But it is no small blunder that this "hip-hop anthem" is coded as an heir to two white men—the latter a slave owner, notorious Native American killer, and land speculator.[19] Nor is it any less of a blunder to omit the fact that *capitalist* reforms are what most decisively fueled the racial inequalities of the Special Period onward—let alone that it is the United States (not Cuba) that has obstructed trade relations between the two nations.

That said, Yotuel's muscular torso in tandem with the braggadocio of his comrades is hard to resist. Dressed in all black and crying out "Se acabó!" (It's over!), they invoke a game of dominoes come to a stalemate, with only two hands left to play: "your five nine" (1959) against "my two two" (2022)—the anachronistic past, that is, versus the hip future. It starts off with a softer tempo and evocations of lament (Yotuel sheds a mournful tear) to a crescendo of harder bass and outrage, all of which builds up to the final chant, "Patria y Vida"—a chant the US press has been eager to echo. National Public Radio's Anamaria Sayre, for instance, teamed up with Miami-based Cuban American musician Lilly Blanco to translate and "explain" the song to English speakers, as if embedded in its lyrics was a complex theory of revolutionary politics or a macroeconomic formula that will solve Cuba's woes. No such revelations are there, of course, which is why much has to be made of the song's "clever wordplay" and its cry for "no more doctrines." Even more has to be made of the rappers' racial identity and their status as "artists," so as to elicit sympathies for (underdog) storylines like the beauty versus politics or the unimpeachable desire for "democracy" and "life" versus a "totalitarian regime."[20]

Cuba's musical retort is not, on that note, as seductive. The song and video "Patria o Muerte por la Vida" (Homeland or death for life), which features Raúl Torres, Annie Garcés, Dayana Divo, Karla Monier, and rapper Yisi Calibre, is lyrically and politically coherent but its music and iconography far less edgy.[21] It calls out Yotuel and his ilk for their hypocrisy and opportunism, with iterations of the refrain "It pays . . ." (*rentabiliza*). It pays to "sing against poverty from your satin sofa" and to "sling mud" at the Revolution. It pays to "confuse the people" and incite "hatred." It is noteworthy that these lyrics are voiced by an ensemble of Afro-Cubans (save for Garcés) and that all are women (save for Torres). They carry themselves with a sense of grace and joy as much as firmness. It is a stark contrast to "Patra y Vida," with an entirely male cast that projects a bravado and aggressivity that, if the tables were turned, would be denounced as "toxic masculinity." It is no small scandal, after all, that so many (American) journalists and academics have conspicuously disregarded the voices of these anti-capitalist and anti-imperialist Afrocubanas. That aside, the song's overall objective is to reconceptualize "Patria o Muerte" as the credo by which the Patria *lives* and the Revolution shall prevail (*vencermos!*). The song saves the best for last, when rapper Yisi takes center stage to rail against "sellouts" (*vendepatrias*) and clarify to the world that this Cubana is not for sale. Nevertheless, the song is not as catchy and the video not as viral-worthy. Its retort may be conceptually sound, but the mouthful "Patria o Muerte por la Vida" is not as chantable. With a combo of violin and son rhythms, moreover, it has melodramatic and festive overtones that seem ill-suited to its content, and its choreographed aesthetic cannot match the aura of underground rebelliousness (and eroticism) that "Patria y Vida" excels at. Whether it will be read as anything other than defensive and state orchestrated is doubtful.

That these protests and (artistic) polemics have emphasized *life* should, nevertheless, be welcomed. For it is an opportunity to, as Bakhtin would say, "novelize" the epic of Cuba Libre—an opportunity to put forth new protagonists and new plots, of which there are auspicious options at hand. As it is, twenty-first-century socialist Cuba has opted for universal health care, medical internationalism, and agroecology. If these are not the criteria by which to judge a politics and economics of *life,* then what are?[22] Nor is it a trifling fact that Cuba has developed its own Covid vaccines, two of which bear names related to none other than the mambí epic: Abdala and Mambisa.[23] Whether or not the Revolution shall survive its latest adversities, thus, it already carries within it a *new story* with precisely the kind of emancipatory promises our times call for: rather than the armed guerrilla or industrial proletariat, a story in which the revolutionary doctor and organic farmer are the heroes. Or more to the point: rather than an epic that romanticizes violence, sacrifice, and death, one that avows care, plentitude, and life. Enrique Dussel, let us recall, proposed that an aesthetics of liberation is an aesthetics in which the beautiful is consonant with "the criterion of life" and "the people" (*el pueblo*). It "obeys" their will to live (*voluntad-de-vida*) and all that is at life's "disposal" (*disponabilidad*). In Cuba, such an obediential epic need not disavow the mambí epic, let alone its barbudo sequel. That (Black) mambisas such as Mariana Grajales and Rosa la Bayamesa were healers who practiced green medicine and that the mambises are closely associated with the guajiro (peasant) who humbly works the land are but two options to *catachrestically* rewrite that epic in closer dialogue with the new myths for social and environmental justice that are so desperately needed.[24] Against the dystopian realities of the capitalist fantasy for "the good life," what this world needs are better stories to live and die by, stories that edify and empower us to take up the heroic vocation at hand and valorize those knowledges we have neglected. For the struggle that lies ahead for a livable and just planet shall no doubt prove *epic,* but that epic calls for heroes that care for, engender, and regenerate life. In this respect, the *decolonial* epic is best understood not as a story about a mythical past inasmuch as about emancipatory futures. And such futures shall rely on stories and storytellers as much as on land and material resources. For as the writer and revolutionary Eduardo Galeano once said, "Scientists say that human beings are made of atoms, but a little bird told me that we are also made of stories."

Notes

Introduction

1. Castro Ruz, *La historia me absolverá,* 88–89; my translation.

2. Ibid., 32. Pericles's funeral oration is found in Thucydides, *The Peloponnesian Wars.* Also see Kantorowicz, "Pro Patri Mori."

3. These wars were the most deadly and destructive in the Americas relative to per capita losses. Pérez, *The Structure of Cuban History,* 22.

4. Even in diasporic communities—not least Miami, Florida—the mambí has been associated with bodegas, restaurants, blogs, tourist companies, social clubs, paramilitary commandoes, periodicals, a radio and television station, and annual parades.

5. To cite only three of the more outstanding historical surveys in English: Foner, *The Spanish-Cuban-American War;* Pérez, *Cuba between Empires;* Tone, *War and Genocide in Cuba.*

6. León Rosabal, *La voz del mambí,* 81.

7. Eliade, *Myth and Reality.*

8. Frye, *Anatomy of Criticism,* 136.

9. Lévi-Strauss, "The Structural Study of Myth," 429.

10. Arendt, *On Revolution,* 29.

11. Arendt speaks of the "plot of freedom," not *liberation.* For her, liberation is a *precondition* for freedom, which she understood as a right to speak freely and deliberately among peers. Given our attentiveness to Third World revolutions, however, it seems apropos to commit to the word "liberation." Ibid., 29–34.

12. Frye, *Anatomy of Criticism,* 133; White, *Metahistory,* 7–10.

13. For an excellent summary, see White, "Interpretation in History." For discussions of tragedy's relation to literature, philosophy, and politics, see Williams, *Modern Tragedy;* Eagleton, *Sweet Violence.*

14. Barthes, *Mythologies,* 109–59.

15. Malinowski, *Myth in Primitive Psychology,* 23.

16. Girard, *Violence and the Sacred.*

17. Eagleton, *Radical Sacrifice,* 56.

18. Sorel, *Reflections on Violence,* 115–18.

19. Ibid., 109–19, 130, 249.

20. Mariátegui, *José Carlos Mariátegui,* 387.

21. Renan, *What Is a Nation?,* 261.

22. Vitier, *Ese sol del mundo moral,* 117.

23. Jameson, *The Political Unconscious,* 64, 278.

24. Bloch, *The Principle of Hope.*

25. Jameson, *The Political Unconscious,* 281–82.

26. Jameson, *Archealogies of the Future,* 12. For an excellent survey and discussion of utopian thought and literature, see Ainsa, *La reconstrucción de la utopía.*

27. Marcuse, *The Aesthetic Dimension,* 48. For a fuller theoretical account of Marcuse's appropriations of Freud to emancipatory politics, see Marcuse, *Eros and Civilization.*

28. Innes, *Epic,* 1.

29. Bowra, *From Virgil to Milton,* 1.

30. Aristotle, *Poetics,* 1460a.

31. For excellent overviews, see Merchant, *The Epic;* Hainsworth, *The Idea of Epic;* J. M. Foley, *A Companion to Ancient Epic.*

32. Meletinsky, *The Poetics of Myth,* 246.

33. D. A. Miller, *The Epic Hero,* 12; Meletinsky, *The Poetics of Myth,* 248.

34. Bakhtin, "Epic and Novel," 15–16.

35. Ibid., 19.

36. Ibid., 21, 31, 37.

37. In the case of Cuba, there is no better example of this than Rafael Rojas, the historical essayist whose prolific work is premised on more or less the same thesis: that the Revolution's "master narrative" does not reflect the plurality of stories that can be told about the Cuban past. It is ironic, to say the least, that Rojas's own work reflects no such "plurality," since it seems only interested in recuperating the history of "constitutional liberalism" in Cuba. Rojas, *Isla sin fin;* Rojas, *La máquina del olvido.*

38. Farrell, "Walcott's Omeros," 274.

39. No doubt Bakhtin would have retorted that in such cases the epic has been "novelized," but that would be to beg the question. McWilliams, *The American Epic;* Ramanujan, "Three Hundreds *Ramayanas*"; Repinecz, *Subversive Traditions;* Roy, *The Postcolonial Epic;* Hammer, *Epic of the Dispossessed.*

40. According to Plutarch, Alexander the Great kept a copy of the *Iliad* under his pillow and claimed to be one of Achilles's descendants. Before his conquest of Persia and Asia Minor, he visited Troy and anointed the classic hero's grave. Alexander's name then inspired Julius Caesar, and Caesar's inspired countless others. The same could be said of Homer and the poet Virgil, whose *Aeneid* situated the Roman elite as descendants of the Trojans and, aesthetically, the *Iliad.* The ancient epic is not, of course, without dissenting voices. According to David

Quint, the prophetic curse of the vanquished is a *topos* of the ancient epic, one that constitutes a "rival narrative of resistance." The Carthaginian queen Dido's prophetic curse in *Aeneid* is a celebrated case in point. But that resistance is, alas, ornamental. The epic's losers are, in Quint's words, "born losers—monstrous, demonic, subhuman—condemned to a futile aimless repetition." Quint, *Epic and Empire*, 4–5, 11.

41. Repinecz, *Subversive Traditions*, 9–10. See also Mignolo, *The Darker Side of Modernity*, 152–58.

42. For an excellent "genealogy" of this problematic, see Escobar, *Encountering Development.*

43. Fanon, *The Wretched of the Earth*, 14–15.

44. Ibid., 240–41.

45. Those influences include the utopian socialist projects of Henri de Saint-Simon, Étienne Cabet, and Charles Fourier; the Revolution of 1848; and the Paris Commune of 1871. For an excellent discussion of the French Revolution and narrative emplotment, see Hayden White's analysis of Jules Michelet, especially his *History of the French Revolution* (1847). White, *Metahistory*, 149–62.

46. Trouillot, "An Unthinkable History." For accounts that complicate Trouillot's thesis, see Buck-Morrs, *Hegel, Haiti, and Universal History;* Kadish and Jenson, *Poetry of Haitian Independence.*

47. Spivak, *Outside in the Teaching Machine*, 71–72, 181–82.

48. Ibid., 67, 335n30.

49. For excellent English-language accounts of the Haitian Revolution, see Fick, *The Making of Haiti;* Nesbitt, *Universal Emancipation;* DuBois, *Avengers of the New World.*

50. Fernández Retamar, *Caliban and Other Essays*, 27–28. For the Spanish edition and a retrospective essay, see Fernández Retamar, *Todo Calibán.*

51. D. Scott, "The Theory of Haiti," 122–25.

52. Breslin, "The First Epic," 223. We should note that Césaire did not, thereby, refer to the *American* Revolution as the first epic of the New World. Césaire also wrote a historical précis titled *Toussaint L'Ouverture: The French Revolution and the Colonial Problem* (1960). James, *The Black Jacobins.* For excellent discussions of C. L. R. James's seminal text, see Forsdick and Hogsbjerg, *The Black Jacobins Reader.*

53. Rabbit, "C. L. R. James's Figuring of Toussaint-Louverture," 118–35.

54. Scott has argued that tragedy attunes us to human fallibility and historical contingency in ways that the romanticism of anti-colonialist narratives do not (or, rather, cannot). D. Scott, *Conscripts of Modernity.* We should note, however, that the majority of Caribbean writers who wrote literary accounts of the Haitian Revolution wrote plays and novels that were anything but romantic: Derek Walcott's *Haitian Trilogy*, Edouard Glissant's *Monsieur Toussaint* (1961), Alejo Carpentier's *The Kingdom of This World* (1949), and Césaire's *The Tragedy of Henri Christophe* (1963) were all decidedly sobering accounts written in the era

of anti-colonial and revolutionary "romanticism." For a different conception of the tragic, see Glick, *The Black Radical Tragic.*

55. Hainsworth, *The Idea of Epic,* 41.

56. Spivak, *Outside in the Teaching Machine,* 175.

57. Iglesias Utset, *Las metáforas del cambio,* 253–55.

58. Dussel, *Twenty Theses on Politics,* 24–29.

59. Ibid., 71–77, 30–35, 80.

60. Ibid., 19.

61. For programmatic statements on the "coloniality of power", see Quijano, "Coloniality of Power"; Mignolo and Walsh, *On Decoloniality.*

62. Dussel, "Siete hispótesis," 7.

63. Ibid., 5–6.

64. I am referring, of course, to the oft-cited passage from Marx's *The Eighteenth Brumaire of Louis Bonaparte* (1852): "Men make their own history, but they do not make it just as they please; they do not make it under circumstances chosen by themselves, but under circumstances directly encountered, given and transmitted from the past" (15).

65. Dussel, "Siete hipótesis," 21.

66. Ibid., 7.

67. The classic Occidental accounts are, of course Burke, *A Philosophical Enquiry;* Kant, *Critique of Judgment.*

68. Again, I am taking the liberty to "translate" Arendt. For her, it would be a new house in which *freedom* can dwell. Justice implies the "social question" (i.e., poverty), which Arendt systematically disavowed as a foul contagion that corrupts all and any revolutions. Arendt, *On Revolution,* 35.

69. Anderson, *Imagined Communities,* 206.

70. Ibid., 10–11.

71. Hubert and Mauss, *Sacrifice,* 99.

72. Examples abound and are cited throughout Vitier's *Ese sol del mundo moral* (1975), from José de la Luz y Caballero's avowal, "the doctrine of sacrifice is the mother of what little we are," to José María de Heredia's verse, "He who knows how to die always prevails," to José Martí's credo, "To die is to live, is to sow. He who dies as he should, is of service [. . .] Serve and you shall live. Love and you will live. Bid farewell to yourself and you will live. Fall [i.e., die] well and you shall rise."

73. Ibid., 92.

74. Ferrer, *Insurgent Cuba;* Prados-Torreira, *Mambisas;* Fornet, *Narrar la nación;* Iznaga, *Presencia del testimonio;* León Rosabal, *La voz del mambí;* Ibarra, *Ideología mambisa.*

75. Iglesias Utset, *Las metáforas del cambio;* Pérez, *To Die in Cuba;* Guerra, *Heroes, Martyrs, and Political Messiahs;* Guerra, *The Myth of José Martí;* Pérez, *The Structure of Cuban History;* Kapcia, *Cuba: Island of Dreams.*

76. Sommer, *Foundational Fictions;* Daut, *Tropics of Haiti;* Figueroa, *Prophetic Visions of the Past;* Kaisary, *The Haitian Revolution;* Puri, *The Grenada Revolution;* Lambert, *Comrade Sister.*

77. D. Scott, *Conscripts of Modernity;* D. Scott, *Omens of Adversity.*

78. Repinecz, *Subversive Traditions;* Roy, *The Postcolonial Epic.*

1. The Epic Marooned

1. Mahler, *From the Tricontinental.*

2. Conjectures do abound. Cuban ethnologist Fernando Ortiz found cognates in African languages such as Kongo, where it means "pernicious," "repulsive," "abominable," or "evil." Historian Manuel Moreno Fraginals wondered whether it was a deformed variant of a Yoruba prefix *mbi.* Cuban maroons (*cimarrones*) called each other, he noted, *ma embi* or *ma m'bi,* which means "my hunted" or "my persecuted" brother (*mi perseguido*) in Afro-Antillean dialects of Yoruba. Nineteenth-century Cuban bibliographer Antonio Bachiller y Morales noted that its possibilities include vulgarized indigenous (Arawak or Taino) words for those who rebelled against chieftains; a species of bird native to the Dominican Republic, one that never leaves the forest; or a tree native to the Dominican Republic, heavily laden with branches that could serve well as cover for guerrilla forces. This latter association was not, evidently, accidental. One account tells us that a Black Spanish officer named Juan Ethnuis Mamby, also known as Eutimio Mambí, defected to the Dominican nationalists in their war (1863–65) to restore national sovereignty. Under his command, a unit of mostly Black and mulatto soldiers wrought havoc and came to be known as the *mambís*—literally, "the men of Mambí." See Ortiz, *Glosario de afronegrismos,* 313–16; Moreno Fraginals, *Cuba/España, España/Cuba,* 291; Steinberg, "Mambises," 366–67; Bachiller y Morales, *Cuba primitiva,* 318–19.

3. That very war had displaced a large number of French planters, engineers, merchants, and overseers to Haiti's neighboring island and sugar-producing successor (Cuba), which thereafter imported enslaved Africans and Haitian seasonal laborers. So it was indeed no idle accusation. See Ferrer, *Freedom's Mirror.*

4. Ferrer, *Insurgent Cuba,* 3.

5. Add to this the fact that Afro-Cuban journalist Juan Gualberto Gómez was by then the chief political coordinator of the war from within the island. Roig de Leuchsenring, *Por Cuba Libre: Juan Gualberto Gómez;* Ferrer, *Insurgent Cuba,* 5.

6. Ferrer, *Insurgent Cuba,* 37.

7. Ibid., 28; R. Scott, *Slave Emancipation in Cuba.*

8. It is little wonder that so many libertos fled insurgent camps and sought refuge in Cuba's elusive *palenques* (maroon communities). Ferrer, *Insurgent Cuba,* 26.

9. Amnesty and freedom were offered only to those Blacks registered with the Liberation Army. Spain also cunningly agreed to emancipate those slaves born

before 1810 and after 1868, which translated into slaves over the age of fifty-eight (a rarity under the circumstances) and the unborn. In other words, nearly all existing slaves remained legally enslaved. Pérez, *Cuba between Empires,* 4–6.

10. Maceo also rejected as "dishonorable" a bounty offered for his surrender and, to Martínez-Campos's plea for Cuba to join the "civilized peoples" of the world, rejoined that Spain had not kept its word to abolish the slave trade or slavery—as the rest of the "civilized" world had already done. Not only a colonial subject, thus, but a man of color had thereby acted out as the true bearer of honor and integrity in the face of he (and they) who ostensibly stood for these very values. Foner, *Antonio Maceo,* 72–87.

11. Gómez, *Diario de campaña,* 219–38.

12. Cruz, *Episodios de la revolución cubana,* 29–32.

13. Ibid., 123.

14. Roa, *Con la pluma y el machete,* 248–49. Legón's story was also recounted in Cruz, *Episodios de la revolución cubana,* 126–27; Sánchez, *Heroes humildes,* 41–43.

15. The practice of *lectura,* a paid reader who would read various periodicals and literature to workers, was well known and valued among Cuban tobacco workers on the island and in Florida.

16. O'Kelly, *The Mambi-Land,* 124.

17. Herrera, *Impresiones de la Guerra,* 18–19.

18. Helg, *Our Rightful Share,* 52.

19. Gonzalez Echevarria, introduction to Martí, *José Martí,* 3.

20. *¡Nubia venció! Muero feliz: la muetre/poco me importa, pues logré salvarla . . . /¡Oh, que dulce es morir cuando se muere/Luchando audaz por defender la patria!* Martí, *Abdala,* 24.

21. Martí, *José Martí,* 320.

22. Ibid., 337–45.

23. Quoted in Ferrer, *Insurgent Cuba,* 123, 133–34.

24. Helg, *Our Rightful Share,* 49.

25. Near the end of 1895, Antonio Maceo's military vanguard enacted a historic march across the island to its farthest westward reaches against a Spanish force decidedly superior in numbers, training, equipment, and funds—a military exploit so audacious and unlikely that the Atlantic press would come to refer to Maceo as a virtuoso the likes of Napoleon, Sherman, and Toussaint L'Ouverture. Yet the Republic in Arms thereafter left Maceo and his elite "expeditionaries" to fend for themselves in the hostile western provinces, where a heavily reinforced Spanish army under the notorious Valeriano Weyler would at last hunt down the "Bronze Titan" in December 1896. Earlier that year, brother José Maceo was relieved of his command of Oriente and replaced by Calixto García. Backed by President Cisneros, García left José Maceo in command of a poorly equipped unit. His request for new arms and munitions was denied, and he died, not surprisingly, in combat against better armed Spanish forces. Foner, *Antonio Maceo,* 252–70.

26. These were the famous words of US secretary of state John Hay.

27. For an excellent account, see Pérez, *War of 1898,* 81–107.

28. On the Philippines, see S. C. Miller, *"Benevolent Assimilation."*

29. Joderías, *La leyenda negra;* B. Miller, *From Liberation to Conquest,* 33–36.

30. Pérez, *War of 1898,* 29.

31. Americans recommended segregated troops, as was the case in the US armed forces. Throughout the republican years (1902–58) the Cuban army's highest posts were consistently held by white officers. Alejandro de la Fuente notes that in 1922 the chief of staff, adjutant general, quartermaster general, and all district commanders were white. Fuente, *A Nation for All,* 132–34.

32. Quoted in Fuente, *A Nation for All,* 155. The *comparsas* were banned between 1917 and 1937.

33. Quoted in Vitier, *Es sol del mundo moral,* 45.

34. This was how it was phrased (and pledged) in the Manifesto de Montecristi, signed by José Martí (as chief delegate of the Cuban Revolutionary Party) and Máximo Gómez (commander of the Liberation Army). Martí, *José Martí,* 337–45.

35. Serra, *Para blancos y negros,* 92. Anarchist and socialist labor radicals in Tampa and Key West dealt with a similar issue: they received no proportionate rewards and representation in postwar Cuba despite their disproportionate financial and propagandistic contributions to the cause and war. Foner, *The Spanish-Cuban-American War,* xxi–xxii.

36. For a fuller account of the PIC's platform, see Fernández Robaina, *El negro en Cuba,* 71–74.

37. Fuente, *A Nation for All,* 66.

38. Helg, *Our Rightful Share,* 193–226.

39. None other than the president of the Republic José Miguel Gómez was a mayor general in the Liberation Army.

40. Miró Argenter was no lay voice. A brigadier general in the Liberation Army, he was chief aide to Antonio Maceo, at whose side he stood in Baraguá and fought with until his fall at Punta Brava. Miró Argenter, *Cuba,* 29. Miró Argenter's *Crónicas* was rereleased in 1909 under the sponsorship of newly elected Liberal Party president José Miguel Gómez, a mayor general of the Liberation Army.

41. The dates of martyrs' deaths in combat were also commemorated: February 27 (Céspedes), May 11 (Agramonte), May 19 (Martí), and December 6 (Maceo). Pérez, *The Structure of Cuban History,* 141–44.

42. A sample of memoir-style chronicles includes Lagomasino Alvarez, *Reminiscencias patria* (1902); Méndez Miranda, *Historia de los servicios prestados* (1928); Consaguerra y Guzmán, *Mambiserías* (1930); Hernández Guzmán, *Memorias tristes* (1934); Izaguirre, *Recuerdos de la guerra* (1936). Texts written by *mambí* officers that were more akin to conventional histories include Mayor

Miguel Varona Guerra's *La Guerra de Independencia* (1946); General Enrique Loynaz del Castillo's *La Constituyente de Jimaguayú* (1952). For more extensive lists, see Pérez, *The Structure of Cuban History,* 304–5n93, 142.

43. The two most influential texts of this early era were those of aide to Antonio Maceo, Brigadier General Miró Argenter, *Cuba: Crónicas de la guerra* (1899) and aide to Máximo Gómez, Brigadier General Bernabé Boza, *Mi diario de la guerrra* (1900). Boza said of the mambí army, "Here nobody cares about the color of a man, but about his talents and his self-respect," 35.

44. We also know very little about the publishers of his unique work. See Mark Sanders's excellent introduction: Sanders, introduction to Batrell, *A Black Soldier's Story,* ix–lxvii.

45. Batrell, *A Black Soldier's Story,* 98, 25, 80.

46. Ibid., 29.

47. Ibid., 141.

48. Sanders, introduction to Batrell, *A Black Soldier's Story,* lv–lvii.

49. Batrell, *A Black Soldier's Story,* 144–47.

50. Ibid., 204.

51. Lyrics can be found in Helg, *Our Rightful Share,* 302. The song is featured in Gloria Rolando's three-party documentary on the PIC and the massacre: *1912: Voces para un silencio.*

52. The body was not exhumed for this express purpose; the whereabouts of Maceo's and Francisco Gómez Toro's bodies were kept a secret throughout the war, for fear that the Spanish would desecrate or throw into a common grave the remains of the national hero and the commander in chief's son. Only after the war did those who know come forth, after which a military committee was commissioned to exhume and rebury the remains with full honors. Montalvo Covarrubias, de la Torre Huerta, and Montané Dardé, *El cráneo de Maceo.* For a scholarly discussion, see Bronfan, *Measures of Equality.*

53. Esténger, *Homenajes a Maceo,* 313. Whenever Maceo's death was commemorated, moreover, so, too, was the death of Captain Francisco Gómez. Gómez, popularly known as Panchito, was son to Commander in Chief Máximo Gómez and aide to Antonio Maceo. At Punta Brava, he tried to recover the fallen Maceo so that his body would not fall into enemy hands. In the act he was wounded, but rather than flee, he stayed by his commander's side. It is said that he was struck down and mutilated by machetes. Panchito's loyalty to his (mulatto) commander would live on in Cuban historiography and oratory as the "earnest consecration of Cuban equality." For those who wished to narrate Cuba Libre and racial democracy as a fait accompli, it was an eloquent and evidently irresistible tale.

54. The original was published in Nicolás Guillén's *West Indies, Ltd.* (1934); for translation, see Guillén, *Man-Making Words,* 67–70.

55. Guillén, *Man-Making Words,* 69.

56. R. Moore, *Nationalizing Blackness,* 191–214, 114–65.

57. In stark contrast to bourgeois "societies of color" such as Club Atenas and Club Minerva, whose Greco-Roman names are telling. Club Atenas catered to the upwardly mobile Blacks and mulattos of Havana. Members had to have a university education, abide by a strict dress code, and pay fees that were cost-prohibitive to lower-middle-class and working-poor Cubans of color. Afro-Cuban music and dance such as the *rumba, mambo,* and *son* were expressly prohibited at their events. One was far likelier to hear and dance to a waltz. R. Moore, *Nationalizing Blackness,* 39, 96, 210.

58. The PCC did at first adhere to a "separate, but equal" Black nation state in Oriente, but this controversial position was later rescinded as going against the national ideology of the multiracial patria. Fuente, *A Nation for All,* 212–22.

59. For the most comprehensive account of 1933, see Soto, *Revolución del 33.*

60. Cinto Vitier, quoted in Pérez, *The Structure of Cuban History,* 186.

61. Guerra, *Heroes, Martyrs, and Political Messiahs;* Castro Ruz, *Historia me absolverá,* 88–89.

62. Fidel Castro, quoted in Pérez, *The Structure of Cuban History,* 202–5.

63. Ibid., 217. Another excellent source on this subject is Guerra, *Visions of Power in Cuba.*

64. The only high-profile Black *barbudo* was Rebel Army commander Juan Almeida.

65. Batista awarded (in 1954) Club Atenas the Order of Carlos Manuel de Céspedes, Cuba's highest medal. Alejandro de la Fuente has pointed out, nevertheless, that the highest echelons of the armed forces where still firmly "white" under Batista. Fuente, *A Nation for All,* 247. It was also the case that Batista's most vociferous critics hailed from the urban white middle classes and routinely used racially inflected graphics and epithets to mock him and his sympathizers. See Guerra, *Visions of Power,* 54.

66. Fuente, *A Nation for All,* 259.

67. For the Spanish and English versions of Guillén's "Tengo," see Randall, *Only the Road,* 24–25.

68. I. Miller, "Religious Symbolism," 30–55; Eckstein, *Back from the Future,* 16.

69. Black commander Juan Almedia comments on this in the documentary *Fidel: The Untold Story* (2001), directed by Estela Bravo. Also see Lillian Guerra's discussion of "black fidelismo" in *Visions of Power,* 150–57.

70. The best example of this is Santiago Alvarez's *Now* (1965). For excellent discussions of the documentary and the larger dynamic of Cuba's appeals to radicals of color in the United States, see Mahler, *From the Tricontinental,* 84–91; C. Young, *Soul Power,* 173.

71. Sawyer, *Racial Politics in Post-Revolutionary Cuba,* 79–101.

72. Davis, *Angela Davis,* 205–10.

73. Fernández Robaina, *El negro en Cuba,* 90–93, 104–9; C. Moore, *Castro, the Blacks, and Africa;* Casal, "Race Relations in Contemporary Cuba," 471–86.

74. Fuente, *A Nation for All,* 280–85.

75. For a fuller account of the Americanization of Cuban culture and identity, see Pérez, *On Becoming Cuban.*

76. For the key theoretic statements/manifestos of Third Cinema, see Martin, *New Latin American Cinema;* for Julio García Espinosa's "For an Imperfect Cinema" and retrospective essays, see García Espinosa, *La doble moral del cine.*

77. For excellent surveys of Cuban revolutionary cinema, see Chanan, *Cuban Cinema;* García Borrero, *Guía críticia.*

78. This was no unambiguous endeavor. One of the most spectacular scenes in the critically acclaimed *Lucía* is that of the naked Black mambises. They are animalistic, as close to "nature" as possible: no saddles, no uniforms, no tactical formalities. They chase Spaniards down, dismount, and pounce on them with raw violence. According to Cuban filmmaker Manuel Octavio Gómez, a historic Black regiment was renowned for riding naked at night to terrify its enemies, who could not see them. But one wonders whether it merely reiterated racist stereotypes that equate blackness with physical prowess and savagery. Chanan, *Cuban Cinema,* 280.

79. For a fuller account of these rebellions, see Childs, *The 1812 Aponte Rebellion.*

80. Carbonell, *Crítica,* especially chapters 3 through 6.

81. Carbonell's *Crítica* would not be available again until 2005, when an online version was authorized under the auspices of Eliades Acosta, director of the José Martí National Library.

82. Suarez's novel was written in 1838 at the request of abolitionist Domingo del Monte for an anthology to be published in London by editor and delegate Richard Madden, who is featured in the film. The works were confiscated, however, and Romero's novel not published until 1880.

83. One of the first acts of the Revolution was to print four hundred thousand copies of Cervantes's *Don Quixote,* available at the meager price of 25 cents. Other important literary and cultural institutes include the Artists and Writers' Union (UNEAC) and Casa de las Américas, which sponsors highly coveted literary awards, symposiums, grants, and cultural events.

84. Fornet, *Narrar la nación,* 80–81.

85. The "testimonial novel" also goes by the name "documentary novel" or "testimonial narrative" in the critical literature. For an important theoretical discussion of the genre, see Beverley, *Testimonio,* especially chapters 1 and 2.

86. Gonzalez Echevarría, "'Biografía de un cimarrón,'" 255.

87. See Barnet's postscript to the Spanish edition: "La novela testimonio: Alquimia de la memoria," *Cimarrón,* 212–15.

88. For Alejo Carpentier's statement on the "genre," see his "De lo real maravilloso americano," published as a prologue to his novel on the Haitian Revolution, *El reino de este mundo* (1949), and anthologized in Carpentier, *Obras completas,* 100–117.

89. Luis, "The Politics of Memory," 477.

90. Barnet and Montejo, *Biography of a Runaway Slave,* 105, 153–54, 193–94.

91. William Luis has pointed out that Esteban Montejo emerges as a character in Barnet's next "documentary novel," *Canción de Rachel* (1969), where he affirms his solidarity with the PIC. Luis, "The Politics of Memory," 487.

92. Mahler, *From the Tricontinental,* 13–14.

93. Fidel Castro's speech was delivered December 22, 1975. Quoted in Waters, *Cuba & Angola,* 31.

94. The acronyms refer to People's Movement for the Liberation of Angola (MPLA); National Union for the Total Independence of Angola (UNITA); National Liberation Front of Angola (FLNA). Namibia's SWAPO (South West African People's Organization) was another relevant constituent. For a comprehensive account, see Gleijeses, *Conflicting Missions;* Gleijeses, *Visions of Freedom.*

95. Gleijeses, *Visions of Freedom,* 426.

96. This Mandela asked at a rally in Matanzas on July 26, 1991, at which he received the Jose Martí Medal, the highest honor conferred on noncitizens by the Republic of Cuba. Waters, *Cuba & Angola,* 71.

97. Cuban Communist Party delegate and the chief ambassador in Angola, Jorge Risquest, does so in the 2007 BBC documentary *Cuba: An African Odyssey,* directed by Jihan El-Tahri, as does Raúl Castro in his May 1991 speech "Thanks to Angola," in Waters, *Cuba & Angola,* 59–72.

98. C. Moore, *Castro, the Blacks, and Africa,* 333. Critics such as Moore argued that the Angolan war and Cuba's African internationalist politics were diversionary tactics meant to draw attention away from Cuba's domestic (racial) woes. Alejandro de la Fuente has argued that these interventions and acts of solidarity nevertheless opened up possibilities for Afro-Cubans in the foreign ministry, press, and armed forces and notably altered stereotypes in Cuba about Africa and its peoples. Fuente, *A Nation for All,* 303. So, too, should it be noted that Cuba's internationalist commitments in Africa did not end in 1991. Their continued civilian service in Africa, especially their internationalist doctors, is featured in the documentary *¡Salud!* (2006), directed by Connie Field. For a fuller discussion of the cultural effects of Angola on Cuban identity, see Peters, *Cuban Identity.*

99. According to *Cuba & Angola,* edited by Mary-Alice Waters, there were 2,077 buried that day, but the overall number of casualties in Angola is much larger, estimated at no less than 5,000 and not officially stated. The EcuRed entry on "Guerra de Angola" does not list overall casualties: https://www.ecured.cu/Guerra_de_Angola.

100. Waters, *Cuba & Angola,* 59.

101. For a nuanced account and analysis of Rectification, see Esckstein, *Back from the Future,* 59–86.

102. The film was a far cry, for instance, from José Massip's *Páginas del diario de José Martí* (1971), an avant-garde film that has received critical acclaim although it was "controversial" in its day.

103. Fuente, *A Nation for All,* 312–13.

104. The twenty-three machetes symbolize the date March 23, 1878, the day Maceo and his forces renewed combat after his famous Protest of Baraguá.

105. An estimated 80 percent of Cuba's trade was with the Soviet Union. The Torricelli and Helms-Burton Acts were thus "timely," designed to render life unlivable for Cubans and to thereby induce rebellions and instability that would justify a "peacekeeping" intervention. The 1992 Torricelli Act, for instance, forbade not only US corporations but also their subsidiaries in third countries from doing business with Cuba—regardless of (or precisely due to) the fact that food and medicine accounted for 90 percent of such trade. It also stipulated penalties for those countries or institutions that granted aid to Cuba—such that if, say, Mexico awarded Cuba $1 million in aid, the US would offer Mexico $1 million less in US aid. The 1996 Helms-Burton Act was no less hostile. Under the guise of standing up for the non-indemnified property rights of exile Cubans and American businesses, it extended US prosecutorial powers against foreign companies that invested in Cuba. So, too, did it renew a budget in the order of tens of millions to fund dissidents and insurrection on the island. For a historical and legal survey of the embargo, see Lamrani, *The Economic War against Cuba.*

106. For nuanced structural analyses of the "Special Period," see Azicri, *Cuba Today and Tomorrow.* For accounts on its cultural effects, see Hernández-Reguant, *Cuba in the Special Period;* Quiroga, *Cuban Palimpsests;* Loss and Prieto, *Caviar with Rum;* Casamayor-Cisneros, *Utopía, distopía e ingravidez.*

107. The US policy at the time enticed precisely such risky ventures. Cubans who reached US waters would be granted permanent residency status in the United States, a policy in place since the 1966 Cuban Adjustment Act (Public Law 89–732) until 2017. And while the United States agreed to grant 27,000 visas a year to Cubans who wished to immigrate legally, its Interests Section in Havana only granted a fraction of that amount per year (i.e., 2,700 in 1993). In other words, it structurally encouraged *illegal* over legal entry to the United States. See Chomsky, *A History of the Cuban Revolution,* 168–71. Also recommended is the documentary *Balseros,* directed by Carlos Bosch and Josep Ma Domeench (2002), which follows the lives of seven of those refugees over a period of seven years and shows the difficulty of life for each in a disaffected, alienating, and work-intensive US economy and culture.

108. For fuller appraisals of the period's reforms, see Azicri, *Cuba Today and Tomorrow;* Eckstein, *Back from the Future.*

109. This has been widely attested to in interviews and research. See Pérez Sarduy and Stubbs, *Afro-Cuban Voices.*

110. Mesa-Lago, *The Cuban Economy Today,* 25.

111. Fuente, *A Nation for All,* 309–11.

112. For the "authoritative" account on the subject, see Morales Domínguez, *Race in Cuba,* which includes most of Morales's seminal study, *Desafíos de la problemática racial en Cuba.* It was an "idealistic error," says Morales, to assume

that structural reforms would suffice to eradicate racism. Morales affirms that racism was a "taboo" subject, not because officials believed it invalid, but because it was deemed a "divisive" subject. Only studies on the history of slavery or folkloric studies on Afro-Cuban cultural practices were thereby tolerated.

113. The 1991 Fourth Party Congress concluded: "The future of the patria will be an eternal Baraguá," a trope that echoed throughout the billboards, posters, and rallies of the 1990s. Pérez, *Structure of Cuban History,* 272.

114. Not unlike the American hip-hop scene, Cuba's embodies many political persuasions, from those that openly decry the socialist state and Communist Party (e.g., los Aldeanos, Orishas) to those that consciously yet critically operate "within" the system (e.g., Anónimo Consejo, Obsesión). Many have been lured away by a combination of lucrative foreign contracts and a locally repressive or less opportune milieu, and some have even been, however unwittingly, exploited by the US State Department and CIA. However, progressive organizations such as the Black August Collective and hip-hop artists such as Mos Def, Dead Prez, and Eryka Badu have also visited Cuba to engender and emulate a politically conscious hip-hop. For scholarly studies on Cuban hip-hop, see Perry, *Negro Soy Yo;* Fernandes, *Cuba Represent!;* Saunders, *Cuban Underground Hip-Hop;* Baker, *Buena Vista in the Club.*

115. For a first-rate study of the Revolution's history, policies, and cultural productions on music, see R. Moore, *Music and Revolution.*

116. For song lyrics, see Rodgríguez Mola and López Cabrera, "Mambí," 205–10. Marc Perry offers an edifying read of this song and Obsessión's work: Perry, *Negro Soy Yo,* 97–104.

117. Rodgríguez Mola and López Cabrera, "Mambí," 209.

118. Perry, *Negro Soy Yo,* 101–2.

2. *¡Empínate!*

1. H. P. Foley, "Women in Ancient Epic," 105–18.

2. Prados-Torreira, *Mambisas,* 6–8.

3. Ibid, 84.

4. Stoner, *From the House,* 28. See also Caballero, *La mujer en el 68;* Caballero, *La mujer en el 95.*

5. Quoted in Pérez, *The Structure of Cuban History,* 94.

6. Ibid., 87–98.

7. Martí, *Abdala,* 14–15, 22.

8. Ibid., 22.

9. These words were published in *Patria* January 6, 1894: *¡Y tú, empínate, porque ya es hora de que te vayas al campamento!*" Quoted in Sarabia, *Historia de una familia,* 104.

10. Prados-Torreira, *Mambisas,* 63–66.

11. Ibid., 65.

12. Ibid., 62.

13. There is the famous Hatuey monument in Baracoa with the inscription "First Rebel of America Immolated in Yara of Baracoa."

14. Leal, *Teatro mambí,* 255.

15. Ibid., 340.

16. Ibid., 339.

17. Ibid., 328, 338.

18. Cruz, *Episodios de la revolución cubana,* 14, 16.

19. Ibid., 18.

20. Such disciplinary actions included court martials. The most notorious case was that of Quintín Banderas. Ferrer, *Insurgent Cuba,* 173–77.

21. The Club Esperanza del Valle petitioned for it, with only ten delegates in favor. Stoner, *From the House,* 55–56.

22. Other significant groups and advocacy included the formation of the National Feminist Alliance and the Havana Lyceum. Ibid., 73–74.

23. Quoted in C. Davis, *A Place in the Sun?,* 15.

24. Their platform included, among other things, a call for free and transparent elections, limits to congressional immunity, open and competitive bids for government contracts, and the eradication of embezzlement or clientelist schemes (i.e., *la botella*). Pérez, *Cuba: Between Reform and Revolution,* 190–92.

25. Ibid.

26. It is said that she seldom affixed her name to her philanthropic works or attended public ceremonies in their honor. Prados-Torreira, *Mambisas,* 110.

27. Stoner, *From the House,* 78–86.

28. Davies, *A Place in the Sun?,* 40–44; Stoner, *From the House,* 89–102.

29. Portuondo Zúñiga, *La virgen de la Caridad,* 223.

30. Ibid., 218–27. The effigy of the Virgen in Santiago de Cuba's St. Thomas church is the one most popularly known as the *Virgen mambisa.*

31. According to the testimony of eighty-five-year-old Juan Moreno, in the version written by the sanctuary chaplain Onofre de Fonseca (1693), the men in the boat were two indigenous (*indios*) and a Black slave boy (Juan Moreno himself), and at least one of them was not named Juan. Schmidt, *Cachita's Streets,* 23–28.

32. Note, however, that the child (baby Jesus) is rarely other than white, which confirms white paternity.

33. In the wake of the 1901 secular constitution and North American Protestant influences, the Catholic Church's power on the island had notably diminished. Its associations with Spain and colonialism were not looked upon kindly. However, the nationalist movement to reaffirm a Hispanic identity (contra Anglo-Saxion superiority) and to reconcile Cuba's racial tensions in the wake of the 1912 massacre created incentives for both Rome and Havana to consolidate the nation under the symbol of the Virgen. Portuondo Zúñiga, *La virgen de la Caridad,* 235–41; Schmidt, *Cachita's Streets,* 54–58, 63–66.

34. Torres Elers and Escalona Chádez, *Mariana Grajales Cuello,* 158. It should be clarified that Mariana's repatriation and burial was the initiative of Santiaguero citizens, not the national government.

35. Teodoro Ramos Blanco would later collaborate on memorials to Juan Gualberto Gómez and at El Cacahual, where Antonio Maceo's remains rest.

36. The lesser-known Mariana monument in Santiago de Cuba was dedicated on Mother's Day (1947), no less indicative of what she and the *mambisa* amounted to in the popular imaginary. It was designed by Santiguera artist Teresa Sagaró Ponce, in an art deco style.

37. Technically, there was the Queen Isabel statue in Havana park, but this was replaced by Martí's monument after independence.

38. Stoner, *From the House,* 148.

39. Davies, *A Place in the Sun?,* 37.

40. Smith and Padula, *Sex and Revolution,* 19–21.

41. Castro Ruz, *Historia me absolverá,* 63.

42. For an excellent discussion of women's roles in the anti-Batista campaigns, see Chase, *The Revolution within the Revolution,* especially chapters 1 and 2.

43. Smith and Padula, *Sex and Revolution,* 22–23.

44. Waters, *Marianas in Combat,* 47–48.

45. Sánchez held her position in the Politburo until her death from cancer in 1980. For a historically rich biography, see Stout, *One Day in December.*

46. The other woman in the Moncada assault was Melba Hernández. Santamaría held her position from Casa's inception in 1959 until her death (by suicide) in 1980. As a woman from rural Cuba with no more than a sixth-grade formal education, Santamaría was not the likeliest choice to head what became the most prestigious literary and cultural institution in the Americas. That she led the institute with a democratic (and internationalist) ethos and without ever reducing the arts to vulgar propaganda made her (and Casa) all the more admirable and consequential. See Randall, *Haydée Santamaría.*

47. The FMC did not come out of nowhere, of course. Its most important predecessor was the Communist Party–affiliated Federacíon Democrática de Mujeres Cubanas. Chase, *The Revolution within the Revolution,* 107–15.

48. Smith and Padura, *Sex and Revolution,* 36–37.

49. Ibid., 39–41.

50. Waters, *Marianas in Combat,* 13.

51. Ibid.

52. Belkis Cuza Malé, quoted in Davies, *A Place in the Sun?,* 120–21.

53. Betancourt's remains were then moved to the site of her historic fame, namely, Guáimaro in 1982, interned in a mausoleum. In 1974 the Order of Ana Betancourt became the highest award conferred by the FMC and in 1979 a state award. The first recipient was Haydée Santamaría.

54. Taylor, "Review of *Lucía,*" 55.

55. Biskind, "Lucía—Struggles with History," 7–8.

56. For other excellent discussions of *Lucía,* see Mraz, "Visual Style and Historical Portrayal"; Chanan, *Cuban Cinema,* 273–88. *Lucía* was followed by three remarkable films on gender and machismo in the contemporary socialist context: Sara Gómez's *De cierta manera* (1974), Pastor Vega's *Retrato de Teresa* (1979), and Tomás Gutiérrez Alea's *Hasta cierto punto* (1983).

57. The thesis that revolutions are tragically necessary and necessarily tragic is corroborated in Lawson, *Anatomies of Revolution,* 17. The notion of "failing better" as a revolutionary credo is consistent with Slavoj Žižek's in *First as Tragedy,* which he credits to a line in Samuel Beckett's *Worstward Ho:* "Try again. Fail again. Fail better." For a similarly nuanced look at revolutions in the Caribbean, see Meeks, *Caribbean Revolutions and Revolutionary Theory.*

58. The poem was originally published in Morejón, *Parajes de una época* (1979). Both the Spanish version and an English translation can be found in Randall, *Only the Road,* 240–44. For an excellent discussion of Morjeón's work, see Cordones-Cook, *Soltando amarras y memorias.*

59. This included an all-women's artillery unit.

60. Stoner, "Militant Heroines and the Consecration," 71–96.

61. Caballero, *La mujer en el 68,* 29.

62. Ibid., 71–75.

63. Caballero, *La mujer en el 95,* 50–52.

64. Ibid., 71.

65. A similar dynamic takes place with Silvio Rodríguez's nueva trova song "Mujeres" (Women) of 1968.

66. Stone, *Women and the Cuban Revolution,* 95.

67. The question of women's entry into the workforce was a complicated issue, one that cannot be simply read as the effect of sexist prejudice and obstacles. In socialist Cuba, families already had health care, affordable housing, and education (including university), and there were relatively few (luxury) consumer items available for purchase. In other words, there were no real structured "incentives" (or necessities) to work outside the home. Smith and Padura, *Sex and Revolution,* 106–11.

68. Ibid., 48–55.

69. Jineterismo can entail an array of illegal and semi-legal activities that service tourists—hustlers, pimps, dealers, unofficial tour guides, etc.—but its most socially stigmatized act (and actress, as it were) is sex work, with the largest share of its workers young low-income women of color. See Fusco, "Hustling for Dollars"; Pope, "The Political Economy of Desire."

70. Cintio Vitier, quoted in Pérez, *The Structure of Cuban History,* 264.

71. Antonio Maceo's godfather, José Ascencio de Ascencio, is also given a good deal of credit. Cupull and González, *Mariana, raíz del alma cubana,* 18–19.

72. Herrera, "El penúltimo sueño de Mariana," 272, 295–97.

73. Ibid., 312.

74. Pérez, *The Structure of Cuban History,* 265.

3. The Epic Travestied

1. Mañach, *Indagación del choteo,* 72.

2. Roy, *The Postcolonial Epic,* 87–91.

3. Propp, *On the Comic and Laughter;* Bakhtin, *Rabelais and His World.*

4. Eagleton, *Sweet Violence,* 72.

5. On bufo see Lane. *Blackface Cuba;* R. Moore, "The *Teatro Bufo*"; Leal, *La selva oscura.*

6. Lane, *Blackface Cuba,* 15.

7. Leal, *La selva oscura,* 31, 159, 174, 274.

8. Ibid., 60–63.

9. Ibid., 275–80.

10. Pérez, *The Structure of Cuban History,* 22–28.

11. Mañach, *Indagación del choteo,* 60.

12. Ibid., 77.

13. Freud, "Mourning and Melancholia." 243–58.

14. Mañach, *Indagación del choteo,* 75. For a contemporary discussion on choteo, see Hidalgo, *Choteo;* Pérez Firmat, "Riddles of the Sphincter.".

15. Other graphic precedents included the works of painter Victor Patricio Landaluze y Uriarte in *El Moro Muza* (1859–77) and *Juan Palomo* (1869–74). Juan, *Caricatura de la República,* 18.

16. Ibid., 45.

17. Ibid., 42.

18. Ibid., 72–73.

19. A February 9, 1913, cartoon has an anonymous "Husband of Tomasa" playfully recite: "I won't tolerate/that damned advancement/that fills with disenchantment/what was once a happy home/I need to have/my Tomasa desist/from this modern conquest;/and have her return to what she was/May she despise the chimera/that is the Feminist Party!" Ibid., 38.

20. Ibid., 30.

21. On messianism, see Guerra, *Heroes, Martyrs, and Political Messiahs.*

22. Guevara, *Che Guevara Reader,* 227.

23. In his roles as president of the National Bank and minister of industries, Guevara's thoughts on the economy were complex and heterodox. See Yaffe, *Che Guevara.*

24. Guevara, *Che Guevara Reader,* 224.

25. Ibid., 213. See also the essays "A New Culture of Work" (1962) and "The Cadre: Backbone of the Revolution" (1962) in Guevara, *Che Guevara, Reader,* 143–57.

26. Blum, *Cuban Youth and Revolutionary Values;* Guerra, *Visions of Power in Cuba,* 227–55.

27. The UPC works with first to ninth graders.

28. This is so despite its decidedly bourgeois and sexist normativity. As Martí said, *Edad de oro* was written for the "gentlemen and mothers of tomorrow." Martí, *Edad de oro,* 15.

29. Guevara, *Che Guevara Reader,* 223.

30. Fidel's 1961 speech known as *Palabras a los intelectuales* is routinely summarized by the quote "Within the Revolution, everything; against it, nothing." On interpretations of this text and the Revolution's cultural policy, see Kumaraswami, "Cultural Policy and Cultural Politics."

31. Gutiérrez Alea, *Dialéctica del espectador.*

32. To this list one could add Alea's later *Guantamera* (1995) and the works of his assistant and prodigy, Carlos Tabío: *Demasiado miedo a la vida* o *Plaff!* (1988), *El elefante y la bicicleta* (1994), *La lista de espera* (2000), and *El cuerno de abundancia* (2008). For a discussion of Cuban cinema and social comedy, see Chanan, *Cuban Cinema,* 437–40.

33. For general information, see EcuRed's "Portal: Elpidio Valdés," https://www.ecured.cu/Portal:Elpidio_Vald%C3%A9s. Also see Planas, "El reverse mítico"; Reyes, "El etnocentrismo blando"; Río, "Elpidio Valdés o la Cubanía Paradigmática."

34. See the retrospective documentary, *Hasta la próxima aventura* (2013), directed by Miguel Torres. Juan Padrón also authored *El libro del mambí* (1985), a graphically rich historical study of the mambí and the wars, with inserts from *Elpidio Valdés* to corroborate the series' fidelity to history.

35. Catalá Carrasco, "From Suspicion to Recognition?," 154.

36. Propp, *On the Comic and Laughter,* 145.

37. Bakhtin, *Rabelais and His World,* 18, 121, 274.

38. I borrow the term "parasocialist" from Laurie Frederik. I prefer it to "postsocialist" and feel it better conveys the ongoing contradictory antagonisms of the Revolution. Frederik, *Trumpets in the Mountains,* 13–14.

39. The *Maine* tragedy is what defined the war for Americans. Although no party's culpability was ever proven, the war's most memorable slogan resounded: "Remember the *Maine,* to Hell with Spain!" Cuban and Spanish (and some American) critics and historians have repeatedly suspected or alleged this was a "false-flag" tactic. See Pérez, *The War of 1898, 57–79.*

40. Kapcia, "Educational Revolution and Revolutionary Morality," 356.

41. Garcia, *Cuban Cinema,* 138–39; Banet-Weiser, "Elian Gonzalez."

42. In this respect, it is perhaps no coincidence that the third series of *Elpdio Valdés* cartoons (four shorts between 2000 and 2003), which were digitally produced and by directors other than Padrón (i.e., Tulio Raggi and Juan Ruiz), fell shy of the "imperfect" mark and were not well received. It is not just the overall polish, however, that has left viewers and critics unsatisfied, if not offended. A couple of new characters resemble the thick-lipped negro bembón of bufo

blackface theater or a gorilla-like imbecile. And this is to say nothing of more predictable and less funny plot lines.

43. Freud, *Jokes and Their Relation,* 123.

44. Bakhtin, "Epic and Novel," 23–24.

45. Pérez Firmat, "Riddles of the Sphincter," 62.

46. White, *Metahistory,* 8.

4. *¡Al machete!*

1. The array of motives cited in war memoirs, diaries, and chronicles is impressive: to feed one's family, to bring honor to one's family name, to impress a betrothed, to prove one's manliness, for liberty, for racial equality, for vengeance, for Patria, or because one had no other choice (e.g., "war finds you" was a refrain). León Rosabal, *La voz del mambí,* 17–21.

2. Masabó denied the charges. Martí, *José Martí,* 396.

3. Ibid., 344–45, 342.

4. Boza, *Mi diario de la guerra,* 120.

5. The US Congress passed resolutions in early 1896 to recognize the Republic in Arms as official "belligerents" in the war, but both President Cleveland and his successor, President McKinley, elided the subject. The PRC hoped that such diplomatic commitments would translate into more easily acquired arms and materiel and to force Spain's hand to negotiate. By late 1897, the PRC was pushing for outright US *military* intervention, not mere belligerency recognition. Pérez, *Cuba between Empires,* 111–12.

6. Boza, *Mi diario de la guerra,* 64.

7. This was usually done in guásima trees, with the judicial act nicknamed *enguasimada.* Tone, *War and Genocide in Cuba,* 66.

8. Boza, *Mi diario de la guerra,* 120.

9. Leal, *Teatro mambí,* 20.

10. Miró Argenter, *Cuba,* 123–24.

11. Boza, *Mi diario de la guerra,* 74.

12. Barnet and Montejo, *Biography of a Runaway Slave,* 161.

13. Tone, *War and Genocide in Cuba,* 125.

14. Ibid., 133–34.

15. Ibid., 77. As Tone astutely explains, the ELC had learned that the most valuable tactic was to only *partially* charge at Spanish troops. Rather than tear Spanish soldiers apart with their machetes, the cavalry would pull away early enough not to fall prey to their foe's Mausers and bayonets. This "taunt," as it were, would cause the Spaniards to form their famous "block" (*cuadro*), which they thought more impervious to cavalry charges, but which likewise rendered them more vulnerable to Cuban rifle fire from concealed positions in the trees and brush.

16. Quesada, *The War in Cuba.*

17. Tone, *War and Genocide in Cuba,* 123–38.

18. By the war's end in 1898, Spain had deployed 190,000 peninsular men to the island and had armed and fielded another 60,000 irregulars from the island. This constituted the largest European armed force (up until then) to be sent abroad to fight a colonial war. Foner, *The Spanish-Cuban-American War,* 16.

19. The Republic in Arms (i.e., the PRC) did assiduously raise funds, purchase arms and supplies, and send out Cuban filibusters in unarmored, but quick schooners from the shores of Florida. Sixty-four expeditions were sent to Cuba throughout the war's three years—twenty-three of which the United States interceded and another four to which either the sea or the Spanish laid claim. All told, only 60 percent of supply expeditions made it to Cuban shores and into the hands of the ELC. Even when supplies did arrive, the lack of standardized weaponry meant that rifles (Springfields, Remingtons, Winchesters) and ammunition were often incompatible and thus worthless, or at least laid fallow until the proper match was made, if ever. Even had they enjoyed a 100 percent success rate to smuggle in supplies, it would not have sufficed to match the Spaniards' capabilities in terms of weaponry, munitions, and supplies. Tone, *War and Genocide in Cuba,* 82; Foner, *The Spanish-Cuban-American War,* 19.

20. Rodríguez Rodriguez, ed. *Algunos documentos políticos,* 10.

21. Foner, *The Spanish-Cuban-American War,* 22.

22. Roig de Leuchsenring, ed. *Ideario cubano,* 68–72. It should come as no surprise, militarily or ideologically, that Gómez and Maceo were decidedly more lenient on Orientales, laborers, artisans, and smaller-scale farmers and ruthless toward the propertied elites and their hired goons.

23. Tone, *War and Genocide in Cuba,* 57–68.

24. Miró Argenter, *Cuba,* 175.

25. Tone, *War and Genocide in Cuba,* 77.

26. By January 1898, in fact, only 50,000 of the 114,000 Spanish forces still on the island were combat-ready. Roig de Leuchsinring, *Cuba no se debe su independencia,* 34–35.

27. Tone, *War and Genocide in Cuba,* 9–11. By contrast, fewer Cuban *mambises* died due to disease (3,437) than to battle or combat-related injuries (5,180). Foner, *The Spanish-Cuban-American War,* 20.

28. Ibid. See also Halstead, *The Story of Cuba,* 122.

29. That mosquitoes were a vector for yellow fever was a theory proposed by the Cuban doctor Carlos J. Finlay as early as 1881; his extensive studies and proofs were, ironically enough, then corroborated by the US Army's Walter Reed Commission in American-occupied Cuba in 1900—the rewards of which the United States would reap in its war in the Philippines.

30. Roig, *Cuba no debe su independencia,* 24.

31. Tone, *War and Genocide in Cuba,* 9.

32. Roig de Leuchsinring, *Cuba no debe su independencia,* 24.

33. I have borrowed this phrasing from Anderson, *Imagined Communities,* 9.

34. Byrne was pushed into exile in 1896 for his nationalist sonnets. He relocated to Tampa, Florida, where he was an active member in the PRC's affiliate and a *lector* to tobacco workers. He returned to Cuba in 1899, and upon entering Havana's port and seeing the US flag in El Moro he penned his most famous poem, "Mi bandera," included in the collection *Lira y espada.*

35. Byrne, *Lira y espada,* 30–31.

36. Plutarch, "Sayings of Spartan Women," 183–93.

37. Byrne, *Lira y espada,* 12–13.

38. Vitier, *Ese sol del mundo moral,* 117.

39. The most famous lines attributed to—and summative of—the 1930s revolutionary movement were the imprisoned Raul Roa's "Tiene la palabra la camarada Mauser" (Comrade Mauser has the word!), a citation of Soviet poet Vladimir Mayakovski's "Leftward March" and, thereby, the Bolshevik epic. For anyone familiar with the mambí epic and the role of the Mauser therein, Roa's choice was not without its ironies! The publication *El Machete* was closely affiliated with the revolutionary Julio Antonio Mella, one of the founders of the José Martí Popular University and of the Cuban Communist Party (1925). Mella was forced into exile and, like Trotsky, was assassinated in Mexico.

40. Rubén Martínez Villena, quoted in Vitier, *Ese sol del mundo moral,* 117. Villena was one of the founders of the storied avant-garde literary group Grupo Minorista and a youth leader in the Veterans and Patriots movement. Later he became, in Mella's absence, one of the key leaders of Cuban Communist Party on the island. He had traveled to Moscow, studied under the Third International, and helped organize the general strike of 1933 that solidified Machado's fall.

41. Ibid., 118. Note, too, that some of the earliest street protests and confrontations with Geraldo Machado's police (i.e., in September 1930) were initiated as if a reenactment of a machete charge: workers and radical students rallied at the call of the mambí bugle. Ibid., 127.

42. Of humble origins, Luna was already a well-known and critically acclaimed poet, whose earlier works included *Corazón Abierto* (1922), *Refugio* (1927), *Surco* (1928), *Pulso y onda* (1936), and *La tierra herida* (1943), among others. Luna collaborated with radicals in the Spanish Civil War, was an active underground militant during the anti-Batista movement, and was a leading figure in the Revolution's press.

43. Navarro Luna, *Obra poética,* 305–6.

44. Ibid., 307.

45. These issues are discussed throughout Che Guevara's *Pasajes de la guerra revolucionaria.*

46. For an excellent discussion on the trials and violence, see Chase, "The Trials."

47. Navarro Luna, *Obra poética,* 467.

48. Roberto Fernández Retamar, quoted in the preface to Navarro Luna, *Obra poética,* 9.

49. Chanan, *Cuban Cinema,* 66–67.

50. In Rocha's cinematic works, *Black God, White Devil* (1964) for instance, there is the repeated use of the outlaw or bandit (*cangaciero*) that retaliates and unleashes his "justice" on landowners and the (petite) bourgeoisie. Rocha, "The Aesthetics of Hunger," 41–45.

51. Originally published in the October 1969 edition of *Tricontinental* (no. 14: 107–32). For a translation, see Solanas and Getino, "Towards a Third Cinema," 33–58.

52. In Cuba, the new cinema was captioned under the title "imperfect cinema," after Julio García Espinosa's 1969 essay "For an Imperfect Cinema." García urged fellow filmmakers to resist the temptation to produce technically elegant films on a par with Hollywood's "perfect" cinema. Cuba's "imperfect cinema" was to be a "popular art," one attuned to the people's vernacular and the Revolution's emancipatory horizons. Rather than pursue artistic mastery, its objective was—like the socialist state—to render itself obsolete. In its wake, the distinctions of filmmaker, artist, critic, and audience would be superfluous, and artistic creation would be the province of all. That García's prose did not resound with militant rhetoric or a visceral tone is perhaps not surprising. It was not written by exiled or underground filmmakers, but by a filmmaker and in a journal (*Cine cubano*) under the auspices of a revolutionary state and its film institute. García Espinosa, *Por un cine imperfecto.* For an English translation by Julianne Burton, see García Espinosa, "For an Imperfect Cinema."

53. Burton, "Democratizing Documentary," 68–69.

54. Sartre, preface to *Wretched of the Earth,* 21–22.

55. Chanan, *Cuban Cinema,* 302–4; Juan-Navarro, "Nación, mito e historia," 179–208; Juan-Navarro, "¿100 años de lucha?," 142–61.

56. Ortiz, *Cuban Counterpoint,* 6–8.

57. Despite the fact that Cubans did produce a record harvest (8.5 tons), it was understood to be a failure with heavy opportunity costs and demoralizing effects. Gott, *Cuba,* 240–43.

58. Since 1898, the United States had militarily intervened in the affairs of Latin American and Caribbean nation states no less than forty times, including the contemporary occupation of the Dominican Republic in 1965. Appleman Williams, *Empire as a Way of Life.*

59. The text was actually an abridged version of the much lengthier *Mis primeros treinta años* (1943). Piedra Martel, *Memoria del mambí,* 71–72.

60. Ibid., 76–77.

61. Ibid. 101.

62. Leal, *Teatro mambí,* 19.

63. Sánchez, *Héroes humildes,* 118; Iznaga, *Presencia del testimonio,* 16–17.

64. Sánchez, *Héroes humildes,* 22–23.

65. Technically, Roa's memoir was limited to the years 1870–71. The full title reads *A pie y descalzo de Trinidad a Cuba, 1870–1871: Recuerdos de campaña.*

66. That Roa refused to fight in the subsequent Little War of 1879–80 and did not return to Cuba to fight in the War of Independence (1895–98) no doubt lent credence to such a read.

67. Martí, "Con todos y para el bien," 704.

68. On this polemic see López, *José Martí,* 258–59; Ferrer, *Insurgent Cuba,* 114–16.

69. As Collazo wrote to Martí, Roa's text was meant not to demoralize but to "serve as experience, so that in the hour of sacrifice [Cubans might] go in full knowledge and with their spirits strong, to avoid regrets." Ferrer, *Insurgent Cuba,* 115.

70. *Episodios de la revolución cubana* was serialized in *El Figaro* in 1893, was read to tobacco workers by *lectores,* and has been republished many times thereafter: 1911, 1943, 1968, 1981, 1990, 2001.

71. Ferrer, *Insurgent Cuba,* 157.

72. Iznaga, *Presencia del testimonio,* 158.

5. The Epic (De)Sacralized

1. I use the grammatically masculine form *reconcentrado* to refer to all "reconcentrated," regardless of sex, age, etc. While this grammatical rule has been rightly called into question, I have elected to stay with the historically accurate phrase to avoid other confusions or anachronisms, but I have made it clear that women and children made up the majority of this category and abysmal reality.

2. *¡Nubia venció! Muero feliz: la muetre/poco me importa, pues logré salvarla . . . /¡Oh, que dulce es morir cuando se muere/Luchando audaz por defender la patria!* Martí, *Abdala,* 24.

3. *No temaís una muerte gloriosa, que morir por la patria es vivir.* Lyrics and sheet music found in appendix of Quesada, *The War in Cuba* (1896).

4. Anderson, *Imagined Communities,* 206.

5. Ibid., 10–11.

6. Valdés-Domínguez, *Diario de soldado,* 1: 35.

7. Salvador Cisneros Betancourt, cited in Pérez, *The Structure of Cuban History,* 20.

8. Ibid., 29.

9. Hubert and Mauss, *Sacrifice;* Brown, *Santería Enthroned.*

10. *El Cubano Libre,* April 15, 1897, 2, my emphasis. Quoted in Pérez, *The Structure of Cuban History,* 29.

11. *La República,* quoted in Pérez, *The Structure of Cuban History,* 81, my emphasis.

12. Céspedes, quoted in "Carlos Manuel de Céspedes," EcuRed, https://www.ecured.cu/Carlos_Manuel_de_C%C3%A9spedes.

13. Leal, *Teatro mambí,* 204.

14. Prados-Torreira, *Mambisas,* 65. Original passage in *Patria* January 6, 1894: *¡Y tú, empínate, porque ya es hora de que te vayas al campamento!"*

15. Prados-Torreira, *Mambisas,* 63–66.

16. Martí, *José Martí,* 414. It would be some time before Martí's remains were buried in the mausoleum at Santa Ifigenia cemetery in Santiago de Cuba.

17. Quesada and Northrop, *Cuba's Great Struggle for Freedom,* 513.

18. Hubert and Mauss, *Sacrifice,* 99.

19. Eagleton, *Holy Terror,* 33.

20. Ibid.

21. Martí, *Jose Martí,* 344.

22. Máximo Gómez, reprinted in Boza, *Mi diario de la guerra,* 285.

23. This is my calculation based on estimates found in Tone, *War and Genocide in Cuba;* Foner, *The Spanish-Cuban-American War;* Pérez Guzmán, *Herida profunda.*

24. Tone, *War and Genocide in Cuba,* 155.

25. Pérez Guzmán, *Herida profunda,* 217.

26. Ibid., 215.

27. Foner, *The Spanish-Cuban-American War,* 34; Roig de Leuchsinring, *Weyler en Cuba,* 71–72.

28. Tone, *War and Genocide in Cuba,* 193–224.

29. For fuller descriptions, photographs, and statistics, see Izquierdo Canosa, *La Reconcentración,* 28–66; Pérez Guzmán, *Herida profunda,* 61–110; Tone, *War and Genocide in Cuba,* 193–224.

30. Izquierdo Canosa, *La Reconcentración,* 28–66; Pérez Guzmán, *Herida profunda,* 61–110; Tone, *War and Genocide in Cuba,* 193–224.

31. Tone, *War and Genocide in Cuba,* 212; Izquierdo Canoza, *La reconcentración,* 36–37. The highest mortality rates were, then, in the west, which may seem counterintuitive given that the west was the haven for Spanish immigrants; but it is easily explained by the fact that the west was far more densely populated, accounting for 74 percent of the island's population.

32. The most rigorous calculations of fatalities can be attributed to Cuban demographers and historians Juan Perez de la Riva, Blanca Morejon, and Julio Le Riverend, who offer the range of 157,000 to 200,000. Tone, *War and Genocide in Cuba,* 209–17.

33. Izquierdo Canosa, *La reconcentración,* 79.

34. According to the census of 1899, only 8 percent of Cuba's population was under five years of age, the lowest such percentage for all other countries in the world for which such data existed. Postwar Cuba also had the highest proportions of orphans and widowed women in the Western Hemisphere. Pérez, *The Structure of Cuban History,* 28.

35. Pérez Guzmán, *Herida profunda,* 217, my emphasis.

36. Agamben, *Remnants of Auschwitz,* 26–27. Agamben points out that early Christians did not agree as to whether these deaths were commendable or senseless (*perire sine causa*). Did they not defy the teachings that Jesus had died for all, and why, after all, would the Lord desire the death of innocents? Out of these

theological disputes emerged a doctrine on martyrdom, citing the Gospels of Luke and Matthew, which made it possible to render the "scandal of a meaningless death" into a divine act. Matthew 10: 32–33: "Whosever therefore shall confess me before men, him will I confess also before my Father which is in heaven. But whosoever shall deny me before men, him will I also deny before my Father which is in heaven."

37. Agamben, *Remnants of Auschwitz,* 26–30.

38. Nancy, "The Unsacrificeable," 27.

39. Agamben, *Homo Sacer,* especially part 2.

40. Arendt, *The Origins of Totalitarianism,* 186–96.

41. Ibid, 299.

42. Senator W. Mason of Illinois was one among many who provocatively avowed: "We [must] take Cuba as the good Samaritan did, and bind up her wounds, furnish her people with something to eat, and clothes to wear; and the nations of the world will say at last, in the beginning of the new century, there is one nation not seeking conquest, not seeking power, but one nation following the Nazarene [Jesus of Nazareth], that has learned the sublime thought, 'Bear ye one another's burdens.'" Quoted in Pérez, *Cuba in the American Imagination,* 47.

43. Witherbee, *Spanish-American War Songs,* 153.

44. Spivak, *Can the Subaltern Speak?,* 244.

45. Witherbee, *Spanish-American War Songs;* Brownlee, *War-Time Echoes.* For a fuller discussion of American and Cuban poetry on the war, see Morales-Franceschini, "Poetry and the Camp."

46. Roig de Leuchsinring, *Weyler en Cuba,* 164–99.

47. Ibid., 179–81.

48. Ibid.; Bozá, *Mi diario de la guerra;* Miró Argenter, *Cuba.*

49. Weyler, *Mi mando en Cuba,* 11.

50. Albeit its polemical tone, one must reckon with the argument as articulated in Izquierdo Canosa, *La reconcentración,* 67–75. This, not least because even President of the American Red Cross Clara Barton writes of how much worse reconcentrados had it under the naval blockade. Barton, *The Red Cross,* 537–39.

51. See chapters on Máximo Gómez and on Valeriano Weyler in Tone, *War and Genocide in Cuba.*

52. Pérez, *The Structure of Cuban History,* 143.

53. Ibid., 142.

54. Machado, *¡Piedad!,* 22.

55. Guerra y Sanchez, *Por las veredas del pasado,* 104–5.

56. Castro Ruz, *La historia me absolverá,* 88–89.

57. Ibid., 66–67.

58. Works consulted on UMAP: Lumsden, *Machos, Maricones, and Gays;* A. Young, *Gays under the Cuban Revolution;* Ros, *La UMAP;* Tahbaz, "Demystifying las UMAP."

59. Tahbaz, "Demystifying las UMAP."

60. Ibid.

61. These practices make them targets in every nation in which they reside, especially in times of war. In both WWI and WWII Jehovah's Witnesses were interned in labor camps in the United States, the UK, and Canada.

62. Kapcia, *Cuba in Revolution,* 70.

63. Guerra, "Gender Policing," 268–89.

64. Guevara, *Che Guevara Reader,* 143–57.

65. Quoted in Guerra, "Gender Policing," 280.

66. According to Lillian Guerra, there was also at least one camp for lesbians and recidivist prostitutes, which she argues attests to their logic as policing of gender normativity, that is, because they interned women who either rejected men as a locus of desire or, as in the case of prostitutes, rejected dependency on the patriarchal state. Guerra, "Gender Policing," 282.

67. The most influential critique came from abroad with the film *Improper Conduct* (1984), directed by Néstor Almendros and Orlando Jiménez Leal. The film features extended interviews with exile literary luminaries such as Guillermo Cabrera Infante, Herberto Padilla, Reinaldo Arenas, Carlos Franqui, and Armando Villadares and draws inflammatory, and rather preposterous, parallels of socialist Cuba and the UMAPs with the Nazi death camps, Stalin's Gulag, Pinochet's Chile, and the Spanish Inquisition. For a critical read, see Georgakas, "Improper Conduct," 45–48. Cuban filmmaker Tomás Guitérrez Alea referred to the film as a "very crude and schematic simplification of reality, very manipulative, like a piece of socialist realism in reverse." Chanan, *Cuban Cinema,* 474.

68. Lumsden, *Machos, Maricones, and Gays,* 65–71.

69. Ibid.

70. Bejel, *Gay Cuban Nation,* 156–61; Chanan, *Cuban Cinema,* 463–74.

71. John Hess has argued that Nancy functions to reign in the homoerotic and emotional "chaos" the film has unleashed and that David, occupying the passivity of a maricón vis-à-vis his relationships to Miguel and Diego, "redeems" himself through Nancy. Hess, "Melodrama, Sex, and the Cuban Revolution," 122.

72. There is something to be said for Germán, Diego's loca friend; Hess has argued that the more flamboyantly loca Germán serves to "normalize" Diego for the film's predominantly heterosexual audience and cultural context. Ibid.

73. Bejel, *Gay Cuban Nation,* 156.

74. Chanan, *Cuban Cinema,* 463.

75. Bejel, *Gay Cuban Nation,* 161.

76. Chanan, *Cuban Cinema,* 474. Alea, to wit, confessed that his film was a cinematic reply to the far less nuanced *Improper Conduct.* In turn, Guillermo Cabrera Infante, the acclaimed Cuban exile writer, also featured in *Improper Conduct,* was signatory to a letter of protest to Jack Valenti, president of the Academy of Motion Picture Arts and Sciences, to block *Fresa y chocolate*'s Oscar nomination. And *Fresa y chocolate* did not get the last word in, for if it was a cinematic reply to *Improper Conduct,* then Julian Schnabel's *Before Night Falls*

(2000), about the highly publicized life and death of gay Cuban writer Reinaldo Arenas, was another iteration in the ongoing polemic.

77. Even the exceedingly judicious Louis Pérez Jr. claims as much. Pérez, *The Structure of Cuban History,* 262.

78. For an excellent survey of the embargo's history, see Lamrani, *The Economic War against Cuba.*

79. For an excellent account of reforms in this period, see Azicri, *Cuba Today and Tomorrow.*

80. Guzmán's *Herida profunda* was, along with Raúl Izquierdo Canosa's *La reconcentración,* the first book-length study published on its subject since Roig de Leuchsinring's 1947 *Weyler en Cuba.* Also in 1998 came Antonio Núñez Jiménez and Liliana Núñez Velis, *La comida en el monte,* which catalogs the various improvised meals (and improvisational ethic) that characterized the nation's historic rebellions and heroes. In their Special Period context, these publications speak volumes. To a hungry Cuban audience, they were not terribly welcome consolations or counsel.

81. Fidel Castro, quoted in Pérez, *The Structure of Cuban History,* 276.

82. Izquierdo Canosa, *La reconcentración,* 67–75.

83. Ibid., 12–13.

84. This latter scenario was what Weyler had hoped for, with amnesty offered to those who surrendered their arms and an even higher price for those who surrendered a horse.

85. Tone, *War and Genocide in Cuba,* 193–224.

86. The best source on this matter, to my knowledge, is Pérez Guzmán, *Herida profunda.*

Epilogue

1. For a compelling and accessible critique of the myth of a "free market," see Chang, *23 Things They Don't Teach You.*

2. Reina María Rodríguez, "—at least, that's the way he looked against the light" (1998). Quoted and translated in Randall, ed., *Only the Road,* 334.

3. Email correspondence with the author, December 5, 2017.

4. Río, "Con los ojos fijos en la altura," 128.

5. On Martí in the early republican imaginary, see Guerra, *The Myth of José Martí.*

6. For a more in-depth analysis of the film, see Bejel, *José Martí,* 67–86; Morales-Franceschini, "The Apostle Desacralized."

7. It is interesting to note, however, the most recent film on the mambí epic, *El Mayor* (2020), is about Ignacio Agramonte, a major general of the Liberation Army in the Ten Years' War renowned for his martial prowess and martyr's death in combat. Directed by Rigoberto López and with none other than Daniel Romero (who played the older Martí in *Ojo del canario*) as Agramonte, the film's trailer and press releases promise a cinematic narrative far more consistent with the

classical epic. Perhaps this is a sign that Cuba (or the PCC) is reassured of itself. We still await a biopic on Mariana Grajales.

8. For information on The Cuban Five, see "Cinco heroes cubanos," Radio Rebelde, http://www.radiorebelde.cu/cinco-heroes/; "Los Cinco Héroes," EcuRed, https://www.ecured.cu/Los_Cinco_H%C3%A9roes.

9. The release of Esteban Morales's *Desafíos de la problemática racial en Cuba* (2007), written by an esteemed economist and published by the prestigious Fundación Fernando Ortiz, and Eric Corlaván's documentary, *Raza* (2008), caused a stir felt among the island's intelligentsia—one of the fruits of which was the creation of the Aponte Commission, which was tasked to review Cuba's educational curriculum, excise any racist discourse, and incorporate Afro-Cuban history.

10. One of the most important such works is Rubiera Castillo and Martiatu Terry, *Afrocubanas.*

11. Castro Ruz, *The Declarations of Havana,* 117.

12. On Venezuela, see Ciccariello-Maher, *Building the Commune.* On *buen vivir/vivir bien,* see Acosta, *El Buen Vivir.*

13. For an informative survey and sympathetic critique, see Harnecker, *A World to Build.*

14. For works regarding Cuban medical care, see Brouer, *Revolutionary Doctors;* Kirk and Erisman, *Cuban Medical Internationalism;* Fitz, *Cuban Health Care.*

15. Some sources say that as much as 90 percent of the fruits and vegetables consumed in Havana are grown locally and organically—an accomplishment that no US city of comparable size could claim. For a nuanced discussion, see Altieri and Funes-Monzote, "The Paradox of Cuban Agriculture." Also see the documentary *Agroecología en Cuba* (2017), https://www.youtube.com/watch?v=O9-awhAqezk&t=2307s. The other noteworthy "green" initiative was the mass distribution of bikes during the Special Period. Were it not for the more readily accessible oil that came from Hugo Chávez's Venezuela, perhaps this, too, would have been better institutionalized.

16. The World Wildlife Fund's 2006 Living Planet Report singled out Cuba as the only country on the planet with high levels of human development that were, at the same time, ecologically sustainable; see also Yaffe, *We Are Cuba!,* especially chapters 4 and 5, and the award-winning documentary, *Agroecología en Cuba* (2017), directed by Juan Pablo Lepore and Nicolas Van Caleon, https://www.youtube.com/watch?v=O9-awhAqezk.

17. Donald Trump's over 240 punitive measures against Cuba made life difficult enough. Then came the pandemic. In the first six months of 2021, Cuba received 90 percent fewer tourists than in the same period the previous year. It also (in January 2021) phased out its dual currency system, which, predictably, has led to runaway inflation (though many hoped it would be temporary). Lopez and Londoño, "Everyone Has a Tipping Point."

18. The video was actually released in February 2021 but only went viral after the July protests. "Patria y Vida," YouTube, https://www.youtube.com

/watch?v=pP9Bto5lOEQ; Cobo, "How 'Patria y Vida' Is Fueling"; Scottie, "How 'Patria y Vida' Became the Anthem."

19. See Dunbar-Ortiz, *An Indigenous People's History.*

20. For the music video "Patria y Vida," released in February 2021, see YouTube, https://www.youtube.com/watch?v=pP9Bto5lOEQ. See also Sayre, "Explaining 'Patria y Vida.'" On US media coverage of the protests, see Macleod, "Media Play Up Protests"; Macleod, "The Bay of Tweets."

21. For the music video "Patria o Muerte por la Vida," released March 1, 2021, see YouTube, https://www.youtube.com/watch?v=Xu4Huw3i-lE.

22. Surely, we would have to add to such criteria a life free of violent repression, a score on which Cuba has been periodically abysmal. But even this would have to be contextualized, whether because the cartel violence that plagues the lives of so many impoverished nations throughout the world is virtually nonexistent in Cuba or because what state violence exists is relatively meek when set against the US-backed coups and dictatorships of the Cold War era or that of police and paramilitary violence throughout the contemporary Americas, but which receive no such unequivocal cries for justice in the US media, academia, or the White House. See Grandin, *Empire's Workshop;* Prashad, *Washington's Bullets.*

23. On the vaccines (Abdala, 92 percent efficacy, and Soberana, 91 percent efficacy) and global pharmaceutical monopolies, see Prashad, "Cuba's Vaccines."

24. A film focused on the infamous murder of eight Havana medical students in 1871, *Inocencia* (2018) could be seen as an attempt to valorize Cuba's revolutionary doctors as heirs to the mambí epic. That said, they did not make it beyond their first year of study, never practiced their trade, and died a martyr's death. Far richer possibilities and stronger candidates are Mariana Grajales and Rosa la Bayamesa, as soldiers, healers, and Black women.

References

Acosta, Alberto. *El Buen Vivir: Sumak kawsay, una oportunidad para imaginar otro mundo*. Quito: Icaria, 2013.

Agamben, Giorgio. *Homo Sacer: Sovereign Power and Bare Life*. Translated by Daniel Heller-Roazen. Palo Alto, CA: Stanford University Press, 1998.

———. *Remnants of Auschwitz: The Witness and the Archive*. Translated by Daniel Heller-Roazen. New York: Zone Books, 1999.

Ainsa, Fernando. *La reconstrucción de la utopía*. Buenos Aires: Ediciones del Sol, 1999.

Altieri, Miguel, and Fernando R. Funes-Monzote, "The Paradox of Cuban Agriculture." *Monthly Review* 63, no. 8 (2012). https://monthlyreview.org/2012/01/01/the-paradox-of-cuban-agriculture/.

Alvarez, Santiago, dir. *Now*. Havana: ICAIC, 1965.

Anderson, Benedict. *Imagined Communities: Reflections on the Origins and Spread of Nationalism*. New York: Verso, 1991.

Appleman Williams, William. *Empire as a Way of Life: An Essay on the Causes and Character of America's Present Predicament, along with a Few Thoughts about an Alternative*. New York: Oxford University Press, 1980.

Arendt, Hannah. *On Revolution*. New York: Penguin Books, 1990.

———. *The Origins of Totalitarianism*. New York: Harcourt, 1976.

Aristotle, *Poetics*. Translated by Malcolm Heath. New York: Penguin Books, 1996.

Azicri, Max. *Cuba Today and Tomorrow: Reinventing Socialism*. Gainesville: University Press of Florida, 2001.

Bachiller y Morales, Antonio. *Cuba primitiva*. 2nd ed. Havana: Libreria de Miguel de Villa, 1883.

Baker, Geoffrey. *Buena Vista in the Club: Rap, Reggaetón, and Revolution in Havana*. Durham, NC: Duke University Press, 2011.

Bakhtin, Mikhail. "Epic and Novel." 1941. In *Dialogic Imagination: Four Essays*, edited by Michael Holquist. Austin: University of Texas Press, 1981.

———. *Rabelais and His World*. Translated by Helene Iswolsky. 1965. Bloomington: Indiana University Press, 1984.

Banet-Weiser, Sarah. "Elian Gonzalez and 'The Purpose of America': Nation, Family, and the Child-Citizen." *American Quarterly* 55, no. 2 (June 2003): 149–78.

Barnet, Miguel, and Esteban Montejo. *Biography of a Runaway Slave.* Translated by W. Nick Hill. Willimantic, CT: Curbstone Press, 1994.

———. "La novela testimonio: Alquimia de la memoria." *Cimarrón.* 212–15. Buenos Aires: Ediciones del Sol, 1987.

Barthes, Roland. *Mythologies.* Translated by Annette Lavers. New York: Hill and Wang, 1972.

Barton, Clara. *The Red Cross: A History of This Remarkable International Movement in the Interests of Humanity.* Washington, D.C.: American National Red Cross, 1899.

Batrell, Ricardo. *A Black Soldier's Story: The Narrative of Ricardo Batrell and the Cuban War of Independence.* Edited and translated by Mark Sanders. 1912. Minneapolis: University of Minnesota Press, 2010.

———. *Para la historia: Apuntes autobiográficos de la vida de Ricardo Batrell Oviedo.* Havana: Seoane y Alvarez, 1912.

Bejel, Emilio. *Gay Cuban Nation.* Chicago: University of Chicago Press, 2001.

———. *José Martí: Images of Memory and Mourning.* Basingstoke, UK: Palgrave Macmillan, 2010.

Beverley, John. *Testimonio: On the Politics of Truth.* Minneapolis: University of Minnesota Press, 2004.

Biskind, Peter. "Lucía—Struggles with History." *Jump Cut* 2 (1974): 7–8.

Bloch, Ernst. *The Principle of Hope.* Vol. 1. Translated by Neville Plaice, Stephen Plaice, and Paul Knight. Cambridge, MA: MIT Press, 1995.

Blum, Denise F. *Cuban Youth and Revolutionary Values: Educating the New Socialist Citizen.* Austin: University of Texas Press, 2011.

Bosch, Carlos, and Josep Ma Domeench, dirs. *Balseros.* Spain: Bausan Films, 2002.

Bowra, C. M. *From Virgil to Milton.* London: Macmillan, 1945.

Boza, Bernabé. *Mi diario de la guerra: Desde Baire hasta la intervención americana.* Havana: La Propagandista, 1900.

Bravo, Estela, dir. *Fidel: The Untold Story.* United States: Faction Films, 2001.

Breslin, Paul. "The First Epic of the New World: But How Shall It Be Written?" In *Tree of Liberty: Cultural Legacies of the Haitian Revolution in the Atlantic World,* edited by Doris Lorraine Garraway, 223–48. Charlottesville: University of Virginia Press, 2008.

Bronfan, Alejandra. *Measures of Equality: Social Science, Citizenship, and Race in Cuba, 1902–1940.* Chapel Hill: University of North Carolina Press, 2004.

Brouer, Steven. *Revolutionary Doctors: How Venezuela and Cuba Are Changing the World's Conception of Health Care.* New York: Monthly Review, 2011.

Brown, David H. *Santería Enthroned: Art, Ritual, and Innovation in Afro-Cuban Religion.* Chicago: University of Chicago Press, 2003.

Brownlee, James Henry, ed. *War-Time Echoes: Patriotic Poems, Heroic and Pathetic, Humorous and Dialectic of the Spanish-American War.* New York: Werner, 1898.

Buck-Morrs, Susan. *Hegel, Haiti, and Universal History.* Pittsburgh: University of Pittsburgh Press, 2009.

Burke, Edmund. *A Philosophical Enquiry into the Sublime and the Beautiful.* New York: Penguin Books, 1998.

Burton, Julianne. "Democratizing Documentary: Modes of Address in the New Latin American Cinema, 1958–1972." In *The Social Documentary in Latin America,* edited by Julianne Burton, 49–85. Pittsburgh: University of Pittsburgh Press, 1990.

Byrne, Bonifacio. *Lira y espada.* Havana: El Figaro, 1901.

Caballero, Armando O. *La mujer en el 95.* Havana: Editorial Gente Nueva, 1982.

———. *La mujer en el 68.* Havana: Editorial Gente Nueva, 1978.

Carvajal, Pedro, dir. *Cuba.* Havana: Anola Films—ICAIC, 1999.

Carbonell, Walterio. *Crítica: Cómo surgió la cultura nacional.* 2nd ed. Havana: Biblioteca Nacional José Martí, 2005.

Carpentier, Alejo. *Obras completas: Ensayos.* México, D.F.: Siglo vientiuno editores, 1990.

Casal, Lourdes. "Race Relations in Contemporary Cuba." In *The Cuba Reader: The Making of a Revolutionary Society,* edited by Phillip Brenner, William LeoGrande, Donna Rich, and Daniel Siegel, 471–86. New York: Grove Press, 1985.

Casamayor-Cisneros, Odette. *Utopía, distopía e ingravidez: Reconfiguraciones en la narrativa possoviética cubana.* Madrid: Vervuet, 2013.

Castro Ruz, Fidel. *The Declarations of Havana.* New York: Verso, 2018.

———. *La historia me absolverá.* Havana: Editorial de Ciencias Sociales, 2007.

———. *Palabras a los intelectuales.* 1961. Havana: Ocean Sur, 2011.

Catalá Carrasco, Jorge. "From Suspicion to Recognition? 50 Years of Comics in Cuba." *Journal of Latin American Cultural Studies* 20, no. 2 (2011): 139–60.

Chanan, Michael. *Cuban Cinema.* Minneapolis: University of Minnesota Press, 2004.

Chang, Ha-Joon. *23 Things They Don't Teach You about Capitalism.* New York: Bloomsbury Press, 2010.

Chase, Michelle. *The Revolution within the Revolution: Women and Gender Politics in Cuba, 1952–1962.* Chapel Hill: University of North Carolina Press, 2015.

———. "The Trials: Violence and Justice in the Aftermath of the Cuban Revolution." In *A Century of Revolution: Insurgent and Counterinsurgent Violence during Latin America's Long Cold War,* edited by Greg Grandin and G. M. Joseph, 163–98. Durham, NC: Duke University Press, 2010.

Childs, Matthew. *The 1812 Aponte Rebellion in Cuba and the Struggle against Atlantic Slavery.* Chapel Hill: University of North Carolina Press, 2006.

Chomsky, Aviva. *A History of the Cuban Revolution*. Malden, MA: Wiley-Blackwell, 2010.

Ciccariello-Maher, George. *Building the Commune: Radical Democracy in Venezuela*. New York: Verso, 2016.

Cobo, Leila. "How 'Patria y Vida' Is Fueling a New Cuban Revolution." *Billboard,* July 16, 2021. https://www.billboard.com/articles/columns/latin/9601996/cuban-revolution-protests-patria-y-vida/.

Collazo, Enrique. *Desde Yara hasta el Zanjón: Apuntaciones históricas*. Havana: La Lucha, 1893.

Consaguerra y Guzmán, Israel. *Mambiserías: Episodios de la Guerra de Independencia, 1895–1898*. Havana: Imprenta del Ejército, 1930.

Cordones-Cook, Juanamaría. *Soltando amarras y memorias: Mundo y poesía de Nancy Morejón*. Santiago, Chile: Editorial Cuarto Propio, 2009.

Cruz, Manuel de la. *Episodios de la revolución cubana*. 1890. 2nd ed. Havana: Miranda, López Seña y Ca., 1911.

Cupull, Adys, and Froilán González. *Mariana, raíz del alma cubana*. Havana: Editora Política, 2017.

Daut, Marlene. *Tropics of Haiti: Race and the Literary History of the Haitian Revolution in the Atlantic World, 1789–1865*. Liverpool: Liverpool University Press, 2015.

Davies, Caroline. *A Place in the Sun? Women Writers in Twentieth-Century Cuba*. London: Zed Books, 1997.

Davis, Angela. *Angela Davis: An Autobiography*. New York: Random House, 1975.

Díaz Torres, Daniel, dir. *Camino al edén*. Havana: Atena 3 Films—ICAIC, 2007.

DuBois, Laurent. *Avengers of the New World: The Story of the Haitian Revolution*. Cambridge, MA: Harvard University Press, 2004.

Dunbar-Ortiz, Roxanne. *An Indigenous People's History of the United States*. Boston: Beacon Press, 2015.

Dussel, Enrique. "Siete hispótesis para una estética de la liberación." *Praxis: Revista de filosofía* 77, no. 1 (January–June 2018): 1–37.

———. *Twenty Theses on Politics*. Translated by George Ciccariello-Maher. Durham, NC: Duke University Press, 2008.

Eagleton, Terry. *Holy Terror*. London: Oxford University Press, 2005.

———. *Radical Sacrifice*. New Haven, CT: Yale University Press, 2018.

———. *Sweet Violence: The Idea of the Tragic*. Malden, MA: Blackwell, 2003.

Eckstein, Susan. *Back from the Future: Cuba under Castro*. 2nd ed. New York: Routledge, 2004.

Eliade, Mircea. *Myth and Reality*. New York: Harper Torchbooks, 1968.

El-Tahri, Jihan, dir. *Cuba: An African Odyssey*. France: ARTE, BBC Films, 2007.

Escobar, Arturo. *Encountering Development: The Making and Unmaking of the Third World*. Princeton, NJ: Princeton University Press, 1995.

Esténger, Rafael, ed. *Homenajes a Maceo: Los discursos de la Cámara de representatnes*. Havana: Editorial Selecta, 1945.

Estudillo, Manuel, dir. *El Edén perdido*. Havana: Atena 3 Television—ICAIC, 2007.

Fanon, Frantz. *The Wretched of the Earth*. Translated by Richard Philcox. New York: Grove Press, 1963.

Farrell, Joseph. "Walcott's *Omeros:* The Classical Epic in a Postcolonial World." In *Epic Traditions in the Contemporary World: The Poetics of Community*, edited by Susanne Wofford, Margaret Beisinger, and Jane Tylus, 270–99. Berkeley: University of California Press, 1997.

Fernandes, Sujutha. *Cuba Represent! Cuban Arts, State Power, and the Making of New Revolutionary Cultures*. Durham, NC: Duke University Press, 2006.

Fernández, Emilio, dir. *La Rosa blanca*. Cuba-Mexico, 1953.

Fernández Retamar, Roberto. *Caliban and Other Essays*. Translated by Edward Baker. Minneapolis: University of Minnesota Press, 1989.

———. *Todo Caliban*. San Juan, Puerto Rico: Ediciones Callejon, 2002.

Fernández Robaina, Tomás. *El negro en Cuba: Colonia, República, Revolución*. Havana: Ediciones Cubanas, 2012.

Ferrer, Ada. *Freedom's Mirror: Cuba and Haiti in the Age of Revolution*. New York: Cambridge University Press, 2014.

———. *Insurgent Cuba: Race, Nation, and Revolution, 1868–1898*. Chapel Hill: University of North Carolina Press, 1999.

Fick, Carolyn. *The Making of Haiti: The Saint Domingue Revolution from Below*. Knoxville: University of Tennessee Press, 1990.

Field, Connie, dir. *¡Salud!* United States: New Paradigms, 2006.

Figueroa, Victor. *Prophetic Visions of the Past: Pan-Caribbean Representations of the Haitian Revolution*. Columbus: Ohio State University Press, 2015.

Fitz, Don. *Cuban Health Care: The Ongoing Revolution*. New York: Monthly Review Press, 2020.

Foley, Helene P. "Women in Ancient Epic." In *A Companion to Ancient Epic*, edited by John Miles Foley, 105–18. Malden, MA: Blackwell, 2005.

Foley, John Miles, ed. *A Companion to Ancient Epic*. Oxford: Blackwell, 2005.

Foner, Philip S. *Antonio Maceo: The "Bronze Titan" of Cuba's Struggle for Independence*. New York: Monthly Review Press, 1977.

———. *The Spanish-Cuban-American War and the Birth of American Imperialism*. Vol. 1. New York: Monthly Review Press, 1972.

Fornet, Ambrosio. *Narrar la nación: Ensayos en blanco y negro*. Havana: Letras Cubanas, 2009.

Forsdick, Charles, and Christian Hogsbjerg, eds. *The Black Jacobins Reader*. Durham, NC: Duke University Press, 2017.

Fraga, Jorge, dir. *La Odisea de General José*. Havana: ICAIC, 1969.

Frederik, Laurie. *Trumpets in the Mountains: Theater and the Politics of National Culture in Cuba*. Durham, NC: Duke University Press, 2012.

Freud, Sigmund. *Jokes and Their Relation to the Unconscious*. Translated by James Strachey. 1905. New York: W. W. Norton, 1960.

———. "Mourning and Melancholia." *The Standard Edition of the Complete Psychological Works of Sigmund Freud*. Vol. 14. Translated by James Strachey, 243–58. 1917. London: Hogarth Press, 1957.

Frye, Northrop. *Anatomy of Criticism: Four Essays*. New York: Antheneum, 1967.

Fuente, Alejandro de la. *A Nation for All: Race, Inequality, and Politics in Twentieth-Century Cuba*. Chapel Hill, NC: University of North Carolina Press, 2001.

Fusco, Coco. "Hustling for Dollars: *Jineterismo* in Cuba." In *Global Sex Workers: Rights, Resistance, and Redefinition*, edited by Kamala Kempadoo and Jo Doezema, 151–66. New York: Routledge, 1998.

Garcia, Enrique. *Cuban Cinema after the Cold War: A Critical Analysis of Selected Films*. Jefferson, NC: McFarland, 2015.

García Borrero, Juan Antonio. *Guía críticia del cine cubano de ficción*. Havana: Arte y Literatura, 2001.

García Espinosa, Julio. "For an Imperfect Cinema." Translated by Julianne Burton. *Jump Cut*, no. 20 (1979): 24–26. https://www.ejumpcut.org/archive/onlinessays/JC20folder/ImperfectCinema.html.

______. *La doble moral del cine*. Havana: Editorial Voluntad, 1995.

———. *Por un cine imperfecto*. Madrid: Castellote, 1991.

Georgakas, Dan. "Improper Conduct." *Cineaste* 14, no. 1 (1985): 45–48.

Gil, Alejandro, dir. *Inoncencia*. Havana: ICAIC, 2018.

Giral, Sergio, dir. *El Otro Francisco*. Havana, ICAIC, 1975.

———, dir. *El Rancheador*. Havana: ICAIC, 1976.

———, dir. *Maluala*. Havana: ICAIC, 1979.

Girard, René. *Violence and the Sacred*. Translated by Patrick Gregory. Baltimore: Johns Hopkins University Press, 1979.

Gleijeses, Piero. *Conflicting Missions: Havana, Washington, and Africa, 1959–1976*. Chapel Hill: University of North Carolina Press, 2002.

———. *Visions of Freedom: Havana, Washington, Pretoria, and the Struggle for Southern Africa, 1976–1991*. Chapel Hill: University of North Carolina Press, 2013.

Glick, Jeremy Matthew. *The Black Radical Tragic: Performance, Aesthetics, and the Unfinished Haitian Revolution*. New York: New York University Press, 2016.

Gómez, Manuel Octavio, dir. *La Primera carga al machete*. Havana: ICAIC, 1969.

Gómez, Máximo. *Diario de campaña (1868–1898)*. Asturias, España: Universidad de Oviedo, 1998.

Gómez, Sara, dir. *De cierta manera*. Havana: ICAIC, 1974.

Gonzalez Echevarría, Roberto. "'Biografía de un cimarrón' and the Novel of the Cuban Revolution." *Novel: A Forum on Fiction* 13, no. 3 (Spring 1980): 249–63.

Gott, Richard. *Cuba: A New History.* New Haven, CT: Yale University Press, 2004.

Grandin, Greg. *Empire's Workshop: Latin America, the United States, and the Making of an Imperial Republic.* Updated and expanded ed. New York: Picador, 2021.

Guerra, Lillian. "Gender Policing, Homosexuality, and the New Patriarchy of the Cuban Revolution. 1965–1970." *Social History* 35, no. 5 (2010): 268–89.

———. *Heroes, Martyrs, and Political Messiahs in Revolutionary Cuba.* New Haven, CT: Yale University Press, 2018.

———. *The Myth of José Martí: Conflicting Nationalisms in Early Twentieth-Century Cuba.* Chapel Hill: University of North Carolina Press, 2005.

———. *Visions of Power in Cuba: Revolution, Redemption, and Resistance, 1959–1971.* Chapel Hill: University of North Carolina Press, 2012.

Guerra y Sanchez, Ramiro. *Por las veredas del pasado, 1880–1902.* Havana, 1957.

Guevara, Ernesto. *Che Guevara Reader: Writings on Politics and Revolution.* 2nd ed. Edited by David Deutschmann. Victoria, Australia: Ocean Press, 2003.

———. *Pasajes de la guerra revolucionaria.* Buenos Aires: Ocean Sur, 2007.

Guillén, Nicolás. *Man-Making Words: Selected Poems of Nicolás Guillén.* 2nd ed. Edited and translated by Roberto Márquez and David Arthur McMurry. Amherst: University of Massachusetts Press, 2003.

Gutiérrez Alea, Tomás. *Dialéctica del espectador.* 1983. Habana: Eds. EICTV, 2009.

———, dir. *Hasta cierto punto.* Havana: ICAIC, 1983.

———, dir. *La Muerte de un burócrata.* Havana: ICAIC, 1966.

Gutiérrez Alea, Tomás, and Juan Carlos Tabío, dirs. *Fresa y chocolate.* ICAIC—IMCINE, 1993.

Hainsworth, J. B. *The Idea of Epic.* Berkeley: University of California Press, 1991.

Halstead, Murat. *The Story of Cuba: Her Struggles for Liberty.* Chicago: Cuban Libre, 1896.

Hammer, Robert D. *Epic of the Dispossessed: Derek Walcott's "Omeros."* Columbia: University of Missouri Press, 1997.

Harnecker, Marta. *A World to Build: New Paths toward Twenty-First Century Socialism.* New York: Monthly Review Press, 2015.

Helg, Aline. *Our Rightful Share: The Afro-Cuban Struggle for Equality, 1886–1912.* Chapel Hill: University of North Carolina Press, 1995.

Hernández, Bernabé, dir. *1868–1898.* Havana: ICAIC, 1970.

Hernández Guzmán, José. *Memorias tristes: Apuntes históricos.* Havana, 1934.

Hernández-Reguant, Ariana, ed. *Cuba in the Special Period: Culture and Ideology in the 1990s.* London: Palgrave Macmillan, 2008.

Herrera, Georgina. "El penúltimo sueño de Mariana." In *Wanilere teatro,* edited by Inés María Mariatu, 277–315. Havana: Editorial Letras Cubanas, 2008.

Herrera, José Isabel. *Impresiones de la Guerra de independencia: Narrado por el soldado del Ejército Libertador.* 1948. Havana: Editorial de Ciencias Sociales, 2005.

Herrera, Manuel, dir. *El Llamado a la hora.* Havana: ICAIC, 1969.

Hess, John. "Melodrama, Sex, and the Cuban Revolution." *Jump Cut* 41 (May 1997): 119–25.

Hidalgo, Narciso. *Choteo: Irreverencia y humor en la cultural cubana.* Bogotá: Siglo del Hombre Editores, 2012.

Hubert, Henri, and Marcel Mauss. *Sacrifice: Its Nature and Its Functions.* Translated by W. D. Halls. Chicago: University of Chicago Press, 1981.

Ibarra, Jorge. *Ideología mambisa.* Havana: Instituto Cubano del Libro, 1972.

Iglesias Utset, Marial. *Las metáforas del cambio en la videa cotidiana: Cuba, 1898–1902.* Havana: Ediciones Union, 2003.

Innes, Paul. *Epic.* New York: Routledge, 2013.

Izaguirre, José María. *Recuerdos de la guerra.* Havana, 1936.

Iznaga, Diana. *Presencia del testimonio en la literatura sobre las guerras por la independencia nacional, 1868–1898.* Havana: Editorial Letras Cubanas, 1989.

Izquierdo Canosa, Raúl. *La reconcentración, 1896–1897.* Havana: Verde Olivo, 1997.

James, C. L. R. *The Black Jacobins: Toussaint L'Ouverture and the San Domingo Revolution.* New York: Vintage Books, 1989.

Jameson, Frederic. *Archaeologies of the Future: The Desire Called Utopia and Other Science Fictions.* New York: Verso, 2005.

———. *The Political Unconscious: Narrative as a Socially Symbolic Act.* New York: Routledge, 1983.

Joderías, Julián. *La leyenda negra: Estudios acerca del concepto de España en el extranjero.* 9th ed. Barcelona: Araluce, 1943.

Juan, Aedlaida de. *Caricatura de la República.* Havana: Ediciones UNION, 1999.

Juan-Navarro, Santiago. "Nación, mito e historia: La guerra hispano-cubano-norteamericana en el cine." *Revista de Humanidades* 37 (2019): 179–208.

———. "¿100 años de lucha por la liberación?": Las Guerras de Independencia en el cine de ficción del ICAIC." *Archivos de la Filmoteca* 59 (2008): 142–61.

Kadish, Doris Y., and Deborah Jenson, eds. *Poetry of Haitian Independence.* New Haven, CT: Yale University Press, 2015.

Kaisary, Philip James. *The Haitian Revolution in the Literary Imagination: Radical Histories, Conservative Constraints.* Charlottesville: University of Virginia Press, 2014.

Kant, Immanuel. *Critique of Judgment.* Translated by Werner Pluhar. Indianapolis: Hackett, 1987.

Kantorowicz, Ernst H. "Pro Patri Mori in Medieval Political Thought." *American Historical Review* 56, no. 3 (April 1951): 472–92.

Kapcia, Antoni. *Cuba: Island of Dreams*. London: Bloomsbury Academic, 2000.

———. *Cuba in Revolution: A History since the Fifties*. London: Reaktion Books, 2008.

———. "Educational Revolution and Revolutionary Morality in Cuba: The 'New Man,' Youth and the New 'Battle of Ideas.'" *Journal of Moral Education* 34, no. 4 (December 2005): 399–412.

Kirk, John, and Michael Erisman. *Cuban Medical Internationalism: Origins, Evolution, and Goals*. London: Palgrave Macmillan, 2009.

Kumaraswami, Par. "Cultural Policy and Cultural Politics in Revolutionary Cuba: Rereading the Palabras a los intelectuales (Words to the Intellectuals)." *Bulletin of Latin American Research* 28, no. 4 (2009): 527–41.

Lagomasino Alvarez, Luis. *Reminiscencias patria*. Manzanillo, Cuba, 1902.

Lambert, Laurie. *Comrade Sister: Caribbean Feminist Revisions of the Grenada Revolution*. Charlottesville: University of Virginia Press, 2020.

Lamrani, Salim. *The Economic War against Cuba: A Historical and Legal Perspective on the U.S. Blockade*. New York: Monthly Review Press, 2013.

Lane, Jill. *Blackface Cuba, 1840–1895*. Philadelphia: University of Pennsylvania Press, 2005.

Lawson, George. *Anatomies of Revolution*. Cambridge: Cambridge University Press, 2019.

Leal, Rine. *La selva oscura: Historia del teatro cubana de 1868 a 1902*. Vol. 2. Havana: Editorial Arte y Literatura, 1982.

Leal, Rine, ed. *Teatro mambí*. Havana: Editorial Letras Cubanas, 1978.

León Rosabal, Blancamar. *La voz del mambí: Imagen y mito*. Havana: Editorial de Ciencias Sociales, 1997.

Lepore, Juan Pablo, and Nicolas Van Caleon, dirs. *Agroecología en Cuba*. Argentina: INCAA, 2017.

Lévi-Strauss, Claude. "The Structural Study of Myth." *Journal of American Folklore* 68, no. 270 (October–December 1955): 428–44.

López, Alfred. *José Martí: A Revolutionary Life*. Austin: University of Texas Press, 2018.

Lopez, Oscar, and Ernesto Londoño. "'Everyone Has a Tipping Point': Hunger Fuels Cuba's Protests." *New York Times*, July 12, 2021. https://www.nytimes.com/2021/07/12/world/americas/cuba-protests-usa.html.

López, Rigoberto, dir. *El Mayor*. Havana: ICAIC, 2020.

Loss, Jacqueline, and José Manuel Prieto, eds. *Caviar with Rum: Cuba-USSR and the Post-Soviet Experience*. London: Palgrave Macmillan, 2012.

Loynaz del Castillo, Enrique. *La Constituyente de Jimaguayú*. Havana: Imprenta El Siglo XX, 1952.

Luis, William. "The Politics of Memory and Miguel Barnet's *The Autobiography of a Runaway Slave*." *MLN* 104, no. 3 (March 1989): 475–91.

Lumsden, Ian. *Machos, Maricones, and Gays: Cuba and Homosexuality*. Philadelphia: Temple University Press, 1996.

Machado, Francisco P. *¡Piedad! Recuerdos de reconcentración*. Sagua, Cuba: Imp. de P. Montero, 1917.

Macleod, Alan. "The Bay of Tweets: Documents Point to US Hand in Cuba Protests." *MintPress News,* July 16, 2021. https://www.mintpressnews.com/documents-point-to-us-hand-in-cuba-protests/277987/.

———. "Media Play Up Protests, Play Down Effect of US Sanctions in Cuba." *FAIR,* July 16, 2021. https://fair.org/home/media-play-up-protests-play-down-effect-of-us-sanctions-in-cuba/.

Mahler, Anne Garland. *From the Tricontinental to the Global South: Race, Radicalism, and Transnational Solidarity.* Durham, NC: Duke University Press, 2018.

Malinowski, Bronislaw. *Myth in Primitive Psychology.* K. Paul, Trench, Trubner, 1926.

Mañach, Jorge. *Indagación del choteo*. 3rd ed. 1928. Havana: Editorial Libro Cubano, 1955.

Marcuse, Herbert. *The Aesthetic Dimension: Toward a Critique of Marxist Aesthetics*. Boston: Beacon Press, 1978.

———. *Eros and Civilization: A Philosophical Inquiry into Freud.* Boston: Beacon Press, 1966.

Mariátegui, José Carlos. *José Carlos Mariátegui: An Anthology.* Edited and translated by Harry E. Vanden and Marc Becker. New York: Monthly Review Press, 2011.

Martí, José. *Abdala*. 1868. Barcelona: Red Ediciones, S.L., 2012.

———. "Con todos y para el bien de todos." *Obras completes*. Vol. 1. Havana: Editorial Nacional de Cuba, 1963.

———. *Diario de campaña*. Havana: Editora del Consejo Nacional de Cultura, 1962.

———. *Edad de oro*. Edited by Eduardo Lolo. 1899. Miami: Ediciones Universal, 2001.

———. *José Martí: Selected Writings*. Edited by Roberto Gonzalez Echevarria. New York: Penguin Classics, 2002.

Martin, Michael, ed. *New Latin American Cinema: Theory, Practices, and Transcontinental Articulations*. Vol. 1. Detroit: Wayne State University Press, 1997.

Marx, Karl. *The Eighteenth Brumaire of Louis Bonaparte*. New York: International, 2015.

Massip, José, dir. *Baraguá*. Havana: ICAIC, 1985.

———, dir. *Páginas del diario de José Martí*. Havana: ICAIC, 1971.

McWilliams, John, Jr. *The American Epic: Transforming a Genre, 1770–1860*. Cambridge: Cambridge University Press, 1989.

Meeks, Brian. *Caribbean Revolutions and Revolutionary Theory: An Assessment of Cuba, Nicaragua, and Grenada*. Kingston, Jamaica: University of West Indies Press, 2001.

Meletinsky, Eleazar. *The Poetics of Myth*. Translated by Guy Lanoue and Alexandre Sadetsky. New York: Garland, 1998.

Méndez Miranda, Fernando. *Historia de los servicios prestados en la guerra de independencia*. Havana: A. Soto, 1928.

Merchant, Paul. *The Epic*. London: Methuen, 1971.

Mesa-Lago, Carmelo. *The Cuban Economy Today: Salvation or Damnation?* Prepared for the Cuba Transition Project, Institute for Cuban and Cuban-American Studies, University of Miami. Washington, D.C.: USAID, 2005.

Mignolo, Walter. *The Darker Side of Modernity: Global Futures, Decolonial Options*. Durham, NC: Duke University Press, 2011.

Mignolo, Walter, and Catherine Walsh. *On Decoloniality: Concepts, Analytics, Praxis*. Durham, NC: Duke University Press, 2018.

Miller, Bonnie. *From Liberation to Conquest: The Visual and Popular Cultures of the Spanish-American War of 1898*. Amherst: University of Massachusetts Press, 2011.

Miller, Dean A. *The Epic Hero*. Baltimore: Johns Hopkins University Press, 2003.

Miller, Ivor. "Religious Symbolism in Cuban Political Performance." *TDR/The Drama Review* 44, no. 2 (Summer 2000): 30–55.

Miller, Stuart Creighton. *"Benevolent Assimilation": The American Conquest of the Philippines, 1899–1903*. New Haven, CT: Yale University Press, 1982.

Miró Argenter, José. *Cuba: Crónicas de la guerra*. Vol. 1. Santiago de Cuba: Imprenta de "El Cubano Libre," 1899.

Montalvo Covarrubias, José, Carlos de la Torre Huerta, and Luis Montané Dardé. *El cráneo de Maceo: Estudio antropológico*. Havana: Imprenta Militar, 1900.

Moore, Carlos. *Castro, the Blacks, and Africa*. Los Angeles: Center for Afro-American Studies, University of California, 1988.

Moore, Robin. *Music and Revolution: Cultural Change in Socialist Cuba*. Berkeley: University of California Press, 2006.

———. *Nationalizing Blackness: Afrocubanismo and Artistic Revolution in Havana, 1920–1940*. Pittsburgh: University of Pittsburg Press, 1997.

———. "The *Teatro Bufo:* Cuban Blackface Theater of the Nineteenth Century." In *Soundscapes from the Americas: Ethnomusicological Essays on the Power, Poetics, and Ontology of Performance,* edited by Donna A. Buchanan, 25–42. Burlington, VT: Ashgate, 2014.

Morales Domínguez, Esteban. *Desafíos de la problemática racial en Cuba*. Havana: Fundación Fernando Ortiz, 2007.

———. *Race in Cuba: Essays on the Revolution and Racial Inequality.* Edited and translated by Gary Prevost and August Nimtz. New York: Monthly Review, 2013.

Morales-Franceschini, Éric. "The Apostle Desacralized: Melancholic Aesthetics and the Specter of Assembly in *José Martí: El ojo del canario*." 60 *Jump Cut* (Spring 2021). http://www.ejumpcut.org/currentissue/Morales-JoseMarti/index.html.

_____. "Poetry and the Camp: Epiphanic Witness and Ecstatic Cry in the Spanish-Cuban-American War of 1898–1898." *Comparative Literature* 73, no. 4 (December 2021): 403–20.

Moreno Fraginals, Manuel. *Cuba/España, España/Cuba: Historian en común.* Barcelona: Críticia: 1995.

Mraz, John. "Visual Style and Historical Portrayal in *Lucía.*" *Jump Cut* 19 (1978). http://www.ejumpcut.org/archive/jc50.2008/Lucia/index.html.

Nancy, Jean-Luc. "The Unsacrificeable." *Yale French Studies* 79 (1991): 20–38.

Navarro Luna, Manuel. *Obra poética.* Havana: UNEAC, 2013.

Nesbitt, Nick. *Universal Emancipation: The Haitian Revolution and the Radical Enlightenment.* Charlottesville: University of Virginia Press, 2008.

Núñez Jiménez, Antonio, and Liliana Núñez Velis. *La comida en el monte: Cimarrones, mambises y rebeldes.* Havana: Fundación de la Naturalez y el Hombre, 1998.

O'Kelly, James J. *The Mambi-Land, or Adventures of a Herald Correspondent.* Philadelphia: J. B. Lippincott, 1874.

Ortiz, Fernando. *Cuban Counterpoint: Tobacco and Sugar.* Durham, NC: Duke University Press, 1995.

———. *Glosario de afronegrismos* Havana: Imprenta Siglo XX, 1924.

Padrón, Juan. *El libro del mambí.* Havana: Casa Editora de Abril, 2002.

———, dir. *Elpidio Valdés.* Havana: ICAIC, 1979.

———, dir. *Elpidio Valdés contra dólar y cañón.* Havana: ICAIC, 1983.

———, dir. *Más se perdió en Cuba.* Havana: ICAIC—Telemadrid, 1995.

Pérez, Fernando, dir. *José Martí: El ojo del canario.* Havana: TVE—ICAIC, 2010.

Pérez, Louis, Jr. *Cuba: Between Reform and Revolution.* Oxford: Oxford University Press, 2014.

———. *Cuba between Empires, 1878–1902.* Pittsburgh: University of Pittsburgh Press, 1983.

———. *Cuba in the American Imagination: Metaphor and the Imperial Ethos.* Chapel Hill: University of North Carolina Press, 2008.

———. *On Becoming Cuban: Identity, Nationality, and Culture.* Chapel Hill: University of North Carolina Press, 1999.

———. *The Structure of Cuban History: Meanings and Purposes of the Past.* Chapel Hill: University of North Carolina Press, 2013.

———. *To Die in Cuba: Suicide and Society.* Chapel Hill: University of North Carolina Press, 2005.

———. *War of 1898: The United States and Cuba in History and Historiography.* Chapel Hill: University of North Carolina Press, 1998.

Pérez Firmat, Gustavo. "Riddles of the Sphincter." In *Literature and Liminality: Festive Readings in the Hispanic Tradition,* 53–74. Durham, NC: Duke University Press, 1986.

Pérez Guzmán, Francisco. *Herida profunda.* Havana: Edicions UNION, 1998.

Pérez Sarduy, Pedro, and Jean Stubbs, eds. *Afro-Cuban Voices: Race and Identity in Contemporary Cuba.* Gainesville: University Press of Florida, 2000.

Perry, Marc. *Negro Soy Yo: Hip Hop and Raced Citizenship in Neoliberal Cuba.* Durham, NC: Duke University Press, 2016.

Peters, Christabelle. *Cuban Identity and the Angolan Experience.* New York: Palgrave Macmillan, 2012.

Piedra Martel, Manuel. *Memoria del mambí.* 1943. Havana: Editorial Nacional de Cuba, 1966.

Planas, Justo. "El reverso mítico de Elpidio Valdés." *Rialta,* June 26, 2020. https://rialta.org/el-reverso-mitico-de-elpidio-valdes/.

Plutarch. "Sayings of Spartan Women." In *On Sparta,* translated by Richard J. A. Talbert, 183–93. New York: Penguin, 2005.

Pope, Cynthia. "The Political Economy of Desire: Geographies of Female Sex Work in Havana, Cuba." *Journal of International Women's Studies* 6, no. 2 (June 2005): 99–118.

Portuondo Zúñiga, Olga. *La virgen de la Caridad del Cobre: Símbolo de cubanía.* Santiago de Cuba: Editorial Oriente, 2011.

Prados-Torreira, Teresa. *Mambisas: Rebel Women in Nineteenth-Century Cuba.* Gainesville: University Press of Florida, 2005.

Prashad, Vijay. "Cuba's Vaccines and the Five Monopolies That Rule the World." *Consortium News,* July 2, 2021. https://consortiumnews.com/2021/07/02/cubas-vaccine-the-five-monopolies-that-rule-the-world/.

———. *Washington's Bullets: A History of the CIA, Coups, and Assassinations.* New York: Monthly Review Press, 2020.

Propp, Vladamir. *On the Comic and Laughter.* Edited and translated by Jean-Patrick Debbèche and Paul Perron. Toronto: University of Toronto Press, 2009.

Puri, Shalini. *The Grenada Revolution in the Caribbean Present: Operation Urgent Memory.* London: Palgrave Macmillan, 2014.

Quesada, Gonzalo de, and Henry Davenport Northrop. *Cuba's Great Struggle for Freedom.* New York: Liberty, 1898.

———. *The War in Cuba: Being a Full Account of Her Great Struggle for Freedom.* New York: Liberty, 1896.

Quijano, Anibal. "Coloniality of Power, Eurocentrism, and Latin America." *Nepantla: Views from the South* 1, no. 3 (2000): 533–80.

Quint, David. *Epic and Empire: Politics and Generic Form from Virgil to Milton.* Princeton, NJ: Princeton University Press, 1993.

Quiroga, José. *Cuban Palimpsests.* Minneapolis: University of Minnesota Press, 2005.

Rabbit, Kara M. "C. L. R. James's Figuring of Toussaint-Louverture: *The Black Jacobins* and the Literary Hero." In *C. L. R. James: His Intellectual Legacies,* edited by Selwyn R. Cudjoe and William E. Cain, 118–35. Amherst: University of Massachusetts Press, 1995.

Ramanujan, A. K. "Three Hundred *Ramayanas:* Five Examples and Three Thoughts on Translation." In *Many Ramayanas: The Diversity of a Narrative Tradition in South Asia,* edited by Paula Richman, 22–49. Berkeley: University of California Press, 1991.

Randall, Margaret. *Haydée Santamaría, Cuban Revolutionary: She Led by Transgression.* Durham, NC: Duke University Press, 2015.

———, ed. *Only the Road/Solo el camino: Eight Decades of Cuban Poetry.* Durham, NC: Duke University Press 2016.

Renan, Ernst. *What Is a Nation? And Other Political Writings.* Translated and edited by M. F. N. Giglioli. New York: Columbia University Press, 2018.

Reyes, Dean Luis. "El etnocentrismo blando en el cine de Juan Padrón: Mambises y vampiros como guerrilla anticolonial." *Rialta,* March 25, 2020. https://rialta.org/el-etnocentrismo-blando-en-el-cine-de-juan-padron-mambises-y-vampiros-como-guerrilla-anticolonial/.

Repinecz, Jonathon. *Subversive Traditions: Reinventing the West African Epic.* East Lansing: Michigan State University Press, 2019.

Río, José del. "Con los ojos fijos en la altura." In *José Martí: El ojo del canario,* edited by Carlos Velazco. Havana: Ediciones ICAIC, 2011.

———. "Elpidio Valdés o la Cubana Paradigmática." *Cuba Cine,* August 14, 2020. http://www.cubacine.cult.cu/es/articulo/elpidio-valdes-o-la-cubania-paradigmatica.

Ríos, Santiago, and Teodoro Ríos, dirs. *Mambí.* Havana: ICAIC—SACEM, 1998.

Roa, Ramón. *Con la pluma y el machete.* Vol. 1. Havana: Academia de la Historia de Cuba, 1950.

———. *A pie y descalzo de Trinidad a Cuba, 1870–1871: Recuerdos de campaña.* Havana, 1890.

Rocha, Glauber. "An Aesthetics of Hunger." In *On Cinema,* edited by Ismail Xavier, 41–45. London: I. B. Tauris, 2018.

Rodgríguez Mola, Alexey, and Magia López Cabrera. "Mambí." Translated by Sujatha Fernandes and Kenya Dworkin. *boundary* 2 29, no. 3 (Fall 2002): 205–10.

Rodríguez Rodriguez, Amalia, ed. *Algunos documentos políticos de Máximo Gómez.* Havana: Biblioteca Nacional José Martí, 1962.

Roig de Leuchsenring, Emilio. *Cuba no se debe su independencia a los Estados Unidos.* Havana: Sociedad Cubana de Estudios Históricos e Internacionales, 1950.

———, ed. *Ideario cubano: Máximo Gómez.* Havana, 1936.

———, ed. *Por Cuba Libre: Juan Gualberto Gómez.* Havana: Editorial de Ciencias Sociales, 1974.

———. *Weyler en Cuba: Un precursor de la barbarie fascista.* Havana: Paginas, 1947.

Rojas, Rafael. *Isla sin fin: Contribución a la crítica del nacionalismo cubano.* Miami: Ediciones Universal, 1998.

———. *La máquina del olvido: Mito, historia, y poder en Cuba*. México City: Taurus, 2012.

Rolando, Gloria, dir. *1912: Voces para un silencio*. Havana: Imagines del Caribe, 2010.

Ros, Enrique. *La UMAP: El Gulag Castrista*. Miami: Ediciones Universal, 2004.

Roy, Sneharika. *The Postcolonial Epic: From Melville to Walcott and Ghosh*. London: Routledge, 2018.

Rubiera Castillo, Daisy, and Inés María Martiatu Terry, eds. *Afrocubanas: Historias, pensamientos y práticas culturales*. Havana: Editorial de Ciencias Sociales, 2011.

Sánchez, Jorge Luis, dir. *Cuba Libre*. Havana: ICAIC, 2015.

Sánchez, Serafín. *Heroes humildes y Los poetas de la guerra*. Havana: Editorial de Ciencias Sociales, 1981.

Sanderman, Alejandro, dir. *Hombres de Mal Tiempo*. Havana: ICAIC, 1968.

Sanders, Mark A. Introduction to *A Black Soldier's Story: The Narrative of Ricardo Batrell and the Cuban War of Independence,* by Ricardo Batrell. Edited and translated by Mark A. Sanders. Minneapolis: University of Minnesota Press, 2010.

Sarabia, Nydia. *Historia de una familia: Mariana Grajales*. Havana: Editorial de Ciencias Sociales, 2006.

Sartre, Jean-Paul. Preface to *Wretched of the Earth,* by Frantz Fanon. Translated by Richard Philcox. New York: Grove Press, 1963.

Saunders, Tanya. *Cuban Underground Hip-Hop: Black Thoughts, Black Revolution, Black Modernity*. Austin: University of Texas Press, 2015.

Sawyer, Mark Q. *Racial Politics in Post-Revolutionary Cuba*. Cambridge: Cambridge University Press, 2006.

Sayre, Anamaria. "Explaining 'Patria y Vida,' the Song That's Defined the Uprising in Cuba." *Alt.Latino,* NPR, July 20, 2021. https://www.npr.org/sections/altlatino/2021/07/19/1017887993/explaining-patria-y-vida-the-cuban-song-defying-an-evil-revolution.

Schmidt, Jalane D. *Cachita's Streets: The Virgin of Charity, Race, and Revolution in Cuba*. Durham, NC: Duke University Press, 2015.

Scott, David. *Conscripts of Modernity: The Tragedy of Colonial Enlightenment*. Durham, NC: Duke University Press, 2004.

———. *Omens of Adversity: Tragedy, Time, Memory, Justice*. Durham, NC: Duke University Press, 2014.

———."The Theory of Haiti: The *Black Jacobins* and the Poetics of Universal History." In *The Black Jacobins Reader,* edited by Charles Forsdick and Christian Hogsbjerg, 115–38. Durham, NC: Duke University Press, 2017.

Scott, Rebecca. *Slave Emancipation in Cuba: The Transition to Free Labor*. Princeton, NJ: Princeton University Press, 1985.

Scottie, Andrew. "How 'Patria y Vida' Became the Anthem of Cuban Anti-Government Protests." CNN, July 20, 2021. https://www.cnn.com/style/article/patria-y-vida-cuba-protests-trnd/index.html.

Sellén, Francisco. *Hatuey.* (1891) In *Teatro mambí,* edited by Rine Leal. Havana: Editorial Letras Cubanas, 1978.

Serra, Rafael. *Para blancos y negros: Ensayos politicos, sociales, y económicos.* Havana: "El Score," 1907.

Smith, Lois M., and Alfred Padula. *Sex and Revolution: Women in Socialist Cuba.* Oxford: Oxford University Press, 1996.

Solanas, Fernando, and Octavio Getino. "Towards a Third Cinema." In *New Latin American Cinema,* edited by Michael T. Martin, 1:33–58. Detroit: Wayne State University Press, 1997.

Solás, Humberto, dir. *Lucía.* Havana: ICAIC, 1968.

Sommer, Doris. *Foundational Fictions: The National Romances of Latin America.* Berkeley: University of California Press, 1993.

Sorel, Georges. *Reflections on Violence.* Edited by Jeremy Jennings. Cambridge: Cambridge University Press, 1999.

Soto, Lionel. *Revolución del 33.* Havana: Editorial de Ciencias Sociales, 1979.

Spivak, Gayatri Chakravorty. "Can the Subaltern Speak?" In *Can the Subaltern Speak? Reflections on the History of an Idea,* edited by Rosalind C. Morris, 237–91. New York: Columbia University Press, 2010.

———. *Outside in the Teaching Machine.* New York: Routledge, 2009.

Steinberg, Arthur. "Mambises." In *Encyclopedia of the Spanish-American and Philippine-American War,* edited by Spencer Tucker, 1:366–67. Santa Barbara, CA: ABC-CLIO, 2009.

Stone, Elizabeth, ed. *Women and the Cuban Revolution: Speeches & Documents by Fidel Castro, Vilma Espín & Others.* New York: Pathfinder, 2004.

Stoner, K. Lynn. *From the House to the Streets: The Cuban Woman's Movement for Legal Reform, 1898–1940.* Durham, NC: Duke University Press, 1991.

———. "Militant Heroines and the Consecration of the Patriarchal State: The Glorification of Loyalty, Combat, and National Suicide in the Making of Cuban National Identity." *Cuban Studies* 34 (2003): 71–96.

Stout, Nancy. *One Day in December: Celia Sánchez and the Cuban Revolution.* New York: Monthly Review Press, 2013.

Tahbaz, Joseph. "Demystifying las UMAP: The Politics of Sugar, Gender, and Religion in 1960s Cuba." *Delaware Review of Latin American Studies* 14, no. 2 (December 2013). http://www1.udel.edu/LAS/Vol14-2Tahbaz.html.

Taylor, A. M. "Review of *Lucía* by H. Solás." *Film Quarterly* 28, no. 2 (1974–75): 53–59.

Thucydides. *The Peloponnesian Wars.* Translated by Martin Hammond. Oxford: Oxford University Press, 2009.

Tone, Lawrence. *War and Genocide in Cuba, 1895–1898.* Chapel Hill: University of North Carolina Press, 2006.

Torres, Miguel, dir. *Hasta la próxima aventura.* Havana: ICAIC, 2013.

Torres Elers, Damaris A. *Maria Cabrales: Una mujer con historia propia.* Santiago de Cuba: Editorial Oriente, 2013.

Torres Elers, Damaris A., and Israel Escalona Chádez, eds. *Mariana Grajales Cuello: Doscientos años en la historia y la memoria.* Santiago de Cuba: Ediciones Santiago, 2015.

Trouillot, Michel-Rolph. "An Unthinkable History: The Haitian Revolution as a Non-Event." In *Silencing the Past: Power and the Production of History.* Boston: Beacon Press, 1995.

Valdés-Domínguez, Fermín. *Diario de soldado.* 4 vols. Edited by Hiram Dupotey Fideaux. Havana, 1973.

Varona Guerra, Miguel. *La Guerra de Independencia de Cuba, 1895–1898.* Havana: Editorial Lex, 1946.

Vega, Pastor, dir. *Retrato de Teresa.* Havana: ICAIC, 1979.

Vitier, Cintio. *Ese sol del mundo moral: Para una historia de la eticidad cubana.* Buenos Aires: Siglo veintiuno editores, 2002.

Waters, Mary-Alice, ed. *Cuba & Angola: Fighting for Africa's Freedom and Our Own.* New York: Pathfinder Press, 2013.

———. *Marianas in Combat: Teté Puebla and the Mariana Grajales Women's Platoon in Cuba's Revolutionary War, 1956–1958.* New York: Pathfinder, 2003.

Weyler, Valeriano. *Mi mando en Cuba: Historia military y política de la última guerra separatista durante dicho mando.* Madrid: F. González Rojas, 1911.

White, Hayden. "Interpretation in History." In *Tropics of Discourse: Essays in Cultural Criticism.* Baltimore: Johns Hopkins University Press, 1978.

———. *Metahistory: The Historical Imagination in 19th Century Europe.* Baltimore: Johns Hopkins University Press, 1973.

Williams, Raymond. *Modern Tragedy.* Palo Alto, CA: Stanford University Press, 1966.

Witherbee, Sidney A., ed. *Spanish-American War Songs: A Complete Collection of Newspaper Verse during the Recent War with Spain.* Detroit: Witherbee, 1898.

World Wildlife Fund. *Living Planet Report, 2006.* World Wildlife Fund, 2006. https://wwf.panda.org/discover/knowledge_hub/all_publications/living_planet_report_timeline/lpr_2006/.

Yaffe, Helen. *Che Guevara: The Economics of Revolution.* New York: Palgrave Macmillan, 2009.

_____. *We Are Cuba! How a Revolutionary People Have Survived in a Post-Soviet World.* New Haven, CT: Yale University Press, 2020.

Young, Allen. *Gays under the Cuban Revolution.* San Francisco: Gray Fox Press, 1981.

Young, Cynthia. *Soul Power: Culture, Radicalism, and the Making of the U.S. Third World Left.* Durham, NC: Duke University Press, 2006.

Žižek, Slavoj. *First as Tragedy, Then as Farse.* London: Verso, 2009.

Index

Italicized page numbers indicate illustrations.

Recent books in the series

New World Studies

Rum Histories: Drinking in Atlantic Literature and Culture
Jennifer Poulos Nesbitt

Imperial Educación: Race and Republican Motherhood in the Nineteenth-Century Americas
Thomas Genova

Fellow Travelers: How Road Stories Shaped the Idea of the Americas
John Ochoa

The Quebec Connection: A Poetics of Solidarity in Global Francophone Literatures
Julie-Françoise Tolliver

Comrade Sister: Caribbean Feminist Revisions of the Grenada Revolution
Laurie R. Lambert

Cultural Entanglements: Langston Hughes and the Rise of African and Caribbean Literature
Shane Graham

Water Graves: The Art of the Unritual in the Greater Caribbean
Valérie Loichot

The Sacred Act of Reading: Spirituality, Performance, and Power in Afro-Diasporic Literature
Anne Margaret Castro

Caribbean Jewish Crossings: Literary History and Creative Practice
Sarah Phillips Casteel and Heidi Kaufman, editors

Mapping Hispaniola: Third Space in Dominican and Haitian Literature
Megan Jeanette Myers

Mourning El Dorado: Literature and Extractivism in the Contemporary American Tropics
Charlotte Rogers

Edwidge Danticat: The Haitian Diasporic Imaginary
Nadège T. Clitandre

Idle Talk, Deadly Talk: The Uses of Gossip in Caribbean Literature
Ana Rodríguez Navas

Crossing the Line: Early Creole Novels and Anglophone Caribbean Culture in the Age of Emancipation
Candace Ward

Staging Creolization: Women's Theater and Performance from the French Caribbean
Emily Sahakian

American Imperialism's Undead: The Occupation of Haiti and the Rise of Caribbean Anticolonialism
Raphael Dalleo

A Cultural History of Underdevelopment: Latin America in the U.S. Imagination
John Patrick Leary

The Spectre of Races: Latin American Anthropology and Literature between the Wars
Anke Birkenmaier

Performance and Personhood in Caribbean Literature: From Alexis to the Digital Age
Jeannine Murray-Román

Tropical Apocalypse: Haiti and the Caribbean End Times
Martin Munro

Market Aesthetics: The Purchase of the Past in Caribbean Diasporic Fiction
Elena Machado Sáez

Eric Williams and the Anticolonial Tradition: The Making of a Diasporan Intellectual
Maurice St. Pierre

The Pan American Imagination: Contested Visions of the Hemisphere in Twentieth-Century Literature
Stephen M. Park

Journeys of the Slave Narrative in the Early Americas
Nicole N. Aljoe and Ian Finseth, editors

Locating the Destitute: Space and Identity in Caribbean Fiction
Stanka Radović

Bodies and Bones: Feminist Rehearsal and Imagining Caribbean Belonging
Tanya L. Shields

Sounding the Break: African American and Caribbean Routes of World Literature
Jason Frydman

The Haitian Revolution in the Literary Imagination: Radical Horizons, Conservative Constraints
Philip Kaisary

CPSIA information can be obtained
at www.ICGtesting.com
Printed in the USA
LVHW042311260522
719869LV00003B/449

9 780813 948157